Aquinas's Philosophy of Religion

Also by Paul O'Grady

RELATIVISM

THE CONSOLATIONS OF PHILOSOPHY: Reflections in an economic downturn (*editor*)

Aquinas's Philosophy of Religion

Paul O'Grady
Trinity College Dublin, Ireland

First published 2014 by
PALGRAVE MACMILLAN

Palgrave Macmillan in the UK is an imprint of Macmillan Publishers Limited, registered in England, company number 785998, of Houndmills, Basingstoke, Hampshire RG21 6XS.

Palgrave Macmillan in the US is a division of St Martin's Press LLC, 175 Fifth Avenue, New York, NY 10010.

Palgrave Macmillan is the global academic imprint of the above companies and has companies and representatives throughout the world.

Palgrave® and Macmillan® are registered trademarks in the United States, the United Kingdom, Europe and other countries

ISBN: 978–0–230–28517–0

This book is printed on paper suitable for recycling and made from fully managed and sustained forest sources. Logging, pulping and manufacturing processes are expected to conform to the environmental regulations of the country of origin.

A catalogue record for this book is available from the British Library.

A catalog record for this book is available from the Library of Congress.

Contents

Preface and Acknowledgements

Aquinas wrote in a world far removed from the twenty-first century and held many assumptions that few now share. He also wrote a great deal – over 8,500,000 words on a recent estimate [McDermott (1993) p. xv]. He wrote in a distinctive academic style, which can seem remarkably limpid once accustomed to it, but is often rebarbative to new readers. Aquinas, therefore, is a difficult figure to write about. Yet despite these difficulties, I have come to appreciate his manner of thinking and his way of arguing more deeply the longer I engage with his work. There is a robust critical intelligence coupled with a deep religious sensibility evident throughout his writings. And even if one comes to disagree with his views, it becomes clear what the issues are and what the philosophical commitments are which underpin the debate.

Aquinas excites strong responses, being sometimes rejected out of hand, sometimes idolized. His own approach is always to seek to understand his interlocutor, to give them the strongest case they have, but to assess critically and without prejudice the strength of the view under scrutiny. Aquinas didn't write in a vacuum, but rather participated in different communities, took part in current debates of the thirteenth century and on occasion wrote at the request of friends and colleagues.

Neither did my own writing of this book take place in a vacuum and its immediate spur was teaching philosophy of religion at Trinity College Dublin, wishing there was a book like this available. My predecessor teaching philosophy of religion there, J.C.A. Gaskin, is well known for his book *Hume's Philosophy of Religion*. It is a model of clarity and solid information on one of the great figures in the history of the discipline and indispensable for anyone teaching it. It served as an ideal for me as I began to write on one of the other great figures in the history of philosophy of religion.

There are different philosophical and intellectual currents behind my writing. In my initial graduate work at University College Dublin I found myself engaging with contemporary analytical philosophy and this led me to Trinity College Dublin to work on Wittgenstein, Carnap and Quine and issues of cognitive relativism – a world far removed from Aquinas in one way, but not in another, as I shall argue in the book. At Trinity I also found a philosophical community distinctive (in Ireland, at the time) for its vigorous atheism. I found myself teaching philosophy of religion in this environment and using Aquinas as a dialogue partner with Flew, Hume, Mackie, Russell and others, where he seemed, ironically, like a counter-cultural figure to the students.

A more distant but still important source in the emergence of this book is the introduction to Aquinas I received from the Dominican Order in the 1980s. The communities I knew were intellectually exciting, places where ideas were exchanged and debated around the clock and where a certain sense of intellectual closeness to Aquinas (known familiarly as Thomas) pervaded. Given there are many different approaches to Aquinas, the one which most influenced me was one which sought to connect his work to contemporary thought, making it something living rather than just from the history of ideas and frequently something rather left of centre. And in the work of writers such as Victor White, Herbert McCabe, Fergus Kerr and Brian Davies (dialoguing with Jung, Marx, Wittgenstein, Heidegger and others) I found an inspiration which has lasted through to this book, despite my subsequent hesitations about religious institutions.

I have been lucky in having a congenial and varied philosophical community in Dublin and in the good interactions between UCD and TCD where we share a taught graduate programme and work-in-progress groups. It is fruitful having scholars of, e.g., Aristotle, Pseudo-Dionysius, Aquinas and Scotus interact with scholars of Kant, Wittgenstein, Quine, Heidegger, Merleau-Ponty among others – challenging each other's presuppositions and methods.

Many people have helped in the process of getting this book to print. I particularly want to mention Lilian Alweiss, Maria Baghramian, David Berman, Vivian Boland, Con Casey, Gerard Casey, Martin Cogan, Donald Collins, Michael Dunne, Philip Gleeson, Richard Hamilton, James Levine, John Littleton, Ciarán McGlynn, Philip McShane, Dermot Moran, Fran O'Rourke, Jim O'Shea, Vasilis Politis, Roger Pouivet, Fáinche Ryan, Peter Simons, Eleanore Stump and Liam Walsh who have all helped me in various ways. Audiences at NUI Maynooth, Blackfriars Oxford, Fordham University, The International Conference for Philosophy of Religion Krakow and the Priory Institute Tallaght have all contributed helpful material. Material from chapter five has already appeared in *The European Journal of Philosophy of Religion*. Susan and Sarah, who sometimes appear in examples in the text, were constantly patient with and supportive of me as I frequently disappeared off to my computer.

There are three people I want to single out for particular thanks. The first is William Lyons, Professor Emeritus at Trinity College Dublin, who has been a mentor, friend and constant support for many years.

The second is Brian Davies at Fordham University who has generously read the entire manuscript and contributed enormously to its finished state. Finally I would like to extend a *go raibh maith agat* to my graduate student Dónall McGinley who meticulously checked the whole thing for conceptual and literary errors with a gimlet eye.

List of Abbreviations

CT	*Compendium Theologiae*
DAM	*De Aeternitate Mundi*
DDN	*Super librum Dionysii De divinis nominibus*
DEE	*De Ente et Essentia*
DPN	*De Principiis Naturae*
In BDH	*Expositio libri Boethii De ebdomadibus*
In BDT	*Expositio super librum Boethii De trinitate*
In DA	*Sententia libri De Anima*
In DC	*Sententia super librum De caelo et mundo*
In DDN	*Expositio super Dionysium De divinis Nominibus*
In Heb	*Expositio libri Boetii De hebdomadibus*
In Met	*Sententia super Metaphysicam*
In NE	*Sententia libri Ethicorum*
In PA	*Sententia super Posteriora analytica*
In PH	*Sententia super Peri hermenias*
In Phys	*Sententia super Physicam*
QDM	*Quaestiones disputatae de malo*
QDP	*Quaestiones disputatae de potentia*
QDV	*Quaestiones disputatae de veritate*
QQ	*Quaestiones quodlibetales*
SCG	*Summa Contra Gentiles*
SS	*Scriptum super libros Sententiarum*
ST	*Summa Theologiae*
Super Heb	*Super Epistemolam ad Hebraeos*
Super Io	*Lectura super Ionannem*

Conventions in Referring to Aquinas's Work

Aquinas wrote in a variety of different genres and his works appear in multiple editions and translations. There is a standard manner of referring to his works, indicating the section of the work in question, rather than giving a page number in an edition.

The *Summa Theologiae* is made up of three parts, the second part being further subdivided in two. References are given initially to the part (First Part, *Prima Pars*, I; First Part of the Second Part, *Prima Secundae* I-II; Second Part of the Second Part, *Secunda Secundae*, II-II; and Third Part, *Tertia Pars*, III). The text is further divided into questions and these questions into articles. So a full reference gives the part, the question number and the article number, e.g. ST 1.8.1 refers to *Summa Theologiae*, First Part, Question 8, Article 1. Articles also have their own internal structure – with numbered objections to the view Aquinas defends, the citation of an authority for the view defended (*Sed Contra*), the body of the article (*Corpus*) and responses to the objections (*ad primum* etc.). Occasionally I will indicate which part of the article is in focus by noting *corpus*, or *ad 1*, *ad 2* etc. Note that beginners reading this work often mistake the initial presentation of an objection for Aquinas's own views.

The *Summa Contra Gentiles* is divided into four books, which are further subdivided into Chapters. References will be to Part and Chapter, e.g. SCG 1.15.

Aquinas's Disputed and Quodlibetal Questions are divided into questions and articles, as is his Commentary on Boethius's *De Trinitate*. His Aristotelian Commentaries are divided into Books and Lectures, while each section in these has also its own number. So in referring to these I shall give Book, Lectures and Section number, e.g. In Met 1.9.134.

1
Philosophy and Theology

1.1 Introduction

Debates about whether religious belief is reasonable or not have much popular currency. A slew of recent best-selling books have argued trenchantly that religious belief is irrational, inviting a variety of different responses. The academic discipline which concerns itself with such questions is philosophy of religion. Sidelined from mainstream analytic philosophy by logical positivism and subsequently methodological naturalism, this field has nevertheless seen a massive flourishing in the last few decades. Drawing on contemporary work in metaphysics, epistemology, philosophy of language and philosophy of mind, those engaged in this discipline address a range of questions such as 'Is it reasonable to believe in God?', 'What meaning does the term 'God' have?', 'What is faith?', 'How does faith relate to reason?', 'What should one make of the plurality of religious beliefs?', 'Does evil count as evidence against religious belief?'. Such a discipline faces challenges from several sides. Some contend that human reason has not the resources to adjudicate such questions. Others maintain that scientific inquiry is the only legitimate mode of answering them. Others again argue that only someone 'internal' to a religious tradition is in an appropriate position to judge that tradition.

One of the most significant figures in the history of this discipline is the medieval Italian philosopher and theologian Thomas Aquinas (c. 1225–1274). He laboured to bring together the best secular thinking of his age with the wealth of religious reflection in Christian, Jewish and Islamic thought. His work is regarded as a masterly presentation of classic Christian belief and is as intricate as it is voluminous. It excites strongly divergent reactions. For some, Aquinas is a party hack, trotting

1

out indefensible doctrine at the behest of one of the most conservative organizations in history, the Catholic Church. Infamously Bertrand Russell dismissed Aquinas, in his *History of Western Philosophy*, as having little of the true philosophical spirit.[1] On the other hand, there are those who treat Aquinas almost as an oracle, who regard him as being right on all essentials and who think that different approaches are irrelevant and can be either ignored or their errors exposed. Neither pole is attractive. Russell's challenge is unfair and biased (and elegantly demolished by Anthony Kenny).[2] Yet defensive 'ghetto Thomism' is at odds with Aquinas's own intellectual liveliness and practice and does not engage with the larger intellectual community. So a way between these is needed, but is hard to chart.

Aquinas lived and wrote in a milieu which is intellectually far away from us. Modern social ideals of democracy and egalitarianism, scientific knowledge of the universe and matter, perspectives on historical development and modern theories of interpretation, psychological accounts of the unconscious and information technology were alien to him. He accepted slavery[3], astrology[4], the inferiority of women[5], monarchy[6] and the right to kill heretics[7]. Despite these differences from present sensibilities, he also had some of the most penetrating reflections on existence, the fundamental structures of reality, the nature of ethics and the nature of human existence produced in the Western philosophical tradition. So Aquinas needs to be understood in his context. This means grasping the conceptual scheme he inherited from ancient philosophy and noting the ways he altered it under the influence of his religious beliefs (for example, how his views on whether the world is everlasting differ from those of Aristotle). In recent years a wealth of important scholarship has been produced seeking to sensitively and accurately understand Aquinas's writings in light of his context, and this work is invaluable for gaining a correct understanding of his views.[8] Yet such scholarship, while necessary, is not sufficient. Aquinas announces an important intellectual goal while commenting on Aristotle's views of the heavens. He notes that 'the study of philosophy is not about knowing what people have happened to think, but rather is about the truth of reality'.[9] Correct historical scholarship is instrumental to the first-order task of trying to find the truth.

To some, this may be a contentious claim, perhaps under the influence of postmodern scepticism about achieving any such truths. But typically such postmodernists tend to confuse making a determinate claim about reality with holding that claim in a dogmatic fashion, mistakenly attacking the latter by abandoning the former (e.g. I can hold that it is raining, and defend it fallibly, but if I leave it open and indeterminate what I mean by it is raining – perhaps in a postmodern space of possibility, drawing on the lexical connections between raining, training, straining etc. to problematize bipolar meaning – I don't seem to be saying anything at all). Another possible objection to bringing Aquinas into a contemporary pursuit of truth is that it invites an ahistorical treatment of Aquinas, attempting to domesticate him, as it were, to the modes and methods of contemporary debate. I would hope to avoid such a distortion, but nevertheless show the relevance of his views to these debates. To deny that such a process is possible seems to commit one to a strong form of cultural or historical relativism, where terms like 'God' or 'nature' are so different as used in different contexts, that engagement across these contexts is not possible.[10] I think Aquinas's own practice of discussing thinkers from very different backgrounds and the presence of Aquinas in contemporary debates speak against the strength of this kind of objection. Therefore, while seeking to give an accurate and sensitive account of various positions held by Aquinas relevant to philosophy of religion, I also want to attempt to assess them. I believe the best way to do that is to bring them into dialogue with contemporary philosophy of religion – to view them in light of the best contemporary reflection on similar issues. Describing how this might be possible and what problems there may be with it is the concern of the rest of this chapter. In the next section I shall discuss the situation of contemporary philosophy of religion, in the following place Aquinas in relation to philosophy of religion and finally discuss various possible objections to Aquinas's philosophy of religion.

1.2 Characterizing philosophy of religion

The academic study of religion includes sociology, psychology, history, comparative religion and theology, among other disciplines. One way in which philosophy of religion differs from empirical and comparative work on religion is in its evaluative stance. This means that the claims to truth made by religious beliefs are scrutinized and assessed and the reasonableness or otherwise of these beliefs is tested. Straightaway this process can be challenged, for example, by those who think it is of the essence of religious belief not to connect to rationality. Some might claim that religious claims are subjective, not answerable to the tribune of reason and therein lies their importance. They say that there is much more to humanity than just reason and that religion inhabits that greater province. Others fasten on to the alleged irrationality of religious beliefs to dismiss them – as in attempts to show they are not scientific and hence dismissable as on a par with fairy stories. Those who contend that religious belief is not scientific tend also to be impatient with philosophical argumentation which does not appeal to observation. Therefore, those who think of religion as essentially subjective, whether positively or negatively, tend to be dismissive of attempts to submit it to rational investigation. Wittgenstein, who valued religious belief highly, was scathing about traditional philosophy of religion, and Dawkins, who does not, says, 'the five "proofs" asserted by Thomas Aquinas in the thirteenth century don't prove anything, and are easily – though I hesitate to say so, given his eminence – exposed as vacuous'.[11]

But the question whether religious belief is essentially subjective, what that might mean and how one might argue for such a claim is exactly the kind of thing which concerns philosophy of religion. There is clearly some overlap in this with theology, but one way in which these disciplines differ is in the resources they regard as acceptable in their pursuit. Theology gives a special role to scriptural resources and a kind of authority to tradition which philosophers, by and large, do not. Philosophers use the resources of conceptual analysis and logical argumentation to carry out their tasks. Historically there has been a greater connection between theology and philosophy than exists currently. There is also the split in contemporary philosophical practice between so-called analytic and continental approaches. Contentious and hard to define as this is, broadly speaking analytical philosophers privilege clarity, explicitness of argumentation, limited goals and have heroes such as Russell and Quine. Continental philosophers challenge assumptions they see implicit in traditional philosophy, seek to overcome the tradition, express themselves in new idioms, address big questions and have heroes such as Hegel and Heidegger (counterexamples to all these claims exist – but I am sketching a general picture). Insofar as contemporary theologians engage with philosophy, it tends to be with continental philosophy. However, in the last number of decades there has been a great deal of activity in analytical philosophy of religion, including discussions of topics which would have been in the tradition remit of theology such as clarifying God's attributes, analysing ways of making sense of the Trinity and suggesting models for the Incarnation. This recent work begins to look very much like the kind of work produced by Aquinas, and these contemporary philosophers of religion begin to look afresh back to Aquinas, Scotus, Ockham, Suarez and others for inspiration.[12]

From its beginning, Western philosophy has engaged with the question of God. The catalogue of great thinkers from classical Greece to the end of the medieval period treated questions about God as central to their project. It was integrated into their general metaphysical debates and connected to questions about knowledge and language. Technical discussions about the nature of knowledge, kinds of causation, scope of knowledge, theories of reference and categories all interconnected with discussions about God. With the rise of modern philosophy, two tendencies worked to undermine this centrality. The first is the advance of natural science, which slowly but inexorably replaced theology as the main dialogue partner for philosophy. The second is the rise of scepticism and atheism as genuine possibilities. By the beginning of the analytic-continental divide (usually held to be the first decades of the twentieth century), the analytic tradition had completely sidelined philosophical interest in God (Frege, Russell, Wittgenstein, Carnap, Quine), while the continental was perhaps more attuned to the impact of God's demise (Heidegger, Sartre, Camus), but God was still intellectually outré.

By the mid-twentieth century, philosophy of religion had retreated to a narrow defensive attempt to show that it actually could exist in the face of challenges which argued it was meaningless. Kenny paints the picture well:

> A chapter of A.J. Ayer's juvenile *Language Truth and Logic* (Gollancz 1936) and four pages on theology and falsification by Anthony Flew called forth a hundred articles of defensive commentary and tentative refutation. But the positivist criteria by which these writers judged theology meaningless had already been abandoned by everyone except theologians.[13]

The demise of positivism led to a renewal of interest in metaphysics in the analytical world. One avenue for this is in 'naturalism', where philosophy allies itself with natural science and seeks interdisciplinary advancement, abandoning claims to have a separate province for itself. Metaphysics, then, arises out of the exigencies of the scientific project. Much of this naturalism is explicitly atheistic, holding that nothing exists beyond the bounds of 'nature', denying any supernatural reality. Those who challenge naturalism and pursue metaphysics in a different way see themselves as having much in common with the metaphysicians of the tradition. For example, two recent opponents of naturalism (who do not concern themselves with philosophy of religion) aligned themselves with the metaphysical views of Plato (J.J. Katz) and Aristotle

(L. BonJour) respectively.[14] This renewal of interest in the metaphysical tradition has helped reverse the kind of defensiveness depicted by Kenny and fostered constructive work in analytical philosophy of religion.

I want to draw attention to three issues in contemporary philosophy of religion which connect directly to Aquinas's work. The first is work on classical theistic argumentation. This means examining the kinds of argument which are given to attempt to demonstrate that God exists. Such arguments have existed since Greek antiquity. One modern issue is the attempt to clarify the status of such arguments. What do they attempt to do? Are they genuine attempts to get any fair-minded judge to accept their conclusion? Are they regarded as dialectically compelling? Are they held to be psychologically compelling? Or are they rational reconstructions of considerations which would render justified beliefs which are held on some other ground? Are they person-relative, or intended as binding on all thinkers? What is their relationship to religious practice and belief? Can they be properly understood in isolation from the kind of culture (form of life) which produced them? Do they have any contemporary validity, or do they belong to the history of (defunct) ideas? Very different views are defended by contemporary philosophers of religion on these issues, and understanding what Aquinas himself thought about them is a matter of interpretative controversy. The most famous and important of these arguments include the ontological argument which seeks to show that God exists using purely a priori argumentation, that is, using concepts solely deriving from logic and language. Aquinas rejected this argument [ST 1.2.1, SCG 1.10–11]. Neither did he deal with issues arising from religious experience as a means of showing that God exists. His favoured means of arguing to God relies on his views about causation, presenting several versions of what is now known as cosmological arguments. He also used the argument to a designer, but one which is importantly different to later famous versions of the same. Contemporary philosophers of religion are also interested in these arguments, not convinced by the general kinds of objections provided by David Hume and Immanuel Kant, and hold that each argument needs to be judged on its own merits. This has occasioned a renewed interest in looking at the specifics of Aquinas's arguments.[15]

Critics of Aquinas note that his arguments tend to end rather quickly with something along the lines of 'and this we call God'. They argue that this is too fast, that even if the arguments are correct, the conclusion may not resemble anything like the classical picture of God. On this Aquinas would agree, but then point to the wealth of argumentation he provides to specify what being God means. This is the domain of discussions of the divine attributes, the second issue to which I want to draw attention and which has seen a significant proliferation of work in the last couple of decades.[16] What is God's relationship to time? Does God change? Does God have parts? How does God know the world? How does God create the world? Is God currently in causal contact with the world? Is freedom possible if God controls the world? What does this say about the existence of evil? These are problems that arise for theists even prior to atheists accusing them of incoherence or posing versions of the problem of evil. Contemporary philosophers of religion who defend theism disagree radically on these issues, and it emerges that Aquinas's views are not widely shared even among theists, who regard them as presenting too austere a conception of divinity.

Finally there is the question of the relationship of faith to reason. This relation depends, of course, on the account one gives of the relata – many different conceptions of faith and of reason have been deployed in these debates. Some want to argue for the strong incompatibility of each side – variously championing one over the other. Rationalistic critics of religion make faith appear irrational, infantile and a kind of dysfunction. Sophisticated critics of reason can appeal to sceptical considerations to deconstruct rationalistic pretensions and hold that faith is more profound and more secure than the illusions of reason. One does not have to be a fundamentalist to challenge reason – legions of philosophers from Sextus Empiricus to Wittgenstein have done so. Aquinas is of interest in wanting to preserve both reason and faith. He gives a detailed account of the nature of faith in such a way that its relationship to reason (or a specific account of reason) makes them compatible with each other. Whether his views on faith, reason and their relations are defensible is an important issue in Aquinas scholarship.

There are other issues in philosophy of religion which are distinctively modern and on which Aquinas has little explicit to say. He does not comment on non-theistic religion (indeed it is likely such an idea would be oxymoronic to him) and the problems of religious pluralism were not his (despite his interaction with Jewish and Islamic thinkers). Yet the foremost modern defender of religious pluralism, John Hick, appeals to Aquinas to explain and defend his views.[17] And recent studies have appeared relating Aquinas to Indian thinkers such as Ramanuja and Nagarjuna.[18] Hence, it seems that Aquinas's thought engages with many layers in contemporary philosophy of religion. Therefore, it is appropriate to examine more closely the writing and context of Thomas Aquinas to see how it relates to contemporary philosophy of religion.

1.3   Aquinas as a philosopher of religion

Aquinas did philosophy in a dialogical manner. Some philosophers meditate in solitude, issuing aphorisms from the mountaintop. Others self-consciously seek to do something new, to break with tradition and establish a new method or even discipline. Aquinas thought the best way of doing philosophy was to engage with his predecessors and contemporaries, whoever they be. He read pagan Greeks, Jewish rabbis and Islamic rationalists as well as a wealth of Christian sources in his search for the answer to the question which, his biographers say, gripped him from childhood – 'what is God?'[19]. He studied, taught and wrote in the context of the new universities and with his colleagues in the Dominican Order, an organization only ten years older than himself, devoted to study and preaching whose motto was '*Veritas*' – truth.

Hence, Aquinas's work is steeped in the tradition of philosophy prior to him. At a time when church authorities regarded Aristotle with suspicion and the Islamic philosopher Ibn Rushd (known to Aquinas as Averroes) with open hostility – Aquinas referred to Aristotle simply and familiarly as 'the philosopher', with Averroes as 'the commentator'. He was immersed in the Bible, the works of the early Christian fathers; he came to know the works of the Eastern Orthodox Church, especially John of Damascus; and was intimately familiar with the works of Augustine and of Pseudo-Dionysius, a fifth-century Syrian who was mistakenly believed to be a figure referred to in the Acts of the Apostles. His work created a pattern in which all these different strands found place.

The size and systematic integration of his work is astounding. He wrote more than eight times the amount Aristotle produced, all of it exhibiting an exactness and concision seldom equalled. A small number of recurring principles and guiding ideas pervade the whole, spanning investigations into language and logic, ethics and politics, psychology and action theory, metaphysics, psychology and of course theology. The mutual support of the parts and suppleness of his use of his intellectual building blocks make the overall work daunting to engage with. Nevertheless it is centrally connected to reflection about God, construed as the source and end of all that exists. His work exhibits a delicate balance between intricate theorizing about God, while at the same time holding to a kind of agnosticism, that we can actually say very little about God. This latter is a useful corrective to approaches which domesticate God, rendering the divinity too familiar by anthropomorphizing it.

Probably the best-known part of his work is a small piece called the Five Ways, in which he offers five brief arguments for God's existence near the start of his major work, the *Summa Theologiae*. In an earlier work, the *Summa Contra Gentiles*, he presented similar arguments in greater detail, and in even earlier works, the *De Ente et Essentia* and the *Commentary on the Sentences*, he presented other arguments. We shall look at these in some detail later on. What they seek to achieve, how to reconstruct them, who influenced them and how successful they are is hotly contested, even among those well disposed towards Aquinas. What is important is to note how integrated these arguments are with Aquinas's discussion of God's nature. It is too limited a perspective to simply judge them without connecting them to his views on simplicity, perfection, goodness and so forth – the kinds of discussions which give content to the very idea of God in his work, a position often labelled 'classical theism'. For example a key claim he makes is that there is no capacity for change in God. Counter-intuitive and limiting as this might appear, it is connected to his views about God's perfection and guides his discussion of God's relation to time, God's manner of causation and how God knows creation. These are issues which will form the core of this book.

At this point I want to say something about how Aquinas thought about the relationship between philosophy and theology. Important as a topic in its own right, it is also important in relation to objections to thinking of Aquinas as a philosopher of religion, which I shall discuss in the next section. The first thing to note is that Aquinas used terminology which does not easily map onto modern usage. While he uses the term *'theologia'*, it has a distinctive meaning for him. Literally it means talk about God of any kind, and Aquinas tends to use the term in this broad manner. So it includes within itself the ruminations of pagan Greeks and Islamic theologians, and can be thought of as part of philosophy. He distinguishes this broader usage from a more specific kind of theology which is distinctive of Christian teaching. For this latter teaching he uses the term *'Sacra Doctrina'*, or sacred teaching. He thinks of this teaching as being directly derived from God through revelation. Indeed at times he uses the terms *'Sacra Scriptura'* and *'Sacra Doctrina'* as interchangeable [see ST 1.1.9]. Yet *Sacra Doctrina* takes as its task the elaboration and clarification of what is expressed in scripture:

> The truth of faith is contained in sacred Scripture, diffusely, under various modes of expression, and sometimes obscurely, so that, in order to gather the truth of faith from sacred Scripture, one needs long study and practice, which are unattainable by all those who require to know the truth of faith, many of whom have no time for

study, being busy with other affairs. And so it was necessary to gather together a clear summary from the sayings of sacred Scripture, to be proposed to the belief of all. This indeed was no addition to sacred Scripture, but something taken from it. [ST 2.2.1.9ad1][20]

Aquinas thinks that revelation has an epistemological superiority relative to the results of human reasoning, since it is the direct authoritative teaching of God, and human reasoning is fallible. I shall discuss various ways of thinking about this in Chapter 3, below. For the moment I am seeking merely to draw the methodological distinction Aquinas makes between *Sacra Doctrina* and philosophy.

In his *Commentary on Boethius's De Trinitate*, Aquinas has a detailed discussion of the nature and division of the sciences. It might seem an odd place for such a discussion, but Aquinas explains that Boethius, having articulated the Christian doctrine of the Trinity, seeks to explore the nature of a science and how a science of such divine truths might be possible [InBDT pars3 pr1]. Aquinas distinguishes between natural science, which requires matter for both the existence of its objects and also for the appropriate kind of understanding; mathematics, which requires material objects for its existence, but which feature is not needed for understanding; and theology or metaphysics, which deals with realities not dependent on matter and whose understanding is not connected to understanding the material realm. Philosophers deal with God in this latter discipline, as the universal beginning of things, whose nature is explored through the consideration of being as such [InBDT 5.4 corp].[21] However, the investigations of philosophers are available only to a minority of people, after much toil, and are riddled with errors [ST 1.1.1; SCG 1.4]. So there is a second way of learning about such truths, which is the way of *Sacra Doctrina*.

> There exist two theologies or divine sciences: in one divine things are not the subject matter of the science but the beginnings of the subject matter, and this theology philosophers pursue and also call metaphysics; in the other divine things are considered for themselves as subject matter of the science, and this theology is the one taught us in holy Scripture. [InBDT 5.4 corp]

Aquinas is clear that *Sacra Doctrina* is superior to the kind of talk about God deriving from metaphysics, because of its clarity, certainty and divinely authorized status. Yet metaphysical reflection on God has its own independent methods and status, and in perhaps a rare autobiographical remark, Aquinas comments on using philosophical reasoning to think about God:

> To be able to see something of the loftiest realities, however thin and weak the sight may be, is...a cause of the greatest joy. [SCG 1.8.1]

The relationship of philosophy to *Sacra Doctrina* parallels at the level of scientific disciplines the relationship of reason to faith in an individual, and I shall explore some of the nuances of Aquinas's account in Chapter 3 below. What I seek to emphasize here is Aquinas's methodological acceptance of the possibility, legitimacy and indeed delight of philosophical inquiry about God, a point to which I will return in Section 1.4 below.

Given that Aquinas recognizes the legitimacy of philosophical approaches to God, I also want to indicate the continuity between Aquinas's interests and methods and those of contemporary philosophers of religion. This is a controversial issue, and I shall discuss objections to it below, but first I want to make the positive case for it. Aquinas does not see the role of philosophy as bringing one to belief in God, being a form of apologetics. That would be a causal story – whether the cause be construed in terms of individual psychology or the subtle workings of divine grace. Instead, philosophy is about the realm of reason – about showing the reasonableness of the beliefs one holds for whatever causal reason. Are the beliefs one might have about God reasonable, defensible by the highest intellectual standards available? And if there are some beliefs for which no reason can be given either for or against (and intellectual work has to be done to show that this is so), can it be shown that the beliefs are not irrational? Again and again we find Aquinas devising arguments, examining objections, making distinctions, clarifying ambiguities to judge the rational status of whatever area of discourse in which he is engaged.

I wish to draw attention to similarities between Aquinas and contemporary analytical philosophers of religion along three themes – firstly topics and areas of interest, secondly methods of argumentation and thirdly his rejection of certain kinds of incommensurability.[22]

Aquinas was interested in discussing the rational status of claims to God's existence. The discussion recurs from his early *Commentary on the Sentences*, through *De Ente Et Essentia*, the *Summa Contra Gentiles* and the *Summa Theologiae* as an explicit study, appropriation and emendation of earlier philosophical treatments of this issue (see Chapter 4 below). He accepted an Aristotelian model of rationality and located the discussion of the demonstration of God's existence within that. The term 'demonstration' had a specific technical meaning, referring to the most secure form of intellectual support a belief might have. Aquinas believed it was possible to produce such an argument. The arguments of Kant to the contrary have been very influential, and I shall discuss them below – but many contemporary philosophers of religion discuss such arguments without Kantian scruples – for example Richard Gale, William Rowe, Richard Swinburne.[23] Aquinas rejects the view that faith is divorced from reason, that they are not capable of engagement with each other. So while having a robust conception of faith, he is not a 'fideist', who like Kant limits reason to make space for faith. Yet this is a subtle issue – since Aquinas does think there are limits to reason. He also rejects the view that there is just no problem about God's existence, that it is some sense obvious.[24] This would seem to put him in conflict with recent epistemologists of religion who maintain that belief in God is 'properly basic', on a par with sense inputs, and like sense inputs not requiring a special defence.[25] His views on God's nature treat of familiar topics such as goodness, knowledge and power, but also more counter-intuitive topics such as timelessness, unchangingness, impassivity and aseity. His integrated treatment of the more and the less familiar amounts to an impressively coherent and comprehensive doctrine of God which stands as a challenge to many contemporary views. He also had discussions of topics such as identity and change, substance, properties, universals, individuals, existence, essence, causation, reference, sense, analogy and many more such which are grist to the mill for contemporary metaphysics. His views are interesting in their own right, but also generally subordinated to the discussion of God and humanity's relationship to God. These are issues which we will examine more closely in the following chapters. The point here is that Aquinas deals with topics which are staples of contemporary analytic philosophy and argues for distinctive positions which can be recognized as similar to some within contemporary debates.

Moreover, the way he argues fits in very well with contemporary analytical philosophical practice. His style is devoid of rhetoric or literary embellishment. Its logical structure is close to the surface, and is readily amenable to formalization in a logical calculus. He is dialogical in that he has mastered a body of texts and engages with them no matter what their confessional provenance. There is no methodological appeal to introspection, to Cartesian-style subjectivity, but rather everything that is material for debate is accessible in linguistic form. There is no appeal to ambiguity, wilful neologism or a desire to throw his interlocutors by exposing hidden assumptions or pathologies in their thinking, say, in contrast to those who see later Wittgenstein or Heidegger as a model. He does not strive to be 'new'. His methods are logical argumentation, appeal to commonplace or scientific examples and appeal to principles which he believes his dialogue partners also hold.

Aquinas is a catholic thinker – meant in the sense of being open to all sources and talking with all comers. His work was regarded with suspicion by some of his theological contemporaries since he engaged with Aristotelian rationalism, especially under the anti-Christian reading yielded by Averroes. He treated the views of Rabbi Moses with respect.[26] He discussed the views of ancient Greek materialists and Irish pantheists.[27] From his position of secure immersion in his religious tradition, he did not think that dealing with diverse traditions contaminated his views, but rather it enriched them. His intellectual practice was of openness to reason, to human experience and all sincere seekers after truth. This did not mean he agreed with them all, or thought that reason did not have limits, but his stance was one in which nothing in principle was beyond the possibility of debate and discussion, even if one recognizes in advance that the object of debate is such that it can never be fully grasped.

That this is important to note is due to a recent trend in Aquinas scholarship to question whether it is appropriate to think of Aquinas as a philosopher. Given that ill-informed dismissals of Aquinas can be frequent enough (see Dawkins above), it is more significant that those who are deeply familiar with his work come to such a conclusion. So I shall now turn to objections to Aquinas's philosophy of religion. I shall start with this fundamental objection that he just is not a philosopher of religion at all and that to read him as such is an anachronism and a mistake. Following this I shall discuss the Kantian objection to the project of natural theology, which persuaded many that an approach such as Aquinas's is mistaken. Then I shall deal with a specific offshoot of the Kantian objection, the challenge that Aquinas is involved in 'ontotheology' and that this is illegitimate, a view made influential by Heidegger. Finally, from a different perspective I shall look at Wittgensteinian-style objections to his approach. Given that such considerations have led many to overlook or dismiss his work, I believe it important to defuse such objections before engaging with his views.

1.4   Objections to Aquinas's philosophy of religion

There are those who argue that Aquinas ought not be classified at all as a philosopher of religion and then those who believe he is, but is deeply mistaken in his views. In this section I wish to discuss both kinds of critic. I might note that this follows Aquinas's own methodology. In many works he begins the discussion of a particular topic with a survey of the opinions and arguments ranged against the view he seeks to defend before articulating his own view and then responding to the objections. Those who deny that he should be read as a philosopher include secular opponents but also theologians who seek to read his work without finding a distinct philosophy there. Among the myriad substantive objections to his views are three general ones (the Kantian, ontotheological and Wittgensteinian) which I would like to address in advance of discussing the details of his views. More specific criticisms will be discussed throughout the book where appropriate (including broadly Humean objections in Section 5.2).

1.4.1   Aquinas was not a philosopher

A familiar objection to Aquinas is that his views are that of the Catholic Church rather than the product of his own authentic reasoning. He knows the answers to his questions before asking them, and is merely the mouthpiece of a conservative institution, seeking rationalizations of the party line. One way of responding to this is to invoke Karl Popper's distinction between context of discovery and context of proof. One may come to hold one's beliefs in a myriad of ways. For example, August Kekulé dreamed about a snake swallowing its own tail, which led him to postulate the circular structure of the benzene molecule. This is how he discovered the belief – but subsequent rigorous empirical work went into demonstrating that it was true.[28] Likewise Aquinas got his basic beliefs through his upbringing and religious education – but whether these beliefs were true was something he devoted his life and writings to exploring. The job of philosophy is to assess and evaluate beliefs, not necessarily to produce and inculcate beliefs.

Less familiar objections come from some scholars deeply immersed in the study of Aquinas who also deny that he should be viewed as a philosopher. Their contention is that he was a theologian first and foremost and therefore any attempt to find a distinct philosophical doctrine in his work is a mistake.It goes against his own intentions and self-understanding. In recent years a significant number of Aquinas experts have advanced views like this, using different arguments and making claims with differing degrees of strength. I shall discuss three such claims. The first argues that Aquinas is not a philosopher because whatever philosophy might exist in his work has been transformed into theology and no longer exists as *philosophy*. The second argues that the correct interpretation of his most famous book, the *Summa Theologiae*, requires that he not be viewed as a philosopher. The third contends that he should not be understood as a 'theist', which is an incorrect description of his specifically Christian doctrine.

(i)   Jordan

Mark Jordan makes a powerful historical case against viewing Aquinas as a philosopher.[29] He notes that by vocation and self-understanding Aquinas was a theologian. The term '*philosophus*' was used pejoratively in the thirteenth century and is never applied by Aquinas to a Christian thinker. The massive focus of his writings is theological; what might be construed as distinctively philosophical involves commentary on other philosophers' doctrines (the Aristotle commentaries), short polemical pieces *De Unitate Intellectu* [On the unicity of the intellect] or *De Aeternitate Mundi* [On the eternity of the world] or brief recapitulations of Aristotelian themes using Islamic commentary *De Ente et Essentia* [On being and essence] *or De Principiis Naturae* [On the principles of nature]. So he wrote no distinctive philosophical doctrine, and such an idea would have been alien to him. In an important metaphor that comes from his commentary on Boethius's work on the Trinity Aquinas says that the water of philosophy has been transformed into the wine of theology [InBDT 2.3ad5]. Jordan takes some case studies of how philosophical material gets changed in theological context into something new and different from its original source, often in Aristotle.

The case is impressive, but not compelling. Firstly one might note that Aquinas accepts that philosophy and theology *do* exist as distinct disciplines – there is no blurring of disciplinary boundaries for him. The distinction is connected to the distinctions between reason and faith and also nature and grace, although not identical with them. Aquinas clearly thinks that the [theology – faith – grace] side of these distinctions is superior to the [philosophy – reason – nature] side. That said, an important principle for him is that grace builds on nature.[30] The action of God in the world does not take away from the proper functioning of the world, even though the proper functioning of the world is itself ultimately dependent on God. Likewise faith does not contradict or obliterate reason. It follows that theology does not wipe out philosophy. While he holds that it is the case that in certain contexts water gets turned into wine, it does not follow that wine and water coalesce in all contexts – they remain separate, and water is not devalued by not being wine. So it is not alien to Aquinas to allow that philosophy exists distinct from theology.

Again, accepting that Aquinas thinks *Sacra Doctrina* is superior to philosophy, this does not invalidate or make impossible the philosophical consideration of important issues – even by Aquinas himself. Indeed one of his major works, the *Summa Contra Gentiles*, has been traditionally regarded as an effort to establish the truth of his beliefs about God from the perspective of reason alone (at least in the first three books). The traditional reason given for writing this book has been to allow for dialogue with Muslims who do not accept Christian revelation.[31] More recent scholarship rejects this account and considers it as an exercise in rational reflection for its own sake.[32] Given his acceptance of the superiority of theology, this does not make redundant the effort to re-examine the same issues using a different methodology.

So I have argued that looking at Aquinas's work as a philosopher is not at odds with his own understanding of reason and the role of philosophy, as a historical claim. But suppose Jordan is correct in his claim that the historical Aquinas did not intend his work to be treated outside of a theological context. Does that mean that philosophers are mistaken in using his work in their debates? This is not at all obvious. Once sufficient attention is given to the context of the work to correctly understand the meaning of the material and the kinds of argumentation involved, it seems that engaging critically with that work is at the heart of the philosophical venture, as distinct from, say, the history of ideas. How can these ideas illuminate contemporary treatments of the issues? What is still viable in them? Aristotle, Augustine, Aquinas, Hume, Nietzsche come from very different cultural and historical contexts which take extended scholarly endeavour to retrieve. Yet they all figure as important thinkers in the discipline of philosophy of religion. It would be a mistake to exclude Aquinas from this discussion and an impoverishment of it.

(ii)   Kerr

Fergus Kerr has devoted his attention to examining different ways of interpreting Aquinas's work.[33] In particular he has looked at the famous five ways, which are the best-known parts of Aquinas's work in the English-speaking world. Typically they are examined by philosophers as stand-alone arguments, and their context is ignored. Furthermore they are construed as foundationalist attempts to provide a rationalistic basis for religious belief – and usually criticized as being inadequate to this task.[34] Among the stock challenges are the charge that the conclusion (this is what we call God) does not follow from the premises and is too big a leap, that they are rooted in outmoded and wrong physics, that the use of regress arguments begs the question against atheism, and so on. Kerr's main target is a rationalistic theological approach associated with certain kinds of neo-Thomism, which stripped Aquinas's work of its mystical and religious content, yielding a kind of positivism 'with no more religious character than the arguments of eighteenth century Deists'[35] [M.D. Chenu, qtd. in Kerr].

Kerr usefully clarifies some of the concepts used in the arguments – noting how the notions of 'cause' and 'substance' in play are different from later usage and involve a much more dynamic picture of the world and of God than the static one usually assumed. He also notes how the whole discussion is shot through with theological assumptions. The very statement of atheism (so unremarkable today) is taken from scripture. The preceding two articles seek to find a middle way between the view that God's existence is transparently obvious to reason, and the view that it is hidden to anything but supernatural faith, a path licenced by appeal to scripture – Romans 1.20. So Kerr's claim is that with the whole text shot through with theological infrastructure, it must be mistaken to treat the arguments as purely philosophical ones.

He endorses a further argument, from Eugene Rogers, which seeks to bring together Aquinas and Karl Barth (the great enemy of natural theology), noting with this that 'the implications for philosophers of religion and their understanding of the Five Ways are obviously important'.[36] He says 'natural knowledge of God's existence independently of the life of grace is not something that Thomas ever imagined'.[37] A key text from Aquinas's discussion of faith is used to make this claim. Aquinas writes, 'believing that God exists is not something that non-believers do under the description of an act of faith; they do not believe that God exists under the conditions which faith determines; and so they do not truly believe that God exists, because as Aristotle says, with regard to simples, defective knowledge is not knowing at all' [ST 2–2 2.2]. This means that when non-Christian philosophers say 'God exists', they mean something radically different from 'God exists' as uttered by a believer. And this is not a matter of differing existential commitment or affective attitude to the belief – it is a matter of the logical content of the propositional belief itself.

So, Kerr contends that the five ways are theological not philosophical arguments, they can only be properly understood in a religious context and a consideration of them unhooked from that religious environment would yield the wrong result anyway – whatever the conclusion might be, it is not the God referred to in Christian discourse.

Taking the last point first – do believers and unbelievers mean different things by God? If they do, then it becomes impossible for theists and atheists to disagree. An atheist can never express the negation of what a theist asserts, since the atheist cannot have access to the logical content held by theists. Or indeed a former theist like Kenny cannot understand what his earlier self believed. It seems clear that Aquinas does not agree with this – since he discusses atheism as a genuine objection to God's existence and canvasses arguments in support of atheism [ST 1.2.3]. Furthermore he discusses mistaken views of God – including the 'very stupid' view of David of Dinant who asserted that God was to be analysed in terms of matter [ST 1.3.8]. He also refers to ancient philosophers' views about God, criticizing their inadequacies.[38] It would not be possible to do this if theists and atheists meant something completely different – indeed he thinks the mistaken views of the ancients were somehow connected to what he calls 'God'. It is clear therefore that there is some level of agreement and some level of disagreement between them.

Aquinas held that language signifies the world as mediated by a mental concept.[39] So the mental concept (*ratio*) fixes the reference of the linguistic term. The same object (*res significata* – signified thing) may have different descriptions associated with it (*modus significandi* – means of signification). Aquinas makes an important distinction between one's ability to refer to an object in the manner of a competent language user and in the manner of one who has detailed knowledge of it.[40] The pet owner and the vet can use the term 'cat' correctly, but the vet has much greater knowledge of it. The vet is able to give a scientific account of the *ratio* of the cat, while the pet owner has different knowledge (probably more detailed, idiosyncratic knowledge of the proclivities of *this* cat). There is nevertheless some basic commonality in their knowledge which allows them to talk about the same thing. In one respect, talk about God is like this. People who disagree about God's existence and God's nature have some basic idea in common (perhaps something like creator, first cause etc.). The theist maintains that something with this description exists, while the theist denies this. Christians obviously think about God differently from the way pagans do, but nevertheless there is some continuity in their thinking. However, an important difference from the cat example is that there is no adequate scientific knowledge of God, for Aquinas. God's *ratio*, a detailed scientific account of God's nature, is in principle unavailable to us. This is because it exceeds our cognitive capacities. There is indeed imperfect and inadequate knowledge and one can discriminate between better and worse accounts, but no full account is available. So the argument that Aquinas's views should not be viewed as philosophical because of a kind of incommensurability in meaning between Christians and non-Christians is implausible in itself, and furthermore does not fit with Aquinas's practice.

What then of the dismissal of attempts to view the five ways as being foundationalist epistemological arguments? It seems right to insist that the meaning of these arguments emerges out of a religious context and that a nuanced understanding of terms like 'cause' is required. But to move from this to suggest that a philosophical consideration of them is mistaken is too great a leap. Foundationalism is one species of epistemological justification, and epistemological analysis is one species of philosophical analysis. Classical foundationalism requires non-inferentially justified basic beliefs (beliefs which are self-justifying in some sense) as the foundation of knowledge. Few accept now that such beliefs exist, but this does not mean the end of epistemology.[41] Issues such as coherence, explanatory power and relation to pre-theoretical intuitions play a large role in contemporary epistemology. So if the five ways are interpreted as having theological concepts built into them, it is still epistemologically interesting to examine their logical structure and relationship to other beliefs. The Carnapian idea of 'rational reconstruction' can play a role here.[42] That is, even though such chains of argument may not psychologically cause belief, it is still worthwhile to examine the logical structure of that belief, how it is supported by other beliefs. This fits well with Aquinas's conception of argumentation about God's existence – a reasoned account is possible, even though it is rarely, if ever, the actual cause of one's belief. Again this raises big issues about the relation of faith to reason, of philosophy to theology, which will be examined more closely in Chapter 3, but for the moment I want to use these considerations as a way of defending a philosophical approach to Aquinas's work.

(iii)   Te Velde

A recent important study of Aquinas argues that he ought not be viewed as a theist.[43] While Rudi Te Velde is not directly claiming that Aquinas should not be read as a philosopher, he seeks to remove him from the battleground of theists and atheists. As surprising as this claim may seem, Te Velde makes a strong case based on extensive textual reference and a compelling interpretation rooted in Aquinas's metaphysics of participation. I wish to characterize Te Velde's general position before examining his specific argument against construing Aquinas as a theist. I shall argue that his reasons for this are not sound.

Te Velde accepts that Aquinas is an outstanding and deep philosopher,[44] but notes a certain tension between Aquinas's public utterances about the separation of philosophy and theology and his actual practice in his writing.[45] In practice, the philosophy has to be retrieved from within the theology. Aquinas is not engaged in the task of providing an epistemological foundation for religious belief – establishing a natural theology onto which revealed theology can be tacked.[46] Rather the role of philosophy is subtler. It allows conceptual clarification of the content of religious belief, but conceptual clarification which roots those beliefs in reality. That is, given that Christian revelation could be construed as simply part of the history of human religious ideas, the philosophical exploration of the intelligibility of the content of those ideas seeks to connect it to the 'Greek' discourse about being.[47] By this, revelation is rooted in reality.

Te Velde notes that theism emphasizes the separation of God from creation – that God is a unique being with special characteristics, including causal powers, timelessness etc. But Te Velde has defended an interpretation of Aquinas in which the participation of all things in God as their principle and end is highlighted, and so thinking of God as a distinct and separate being is mistaken – 'Thomas seems to favour the language of participation in which distinction and identity are found inseparably linked together'.[48] Does that make Aquinas a pantheist? No, Aquinas thinks of God as independent, but the conditions under which we think about God always involve the world. Te Velde emphasizes the *triplex via* of causation, negation and eminence in Aquinas's talk about God. That is, God is first established as the cause and principle of all that exists, but then shown to be utterly different to anything else that exists by negation and finally shown to exist in a perfect manner by eminence. Thus the intelligibility of God is linked to creation – humans access and think about God through creation.

Given that Aquinas is not a pantheist and indeed demands the genuine distinction between God and creation, why is it not appropriate to call his views theistic? Te Velde holds that theism entails thinking of God as an entity with certain specific features and requires one to use a representational mode of thinking which accurately captures and described those features. In contrast, Aquinas does not think of God as an entity, does not believe we can articulate clear features possessed by God and does not believe God can be described in representational language. Hence Aquinas is not a theist.

One of the puzzles in this discussion is about the question whether God is independent or not. It seems that this question is ambiguous. If dependence means some lack or need or imperfection, then it is obvious that God is independent – one might think of this as ontological independence. However, if dependence is taken in a more epistemological sense, then thought about God is dependent on thought about the world. Thought about God only gets purchase through reflection on the cause and principle of what exists. So God is ontologically independent while epistemologically dependent (the latter, of course, saying nothing about God, but about knowledge of him). Theism can accept this distinction without qualm. But is theism committed to the view that God's ontological independence is as an independent *entity*? It is clear that some theists hold this view – but it does not necessarily follow for all theists. Theism is committed to the ontological independence of God, as stated above, but how this ontology is to be explained is an open question. That God is not an entity like any other, that divine simplicity demands a lack of distinction between essence and existence, is a specific kind of theism, namely Thomistic, which differs from other kinds, say, Scotistic theism. So to insist that theism must be committed to the view that God is a superpowerful entity is stipulative and generates a straw target. This is not to say that distinguishing Aquinas's theism from other forms is not important, but to infer from this that Aquinas is not a theist is too big a leap.

What about representational thought? It is clear that Aquinas holds that we do not know God's essence. Yet we do know that God exists. So to speak about God is to refer to something which we do not fully know. Indeed he thinks our knowledge of God is extremely slight, insofar as God's intelligibility exceeds human knowledge and we are as bats blinking in the sunlight [ST.1.1.5ad1]. Yet it is also clear that some things can be said – that God exists as the ultimate cause of things, what God is not and how God exceeds other things in perfection (involving the *triplex via* of causation, negation and eminence).[49] There is an indirect means of making statements about God, which Aquinas exploits and which Te Velde has carefully elucidated.

But Te Velde's account of how reference to God is possible is troubling where he seems to suggest that we both do and do not have concepts of God. While he argues that no concept captures God's essence, this is compatible with using concepts to indirectly approach God's essence, as in the *triplex via*. So concepts are of use in indirectly allowing reference to God. It seems that Te Velde thinks of 'description' and 'representation' as involving full and complete grasp of the object of thought, which is what he objects to. Yet, for example, the description 'the proof reader of this book' picks out and refers to an individual under a description, but leaves much more besides opaque. So descriptions do not fully describe. However, it may be that he thinks that descriptions are used of distinct individuals (entities), while this is not appropriate for God, who is not to be understood as an entity. I do not see why this follows. 'First cause', '*ipsum esse subsistens*' and 'God of Abraham, Isaac and Jacob' refer to the same reality, but partially and incompletely. They are referring phrases, and since they differ from each other in terms of intelligible content, it seems right to characterize them as being different descriptions, albeit incomplete descriptions. To insist that descriptions cannot be used in relation to God seems unwarranted, confusing full and partial descriptions. So the case that representational or descriptive language is not possible in relation to God is unproven. What is clear is that God remains mysterious, unlike anything else and never fully grasped by human intellect. Human efforts to talk and understand are conducted in language – which is exactly what theism attempts. Distinguishing between approaches to God which domesticate God and make the divinity into a superbeing is important, but to claim that no representation or description is possible is to overstate the case.

So these objections to reading Aquinas as a philosopher are useful in terms of clarifying his aims and methods, correct in replacing certain kinds of overrationalistic readings and important for a sensitive historical retrieval of his work. But they overstate the case against fruitfully bringing his work into the ongoing philosophical discussion. I now turn to the kind of objection which accepts Aquinas's philosophical credentials, but thinks he is simply mistaken.

1.4.2   Aquinas's philosophical approach is mistaken

(i)   The Kantian objection

Kant's influence has been profound in rendering unpalatable to many the kind of metaphysical philosophy seen in Aquinas. For a large swathe of 'post-Kantian Continental philosophers', it goes without saying that the kind of realism associated with Aquinas is naïve and pre-critical. Many theologians have also been influenced by this approach, thinking that Aquinas's approach to theology is too wedded to Greek metaphysics and has been superseded by more modern developments. However, there are reasons to doubt the broad consensus seen here. A first move is to comment on the tensions internal to Kant's position itself. It is not free from difficulty. A second is to look more closely at Kant's own approach to religious belief and theology, which seems to differ from the popular conception of his impact. Thirdly, one might note the way in which metaphysicians in the analytical tradition have felt free to do philosophy in a manner similar to Aquinas, unconstrained by the Kantian scruples many think effective against Aquinas. I shall discuss each point in turn.

The term 'transcendental' is very much associated with Kant, and for him the term is synonymous with the notion of a precondition.[50] If something is transcendental, it is a precondition for another thing. He argued that many of the features taken for granted as real features of the world are, in fact, supplied by the mind. That is, they are not there as part of how the world really is, but are preconditions of the process of knowing. A modern analogy often used to describe this is that of sunglasses which shade the world in a distinctive colour. The human mind supplies features of experience which yield the world as coloured in a certain way. What are these features? Kant argues that the notions of space and time are not 'out there' as part of the world.[51] That we understand space in terms of three dimensions, and can even add duration as a fourth dimension, is not necessarily how the world really is. For Kant, the world is not available as it really is in itself, and so it can only ever be experienced in space and time. Kant introduces a distinction between what he calls 'phenomena' and 'noumena' to make sense of this.[52] Phenomena are those things in the world as experienced, clothed in space and time, as it were. Noumena are those things as they really are in themselves. Humans postulate the existence of noumena, but can never really know them. There are features of the world other than space and time, which are also part of the human way of experiencing the world, but which are not part of the world in itself. Causation is supplied by the mind, but does not exist in the noumenal realm. So too is the idea of substance, the underlying stable basis of properties.[53] The upshot of this for metaphysics is profound. Traditional metaphysics seeks to articulate truths about the world as it really is in itself, in its most fundamental features. It supplies accounts of substance, causation, properties, universals etc. Kant has argued that such accounts are, at best, misleading. Rather than being of the basic features of reality, they are tracing the lines on the spectacles by which humans view the world.

Kant is challengeable on the intelligibility of this position. One argument is that the distinction between phenomenon and noumenon is not one that Kant can himself draw. On the one hand, he wants to say that we cannot say anything about how the world really is, and on the other hand, he wants to draw a distinction between appearance and reality, between phenomenon and noumenon. The very act of drawing this distinction is, in itself, a way of tracing the ultimate way the world is, of doing what Kant says is not possible. So his position denies that talking about the ultimate way the world is, is possible, and yet he has to talk about the ultimate way the world is to make his claim. Kant wanted to retain the notion of noumenon in order to keep hold of the idea of a reality independent of human construction. To drop this idea would be to hold an extreme form of idealism – where the mind creates everything. To accept the idea of noumenon, however, seems to accept the very possibility of doing metaphysics – to talk about how the world is in itself. The important lesson that can be learned from Kant is that one should be aware of what the mind adds to our picture of reality. However, it seems possible to accept this lesson and still think that one is giving a modest, fallible account of how reality actually is, including potentially saying something true about God in the process.

The second consideration is that Kant himself seems to allow space for discussions of God, religious language and the interaction of theoretical and practical reasons in ways which a hard-line reading of Kant's rejection of metaphysical theology cannot explain. There is not sufficient space here to develop this line of argument, but I am impressed by recent studies making this case.[54] Finally, one might note the renewal of robust realistic metaphysics within the analytical tradition and the combative assault on Kantian constructivist positions by a multiplicity of contemporary philosophers (Kant is discussed on 7 of the 724 pages of the recent *Oxford Handbook of Metaphysics*).[55] While many of these might well disagree with Aquinas on other grounds, it is not because of Kantian scruples. So there are reasons to doubt the compelling nature of the Kantian objection.

(ii)   The ontotheological objection

A more specific objection to classical theism is associated with the term 'ontotheology'. This has had wide influence in making theologians sceptical of attempts to give rational grounding to belief in God and has tended to support a Barthian fideistic approach to religious belief.[56] Despite the wide success of this objection, the actual substance of it can be quite obscure. The origin of the term lies with Kant, it has been popularized by Heidegger, and recently deployed by thinkers as varied as Jacques Derrida and Jean-Luc Marion.[57] There seem to be two core aspects to this position. The first is that attempts to rationally demonstrate the existence of God result in removing God from the realm of religion. God becomes a rational explanatory posit, like that of the eighteenth-century Deists. It is then claimed that such an intellectual construct is far removed from the God of genuine piety and religious sentiment. The second is that such approaches remove God's mystery.

God is domesticated, so to speak, and placed within a larger conceptual scheme, since the ontotheological philosopher has a system, with a place for God within that system. So while God might be construed as a supreme being, as very important indeed, this still places God within a context which just fails to be true to the awesome otherness of the deity. The work of Aquinas and other medieval philosopher-theologians is often cited as a prime example of such ontotheology.

The term itself seems associated by Kant with deism.[58] The deism which uses cosmological-type arguments is 'cosmotheology', and the deism which uses ontological arguments is 'ontotheology'. However, Kant thinks that typically those who use cosmological arguments covertly bring in the ontological argument to show that the first cause arrived at is really God, the most perfect being. So perhaps all forms of such deism are 'ontotheological'.

A first remark about this is that it seems to rely on a Kantian approach to knowledge and reality. There is a fundamental commitment to agnosticism about the deep nature of reality. While such a commitment may be justifiable, it is usually assumed rather than argued for by those who advance the ontotheological objection, just as it is also assumed by those who defend Barthian fideism. It is clear that a wide sweep of contemporary philosophers, unconnected to philosophy of religion, no longer accept this Kantian agnosticism and believe in the possibility of making claims about the fundamental nature of reality. So uncritical acceptance of Kant's worries about natural theology serve to make this objection more plausible than it might otherwise be.

Furthermore, it is clearly problematical to assimilate Aquinas's views to that of Deism. In his system, God is not a being, not even the most powerful being. God is understood as being itself, self-subsisting being. If Heidegger contends that the history of Western philosophy has involved the forgetting of being, it is hard to square that with Aquinas's insistence on distinguishing Being from beings.

As noted above, a deeply important aspect of Aquinas's account of God is that humans do not understand God's essence, that there is not a *ratio* about God. The reality of God is too great for us; it far exceeds our mental capacities. So God is not captured within a system, or made part of a greater whole. Aquinas constantly reiterates how God exceeds human cognitive capacities. Some things can be said about God which are indeed true, but many of these are negations, pointing out wrong ways of talking about God. For example, to say that God is eternal is to deny that God exists in time. Since humans live and think in time, it is hard to make sense of a kind of existence which is timeless. Yet something true is said when God is called eternal, despite the fact that the speaker has little grasp of the real content of it.

Thus, while Aquinas thinks that we can rationally manage to say some truths about God, there is an infinity more besides, which we fail to get. So in no sense is God reduced to an explanatory posit or to a supercog in a conceptual system. Yet are Aquinas's alleged truths merely about the God of the philosophers, while the God of Abraham, Isaac and Jacob completely eludes his grasp? A truism of medieval logic, reiterated forcefully by Frege in the nineteenth century, is that the very same object can be given quite different descriptions. Aquinas's claim is that the God yielded by natural theology is the very same God as that of revelation. Not everything we know about that God comes from reason (indeed comparatively little comes that way in Aquinas's view), yet his laconic 'And this we call God' which completes his arguments in ST 1.2.3, indicates that the reality made available by reason is also the reality known in religious tradition.

Obviously this ontotheological objection has no weight for naturalists or atheists, but it has inspired a great number of Christian thinkers to be sceptical of Aquinas's views. Accepting it as an objection requires a commitment to Kantian epistemology and characterizing Aquinas as a deist. While Aquinas is definitely not a deist, the cogency of Kantian epistemology is a genuinely open issue in contemporary epistemology and metaphysics. To side with Aquinas in this is also, as noted above, to side with many contemporary metaphysicians, most of whom cannot be accused of special pleading for religious purposes.

(iii)   The Wittgensteinian objection

Wittgenstein wrote little about religious belief in his major works, and what he did write was scattered through various notes, conversations and lecture reports, many of them redacted by friends and students. He mentions God four times in the *Tractatus Logico-Philosophicus*, but seems to equate 'God' with the meaning of life rather than anything specifically connected to theistic belief.[59] In conversations with his friends he reveals the importance of religious issues in his personal life. He read the New Testament, Søren Kierkegaard and Augustine assiduously – indeed he got rid of his personal fortune after reading the parable of the rich young man whilst a soldier, in 1916. He regarded religious issues as supremely important but also as personal and subjective, and had little truck with dogma or religious affiliation. While he persuaded his friend Drury not to be ordained an Anglican priest, he also suggested he attend mass daily to see its effect on his mood. He reported that he was glad to be made go to church whilst a prisoner of war in Italy, briefly considered becoming a monk and professed to Norman Malcolm that he saw everything from a religious point of view. Yet the bulk of his writing has to do with logic and language, mathematics and psychology, and his name is associated with distinctive and revolutionary views in the philosophy of these areas.

Despite the paucity of his written work on it, he has had a significant impact on philosophy of religion, not least in suggesting that the kind of work done by philosophical theologians is deeply mistaken and indeed superstitious rather than genuinely religious.[60] The position most associated with his work has been labelled Wittgensteinian Fideism by Kai Nielsen, an atheistic critic of it. Whether Wittgenstein actually was a fideist is controversial, but his work has been developed by Welsh philosophers, including D.Z. Phillips and Rush Rhees, in that direction. The basic idea is that Wittgenstein's famous notions of language game and form of life can be applied to the phenomenon of religion. A language game is a mix of action and linguistic usage associated with a certain way of living. Language games are autonomous and establish their own rules – it is a conceptual error to critique one language game using the criteria of a different game. Thus, to challenge the language game of religion using the criteria of science, for example, is an example of such an error.

Objections to this approach include the worry that 'religion' is too huge a phenomenon to be adequately described as a language game. Wittgenstein's own examples of language games are very small scale – for example, builders with four words or tribes using counting words. Rather than being a general theory of language use, Wittgenstein uses the twin notions of language game and form of life to draw attention in specific instances to how language is actually used and to disabuse one of mythologies or fixed ideas about how it ought to work. To generate a position like 'Wittgensteinian Fideism' is too constructive and too much like traditional philosophy to fit well with Wittgenstein's approach.

Nevertheless, Wittgenstein does make certain claims which fit well with such a view. He thinks that religious belief cannot have a rational justification, and is rather better understood as something like a passionate commitment to a frame of reference. As one uses certain kinds of language (say talk about the Last Judgement), it provides a means of representation for making sense of the world and one's life. It does not rest on anything more fundamental and any attempt to provide such a justification is a kind of superstition. Thus he thinks that natural theology of the kind produced by Anselm or Aquinas is just mistaken, and is scathing about philosophers such as Copleston or a certain Fr O'Hara, who attempt to show the reasonableness of Christian belief. Such an attitude has been quite influential. Here is Robert Arrington:

> With regard to religious discourse, the philosophers themselves, or at least Anselm and Aquinas, would be held responsible by Wittgenstein for much of the confusion that surrounds the question of the existence of God. These 'metaphysical' theologians would be guilty in his eyes of the same confusion he attributes to metaphysicians in general, namely that of confusing conceptual and factual inquiries...such philosophizing is a perfect example of a confusion of the grammatical and factual realms.[61]

Wittgenstein held that metaphysics was generated by mistaking choices about a system of representation for a factual question – rather like wondering whether a certain distance was really five miles or eight kilometres. The distance is factual, but the difference between five and eight units of measurement is conceptual and not determined by the factual element. Metaphysics consists of instances of such confusions.

Wittgensteinians try to impress on their opponents the obviousness and truistic nature of their views, and counsel a 'just look' approach, rather than advance countervailing philosophical theses. This facet of Wittgenstein's approach has had little impact in the practice of contemporary philosophies of language, logic, mathematics and mind, and in my opinion it should have little in philosophy of religion either. The distinction between conceptual and factual discourse is not a simple, naïve or neutral one. It connects to debates about the epistemological distinction between a posteriori and a priori beliefs (between beliefs justified with and without experiential input) and debates about the semantic distinction between analytic and synthetic propositions (between ones which are true by virtue of meaning and those true by virtue of the world). How Wittgenstein's views relate to these debates is complex, as is the question whether he espoused epistemological conventionalism (that we are free to choose whatever system of representation we wish, including logic and maths) and how his focus on the natural history of humanity might curb the wildly counter-intuitive freedom his position seems to advocate. These are issues which I will examine more closely in Chapter 5 below. Furthermore, while some of Wittgenstein's oracular utterances are acute and provoke further thought, some seem just daft and should be dismissed, even if Wittgenstein happened to say them (for example 'if Christianity is the truth then all the philosophy that is written about it is false', Wittgenstein [1980] p.83). The upshot is that it is by no means obvious that the kind of philosophy of religion articulated by Aquinas has been shown to be incoherent (*pace* Arrington), and indeed writers such as Kenny and Herbert McCabe have shown fascinating points of convergence between the two.[62]

Conclusion

This chapter has sought to motivate an examination of Aquinas's work by pointing to the perennial interest in the kinds of topics he explored, the value of the approach of philosophy of religion and a characterization of his work as contributing to an ongoing debate in philosophy of religion. The final section broached important kinds of objections to viewing his work in this way and attempted to show that the objections are less powerful than they have been taken to be. So where to now?

In the next chapter I wish to supply some context to Aquinas's work to allow an adequate interpretation of it to emerge. It has to be understood in the intellectual context of the mid-thirteenth century – so I wish to discuss some of the main streams of thought influencing Aquinas, examine the development of his own thought and then focus on a number of key themes which serve as structural principles in his work. In Chapter 3, I shall discuss his views on faith and reason, contrasting them with different approaches and suggesting ways in which his views on reason might be adjusted. Chapter 4 examines the chief arguments advanced to show that God exists and situates them in relation to the contemporary discussion, while Chapter 5 looks at his treatment of two key objections to theistic belief – the problem of evil and science rendering religious belief redundant. Chapter 6 looks at the way of characterizing what God is like using the way of negation, while Chapter 7 explores the way of eminence, further trying to clarify talk about God.

2
Aquinas's Contexts

Given the intellectual distance between Aquinas and the present, I want to approach Aquinas via a sequence of ever-narrowing contexts. Starting at the broadest level, I want to look at the general intellectual context of the thirteenth century, discussing the environment in which Aquinas wrote and examining the influences on him. After a brief biographical sketch, I shall then survey his writings, noting their genres and issues about interpretation. Finally, I wish to present three structural principles which pervade his work and which require clarification, before moving on to specific issues in philosophy of religion in the following chapters.

2.1 Intellectual context

Born at the end of the first quarter of the thirteenth century in Italy, Aquinas entered a world where large-scale conflicts marked Christendom from within and without.[1] Europe was Christian throughout, and political, social and religious identities were closely entwined, but tension existed at the top of this edifice between the Pope and the Holy Roman Emperor for political dominance. Aquinas's own family was caught up in these disputes, with his early education affected by political instability. A schism existed between the Eastern Church based at Constantinople and the Rome-based Western Church, while wars were waged between Christians and Moslems. New religious movements preaching reform and critical of institutional religion regularly sprang up and were ruthlessly put down as a threat to social stability. While the masses were illiterate, a thriving intellectual culture came to fruition with the founding of the universities in the two decades before Aquinas's birth.

In the eight hundred years between Augustine (354–430) and Aquinas (1225–1274), Neoplatonism was the dominant form of philosophy. This later Greek (Hellenistic) school of philosophy sought to systematize and unify the work of Plato and Aristotle, with a definitely Platonic emphasis. Among the reasons for its dominance was the fact that most of the works of Aristotle were not available in Western Europe up to the twelfth century. Plato's school, the Academy in Athens, was closed by the Christian Emperor Justinian in 529, and the scholars took the Aristotelian texts eastwards with them, eventually to Persia, where they were later absorbed into the new Islamic culture of the seventh century. Great Islamic thinkers such as Al Farabi (c. 870–950), Al Kindi (801–873), Ibn Sina (Avicenna) (980–1037) and Ibn Rushd (Averroes) (1126–1198) were to develop an approach to Aristotelian scholarship which was deeply influenced by Neoplatonism. Mathematics, medicine, astronomy and philosophy flourished under Islamic rule, and voluminous commentaries on Aristotle's works were made. None of this was available to Western Europe until the twelfth century, when Christians, Jews and Arabs began to exchange and translate texts in Spain. By the beginning of the thirteenth century, a flood of Aristotelian scholarship came to the West and constituted a rival way of doing philosophy to the more traditional Neoplatonic approach.

In the early Middle Ages in the West the only centres of learning were monasteries. Monastic learning was conservative, in the literal sense, in that it eschewed novelty and attempted to conserve the glories of the past. Rhetorical and literary studies, scriptural studies and patristic studies flourished in this environment, but it was not particularly conducive to philosophical development. By the eleventh century, a number of changes were in evidence. With the growth of cities, society was beginning to change. Often a city would develop around an ecclesiastical centre – particularly one where there was a powerful or influential bishop. Schools, built up to service the cathedrals, were an educational innovation. The liberal arts (rhetoric, grammar, logic, astronomy, geometry, arithmetic and music) were taught as the basis for further studies in theology. The court of Charlemagne (742–810) had begun to foster this kind of education in the ninth century.

However, by the beginning of the twelfth century, philosophy was beginning to have an impact, again, on theology. Anselm of Canterbury (1033–1109), a Benedictine monk, articulated the intellectual method of the High Middle Ages in the motto "Faith Seeking Understanding" (*Fides Quaerens Intellectum*). The starting place for inquiry was a firm commitment to inherited religious belief, but that was compatible with a lively intellectual probing of that belief. In the middle of the twelfth century, the logical works of Aristotle stimulated logicians such as Peter Abelard (1079–1142) to develop a new approach to theology. Instead of the rather meditative approach of the Christian Neoplatonists, this theology was more systematic and hard headed. It revelled in distinctions and arguments, and it staked out and defended clear positions. It also met with great resistance. The founder of the Cistercians, Bernard of Clairvaux (1090–1153), pursued Abelard through various Church councils, condemning this approach. However, the tide was inexorable. By the start of the thirteenth century there were flourishing schools of logic in many different places. The teachers in Paris banded together to form a corporation, establishing qualifications, courses and structures. This was to be the start of the university there. Subsequently, in the thirteenth century universities flourished at Oxford, Bologna and Montpellier among other places. However, the University of Paris had pre-eminence for philosophy and theology.

The University of Paris had Arts as its basic faculty, and as the century advanced, the course in the Arts faculty came to be nearly completely Aristotelian. The influx of Aristotelian texts, newly translated into Latin, seized the imagination of the thirteenth-century scholars. Logic, physics, ethics, metaphysics and biology were all investigated using Aristotle's texts. The higher faculties were Law, Medicine and Theology, and Bologna, Montpellier and Paris were eminent in each of these respectively. Despite the enthusiasm for Aristotle in the Arts faculty, the Parisian theologians were still very much under the influence of an Augustinian style of theology and were very wary indeed of the Aristotelian influx. They were worried for a number of reasons. Aristotelian thought seemed secular and to be incompatible with Christianity in some respects. For example, it appeared to defend the eternity of the world, the lack of personal immortality and a view of a God who was remarkably uninterested in anything other than the divine self.

Hence, in the latter part of the thirteenth century, there were great intellectual battles over the role of Aristotelian philosophy in the university. An old guard attempted to keep it out, while a new guard tried to show how it might cohere with Christian teaching. A further complication was an active group of philosophers in the Arts faculty, variously labelled 'radical Aristotelians' or 'Latin Averroists', who defended a strongly rationalistic reading of Aristotle. Fear of this group was what largely motivated the anti-Aristotelianism of the Theology faculty.

Looking at the sources of Aquinas's thought, one has first of all to acknowledge the pre-eminence of Christian revelation, with the commentaries on this by early Christian theologians. This was the fundamental world view from which all his philosophical work flowed. However, his understanding, development and defence of that world view were deeply influenced by different philosophical currents. I have mentioned above the historical interweaving of Neoplatonism and Aristotelianism in the centuries prior to Aquinas's work, and here I wish to discuss them in terms of their differences in approach.

Neoplatonism is usually held to have begun with the Egyptian philosopher Plotinus (200–270) (we have no record of the work of Ammonius Saccas, his teacher). His writings were edited by his student Porphyry, and put together in six collections of nine treatises, called the *Enneads*. This work articulated a philosophy in which the physical world is the lowest level of reality, on the verge on non-existence, with non-physical levels arranged hierarchically above that. The goal of the philosopher, through a process of rigorous moral and intellectual purification, was to raise his mind to attempt to pierce the higher realms, ultimately seeking union with the source of all reality, known to Plotinus as 'The One'. Porphyry reports that Plotinus experienced such union on a few occasions during his life – a union which transcended intellectual knowledge, but which could only be achieved through the mental discipline of philosophical study. The One was beyond all description and categories – it could not even be placed in the realm of being, since that would be to limit it in our conceptual framework. While this philosophy has obviously religious aspects, Plotinus had no truck with religious ritual or prayer, which he regarded as useless. The path to union was through philosophy.

Augustine (354–430) was introduced to the writings of Neoplatonists in Milan. His own intellectual development was complex, as he relates in the *Confessions* – from early lukewarm Christianity he moved to Manichaeism (a new religious movement with roots in Persia which advocated a strong dualism between body and spirit). Abandoning this, he embraced scepticism, which counselled a rejection of all such views as the path to happiness. Drawn back to Christianity, he found both intellectual and moral difficulties in accepting a Christian form of life. Neoplatonism was to provide him with an intellectual scheme in which he could resolve his doubts. On overcoming his moral hesitation and endorsing Christianity, Augustine was to bring together the Greek discussion of being with the God spoken of in Christian scripture. He believed that an important text from Exodus, where God spoke from the burning bush and called himself 'I am', signalled the connection between theistic belief and the Greek discussion of being [*Exodus* 3.14].

Augustine's adaptation of Platonic philosophy, with a hierarchical conception of reality, a theory of knowledge which requires God's active illumination of the human mind and a dualistic view of the relation of soul to body, were profoundly influential on subsequent Christian thought.

Yet, another Neoplatonist thinker was to have a deep impact on Aquinas, for odd reasons. A Syrian of the sixth century wrote a number of books which came to be attributed to a certain Dionysius the Areopagite, a philosopher supposedly converted by St Paul in Acts 17. Given the quasi-biblical authority of such a figure, his work was treated with great seriousness. As the real story of the authorship emerged, modern scholars came to call him Pseudo-Dionysius the Areopagite, or Denys the Areopagite. Two key ideas of his deeply influenced Aquinas. The first is the Neoplatonic emphasis on a hierarchical ordering of reality, which he also got from Augustine. The One is God, Platonic ideas become God's ideas, intelligences become angels. Humans are metaphysical amphibians, partly in the realm of mind and partly in the realm of matter, but finding their place in the hierarchy. The other idea played an important structural role on Aquinas's thought – how to name God. Denys emphasized the way in which God transcends our cognitive capacities. He elaborated a triple way (*triplex via*) of having knowledge of God. Firstly, one affirms God as cause – this is the basic relation of God to creation (the way of causation *via causationis*). Then one shows the difference between God and everything else, denying many features of creation in God (the way of negation, *via negationis*). Finally there is the way of showing how some features of the world exist in God in a supreme way (the way of eminence, *via eminentionis*). This means of approach helped Aquinas structure his own work, as we shall see below.

Given his rootedness in the Neoplatonic world of Augustine and Denys the Areopagite, there is also the great importance of Aristotle along with the Arab and Jewish commentators of that tradition. While Neoplatonists wanted to harmonize Plato and Aristotle, many historians of philosophy see a deep difference in mindset between them. The stereotypical differences are that while Plato is mystical, religious, idealistic and otherworldly, Aristotle is hard headed, rationalistic, scientific minded and this-worldly. While scholars dispute this characterization, there is some truth to it, and it is certainly how it seemed to Aquinas's contemporaries. Aristotle developed treatises on meaning and logic, physics, meteorology, biology, psychology, ethics and politics and metaphysics, or theology, as he called it himself. So encyclopedic was his knowledge that Dante Alighieri referred to him as 'the master of those who know'.[2] In his method there is a constant start in observation, in gathering agreed data about the world, followed by a move to analyse this in terms of underlying structure.

Aristotle talked about God, but his God was a rational posit with no religious dimension – God had no interest in what happens in the world, and prayer to such an entity was useless. The physical world coexisted with God from all eternity, which clashed dramatically with theistic views on creation. On death there was no personal immortality, which clashed with theistic views on afterlife. It was little wonder that Neoplatonic-inspired theology would react negatively to Aristotle. Furthermore, Aristotle was mediated through Islamic thinkers who developed his work in different ways. Avicenna used some of Aristotle's ideas to think about God and develop an argument for God's existence using ideas of necessity and existence, which was to influence deeply Aquinas's own thought on this. Averroes wrote lengthy technical commentaries on Aristotle which shaped how Aristotle had been received in the West. His views on mind, which resolutely opposed personal immortality, and on the relation of philosophy to revealed theology (the former superior to the latter, which was for those incapable of abstract thought) provoked as much hostility among Islamic theologians as among Christians. One of Aquinas's tasks was to argue painstakingly that Averroes's view of Aristotle was mistaken, embarking on his own lengthy project of commenting on Aristotle's work. What was unusual about this task was that it would have been a job for a teacher in the Arts faculty, but Aquinas worked in the Theology faculty of the University of Paris at the time. Many scholars note this as evidence for Aquinas's commitment to the importance of philosophy. The project, which remained incomplete at his death, was undertaken while writing his incomplete major work, the *Summa Theologiae*. Nineteenth and early twentieth-century scholarship tended to ignore the Neoplatonic strands at the expense of Aristotelian rationalism, while recent work seeks to attempt to get the balance right between these two aspects.

A final influence who should be mentioned is the Jewish philosopher Moses Maimonides (1138–1204). Writing in Spain, his main work is the *Dux Dubitorum*, or *Guide for the Perplexed*, which is best known for a resolutely negative approach to God. Maimonides denies that anything positive can be attributed to God, but we can go a long way using the method of negation. While Aquinas ultimately rejected the strict line advocated by Maimonides, there is a strong apophatic dimension to Aquinas's work – he consistently notes that our knowledge is limited and defective.

2.2   Biographical context

Aquinas was born in a village called Roccasecca, north of Naples, south of Rome, around 1225.[3] His family was noble, and at an early age Aquinas was sent to the nearby Benedictine monastery of Monte Cassino for education. His status was that of an 'oblate'. It was probably hoped in his family that he would become a Benedictine monk and thus secure an alliance between the Aquino family and the powerful and wealthy monastery. However, history intervened. Political unrest led Aquinas's family to move him to the newly founded University of Naples to continue his education. As noted above, an uneasy relationship existed between the Pope and the Holy Roman Emperor. In Aquinas's youth, the emperor was the German Frederick II (1194–1250), who was engaged in a power struggle with the papacy. He had set up the University of Naples, and the Arts Faculty there was strongly influenced by Averroistic readings of Aristotle. One characteristic of such an approach was that it was very much text based, and so provided students with a very detailed knowledge of Aristotle's works. Whilst in Naples, Aquinas came in contact with the newly founded Dominican order. It had been established in 1216 in the south of France as a group of itinerant preachers, and like its contemporary organization, the Franciscans, proved very successful. The Dominicans were especially dedicated to preaching, study and poverty, and this proved attractive to Aquinas. However, his family was horrified. They had envisaged a distinguished ecclesiastical career for him, and instead he was heading off with what would have been regarded as dubious vagabonds, hardly distinguishable from the myriad heretical bands of the era. So family members kidnapped him in an attempt to get him to see sense. Enduring a year of house arrest, Aquinas finally convinced them that his resolve would not be broken, and so was sent to Paris around 1246.

The Dominicans had attached themselves to the universities and, especially at Paris, had attracted into their number many of the leading teachers at the university. One of these was Albert the Great (1206–1280; Latin: *Albertus Magnus*), a German. He took on Aquinas as his student, and brought him to Cologne where he was charged with setting up a new *Studium* (house of studies) for the order. Albert was a champion of Aristotle, and he continued the work, begun in Naples, of inducting Aquinas into Aristotelian philosophy. Aquinas returned to Paris in 1252 to study for the Mastership in Theology, which was the highest award of the university. He lectured on biblical texts and on Peter Lombard's *Sentences*, the main textbook of medieval theology. He was made Master of Theology in 1256, in acrimonious circumstances. This degree was, in effect, a license to be a teacher, and the Dominicans were anxious to train as many of their members as possible in this fashion. There were a limited number of places for masters available in the university, and the new mendicant (begging) orders – Franciscan and Dominicans – operated a closed shop on the teaching positions they controlled. This led to great resentment in the university at large, as a result of which Aquinas's inaugural lecture in 1256 was held under the protection of archers who maintained the fragile peace of the university, which was liable to break into violence. Aquinas taught for three years at Paris and was then requested to travel to Italy, where he resided for the next ten years, at different places, but mainly Orvieto and Rome. He was charged with helping set up some internal Dominican theological houses of study and also wrote his major works, the great *Summa*'s. In 1269 he was recalled to Paris.

This was a most unusual move. Since the Dominicans wanted to qualify as many masters as possible from Paris, why invite back someone who was already conferred with the degree? The main reason was that the mendicant orders were under threat from secular masters at the university, and Aquinas was recruited to fight for the Dominicans (the secular masters were clerics who were not members of religious orders). However, there was also a great intellectual crisis taking place in the university. The rise of Radical Aristotelianism had provoked a strong reaction in the Theology faculty. Aristotle was regarded with deep suspicion. Moves were even afoot to ban the use of Aristotle in the university, and Aquinas engaged in defending the use of Aristotle. He fought on two fronts. Against the radical Aristotelians he presented what he regarded as a correct interpretation of Aristotle. Against the conservative theologians he defended what he regarded as the truth and validity of the Aristotelian approach. To do this he embarked on a sequence of commentaries on Aristotle's works. At this time he also continued to work on his masterwork, the *Summa Theologiae*, and returned to Italy in 1272, teaching in Naples.

Aquinas is represented in art as a large presence. He was very heavy and also notoriously silent. Yet he walked everywhere (as set down by the rules of his order: Naples – Paris – Cologne – Rome). He also wrote copiously. His memory was prodigious. But in late 1273 something happened to him. He was saying mass and reported to his friend, Reginald, that he had seen something astounding. The pious reading of this is that he had a mystical experience, while the more secular reading is that he had a stroke. Whatever the cause, he fell into ill health and never wrote again. In the spring of 1274, however, he took to the road one last time to go to Lyons, where a Church council was being held, exactly on the issue of the use of Aristotle. Aquinas went to defend the legitimacy of Aristotle. His former teacher and ally, Albertus Magnus, then in his mid-seventies, also took to the road to support his greatest student. However, Aquinas never made it. In March 1274, he took ill on the way to Lyons and died in the Cistercian monastery of Fossanova.

The Arts Faculty of the University of Paris requested his body, such was the regard in which he was held. After his death, his work was defended by the Dominican Order (and was subjected to much attack by the Franciscans). Two condemnations were issued by the Archbishop of Paris (in 1270 and 1277) of views advanced by the radical Aristotelians and held to be heterodox. Some views held by Aquinas were included in the reproof, although when he was canonized some 50 years later his views were taken as acceptable. The complex world of late medieval philosophy is characterized by savage debate among rival schools. The Thomists were mostly Dominicans, opposed by followers of Duns Scotus (Scotists) and William of Ockham (Ockhamists). The point being made here is that Aquinas was by no means universally regarded as being correct in his views and was robustly attacked by subsequent genera-tions of medieval thinkers. Yet in the intervening centuries he has come to be seen as one of the greatest medieval thinkers, famously influencing Dante (1265–1321), as well as numerous later philosophers.

2.3   Works

Aquinas's writings are characterized by a distinctive style, which usually reflects the practices of the medieval university. The two main forms of instruction were lecturing and disputation. To lecture, as the etymology suggests, is to read some other text and comment on it. Aquinas's main responsibility as a master of theology was to comment on the Bible, and he produced specific commentaries on several books. After the Bible, the main text for theological study was the *Sentences* of Peter Lombard (1155), and as an apprentice master in theology, Aquinas wrote his lengthy *Commentary on the Sentences*. The *Sentences* itself was a system-atization of the teaching of patristic theologians. In his commentary, Aquinas discusses themes and questions arising from the text, which will recur and receive developed treatments in his subsequent works.

The *quaestio* is a genre which arises from the practice of disputation. A disputation involves treatment of a specific issue, with examination of arguments for and against. Typically, it was an exercise in which graduate students tested their argumentative skills, pitting arguments against each other, with the debate moderated by a master. However professors of the university engaged in disputed questions on specific topics, which were then written up (for example, Aquinas conducted disputed questions on Truth, Evil, the Virtues, the Soul). There were also quodlibetal questions, where the professors allowed questions from the audience, which they treated extempore, in open debate. Aquinas seems to have relished this and used whatever opportunities for quodlibetal debate offered themselves (such debates occurred twice a year and were a festival occasion). When these were written up, they included a miscellany of issues, not necessarily thematically linked. The dialectical discipline of disputation marked Aquinas's writings profoundly. He frequently follows the disputational style of argument, starting with counterarguments to his own preferred position, citing authorities for his view, articulating his own argument and then responding to the counterarguments. In his published disputed questions, the to and fro of argumentation is quite complex and dense, with nested series of arguments and responses embedded in a single question. His great *Summas* do not exactly follow that genre, but the *Summa Theologiae* can be regarded as having a modified and simplified structure deriving from it.

It is difficult to put exact dates on Aquinas's writings. However, the general chronology is clear. In the period when he was graduate student and then a master at Paris (1252–1259), he wrote the *Commentary on the Sentences*, the *Disputed Questions on Truth*, about half his *Quodlibetal Questions*, various Biblical commentaries and two short treatises, *On Being and Essence* and *On the Principles of Nature*. These last two are of special philosophical interest, insofar as they set out his interpretation of key issues in Aristotelian philosophy, influenced by Avicenna's reading of it. Tradition suggests he was requested to do so by his Dominican confreres (although this is rejected by scholars). Much of his writing was either occasioned by demands of teaching or requested by his colleagues for clarificatory purpose, although there is also his massive project of commenting on Aristotle, which seems to have been inspired by a desire to understand Aristotle better.

In the period 1260–1265, he worked in different Italian cities teaching young Dominicans and wrote the *Summa Contra Gentiles,* begun in Paris. The work is divided into four books. The first deals with God; the second deals with creation; the third deals with providence and morality; and the fourth deals with salvation, and so is specifically Christian. Hence, in the end, it does use resources from scripture and tradition. A recent scholar has stated that

Aquinas's ambitious project in *Summa Contra Gentiles* Books I–III is the most fully accomplished and most promising natural theology I know of.[4]

As noted, tradition held that it was written for Dominicans engaging with Moslems, and so mostly appealed to philosophical argument, instead of scripture. Recent scholarship has challenged this view, and suggests it shows Aquinas reflecting on the rational presuppositions and intellectual structure of his faith.

In 1265, Aquinas was called from Orvieto to Rome to establish an advanced house of study for Dominicans, which seems to have been set up especially for him. There he began his *chef oeuvre*, the *Summa Theologiae*. The motivation for the work was to clarify, simplify and rationalize the course of study. The students he taught would have completed studies in the Arts faculty and been familiar with Aristotelian and Biblical thought; hence, the puzzling opening of that work, where it speaks of being directed at beginners in theology. Such beginners were graduate students working in a higher faculty and already immersed in an intellectual culture – and it explains the feelings of disorientation and puzzlement many a modern 'beginner' has experienced on attempting to read the text.[5]

This work is unfinished. Begun in Rome, it was continued while Aquinas was in his second residency at the University of Paris. The *Summa Theologiae* is divided into three parts. The first part (*Prima Pars*) deals with God and creation. Included in this are discussions of the nature of theology, the existence of God, God's nature, the Trinity, creation in general, angels, humanity and providence. The second part is divided in two. The first part of the second part (*Prima Secundae*) deals with general theoretical issues in ethics. It examines the goal of human life, happiness, and then examines the nature of human action, for example, how do will and intellect interact in human activity and what is the nature of human emotion? He then discusses the nature of dispositions, or habits, followed by a discussion of good habits, or virtues. Finally, Aquinas discusses grace, which is an integral part of the moral life, on his account. The second part of the second part (*Secunda Secundae*) deals in more detail with specific virtues, including the theological virtues faith, hope and charity and also with states of life. The third part (*Tertia Pars*) deals with specifically religious themes such as the Incarnation, the sacraments and the life of Christ. There is a specific system of abbreviation for references to the *Summa Theologiae*. The *Prima Pars* is usually designated S.T.Ia, the *Prima Secundae* is S.T. I-IIae, the *Secunda Secundae* is II-IIae, whilst the *Tertia Pars* is S.T. IIIa. Then the question number is given, followed by the article within the question. So Aquinas discusses the issue of whether law is always related to the common good in the *Prima Secundae*, question 90, article 2. This is referred to as S.T. I-IIae, q.90, a.2.

The overall structure of the *Summa Theologiae* is often presented as reflecting a pattern of outflow from God and return to God. This is held to be a Neoplatonic theme, and is expressed in Latin as *exitus-reditus* (going out and return). It begins with God's existence and nature, moves to creation, then moves to the life appropriate to human union with God and finishes with the means to achieve that. Whether this schema accurately captures the structure has been recently challenged.[6] As mentioned above, Aquinas never completed the work, and so the *Tertia Pars* is incomplete.

While Aquinas was teaching for his second period in Paris (1269–1272), he embarked on a series of commentaries on Aristotle's works. This was unusual for a Master of Theology. It would normally have been the work of a Master of Arts, which was regarded as a lower faculty. However, Aquinas was convinced that a proper understanding of Aristotle was vital to the correct development of theology, so he produced detailed commentaries on 13 of Aristotle's works. He also wrote two important polemical works. *On the Unity of the Intellect against the Averroists* interprets Aristotle's difficult *De Anima* in such a way as to show it compatible with Christian views on a personal afterlife. It seeks both to give an accurate reading of Aristotle and to offer substantive rebuttals of Averroistic denials of the possibility of personal immortality. *On the Eternity of the World* is very interesting in that it controversially maintained that it was not possible to show rationally that the world had a beginning in time. Aquinas, of course, believed that God created the world and time with it, but did so for religious reasons, drawn from scripture. Unlike many of his contemporaries, he maintained that the arguments which sought to prove this philosophically were defective – as were the ones which sought to disprove it. Either option is rationally possible. This text shows the importance Aquinas attached to intellectual honesty and the importance of clarifying the exact intellectual status of one's beliefs. It would have been convenient to have such an argument – but Aquinas believed such was not possible and it was important to highlight this.

Aquinas's written output was prodigious. Dead probably before 50, he had written a vast corpus – the *Summa Theologiae* alone is over two million words. Given that he presupposed a certain familiarity in his readers with Aristotelian modes of thought, in the final section of this chapter I wish to discuss three key structural features which recur through all his treatments of diverse issues, including God's existence and nature.

2.4   The conceptual scheme

Aquinas's work is remarkably systematic, in that a small number of structural principles constituting a basic conceptual scheme are used with great ingenuity to investigate and clarify a wide range of diverse issues. These principles find their origin in Aristotle's work, but are developed beyond the bounds of the Aristotelian world view. Aquinas assumed familiarity with such principles in his readers, as they pervade his works. He wrote two short pedagogical treatises – *On the Principles of Nature* and *On Being and Essence* – to expound these views. I shall focus here on three distinctions which constitute in turn a theory of explanation, a theory of change and a theory of things respectively. These are the matter/form, potency/act and essence/existence distinctions. They appear throughout his work, and a grasp of them is required before advancing into specific issues in his work. Nowadays we are perhaps more accustomed to think of our basic theories in terms of natural science – looking for the fundamental particles making up reality, or perhaps a grand unified theory. For Aquinas, a metaphysical account of reality is even more fundamental than a scientific one – looking at questions about identity, change, causation and universals. Even if one holds to a physicalistic view of reality (i.e. holding that what ultimately exists is what is expressed in our physical theories), this is a metaphysical theory, answering questions which are not scientific in nature, that is, which are not to be answered by appeal to empirical observation. Hence his conceptual framework provides tools with which he will analyse both the physical world about us and also the non-physical world, which he regards as more real than the world evident to the senses.

2.4.1   A theory of explanation

A theory of explanation sets out the conditions and features of any adequate explanation. One can ask a multitude of questions – think of a toddler's insistent use of 'why?' – but only some questions seek genuine explanations for things in our experience. Aquinas held that exploring the causes of a thing is the key to understanding it; hence, his theory of explanation can be classified as a causal theory. However, his understanding of the notion of 'cause' is wider than the typical modern use of the term. Following Aristotle, he distinguishes four kinds of cause. One of these, the efficient cause, is closest to the modern notion of cause, being a maker or an agent. The efficient cause of the chair is the carpenter, and the efficient cause of the lamb is its parents. Yet merely to identify the efficient cause leaves out a lot of other explanatorily important material. Anything we come across has a structure, a distinctive way of being. This is so for things such as chairs or lambs, but also so for features of things such as colour, temperature or texture. Aquinas calls this structural aspect of things 'form', and form is also understood as a kind of cause. In material things form is always instantiated in something – the form of lamb in this bundle of flesh and blood is different to the form of puppy in that bundle of flesh and blood (simplifying for a moment by speaking of physical things). That in which form is instantiated is also considered a cause, called the material cause. Finally, the purpose of a structure, for example, the pumping action of the heart, is also a cause, called the final cause. Taken together, these four causes constitute an integrated theory of explanation. While Aristotle first articulated these distinctions in his *Physics*, Arabic philosophers, especially Averroes in his Aristotelian commentaries, explored and developed them.

Aquinas investigated the relations between such causes, distinguishing intrinsic from extrinsic causes, and the kinds of priority they might have to each other. Material and formal causes were held to be intrinsic, while efficient causation and final causation are extrinsic – because matter and form are inner and constitutive, not requiring a relationship to anything else to exist, whereas efficient and final causation are external. The efficient cause is the maker, while the final cause is a goal – both extrinsic features. A cause is prior to its effect in an explanatory sense – for example, the hot drink scalds my tongue; it is not my scalded tongue which makes the drink hot. Thus there is a direction to causal explanation, or an asymmetry between cause and effect. Yet the relation of cause to effect is subtle – things can be both cause and effect of each other, but in different respects, that is, relative to different kinds of causation. Efficient causes *produce* goals, but goals *direct* efficient causes. For example, a doctor helps bring about health in her patients, but the goal of health directs the activity of the doctor. Each is cause and effect, but relative to different kinds of causation. Hence simple causal priority operates in a single notion of cause (an efficient cause is always prior to its effect), but priority may be more complex across different kinds of causes (an efficient cause may be prior to a final cause in one sense, but the final can be prior in another). This is because one can distinguish between priority in time and priority in being. Causes can be related in both these ways. That is, children precede adults in time, but a grown adult is a more developed organism than a child. So the child exemplifies priority in time, but the adult priority in being. Applying this distinction to matter and form, matter precedes form in time, in that the form is received in matter, but form precedes matter in being (that is, in existence, or instantiation). Similarly with efficient and final causation, efficient causation precedes the goal in time, but the goal, which governs which action is taken, precedes the efficient in being.

Aquinas thinks that the final cause has a certain kind of overall priority. It is what directs the causation of the efficient and formal causes. The final cause of a cat is its flourishing as an organism. Its efficient cause (its parents' reproductive activity) is directed to this end, and its formal cause (all its feline characteristics and organs) is also shaped by this. Hence the end has an explanatory function even in relation to formal and efficient causation. While these roles are conceptually distinct, they may coincide at times in an individual. Aquinas's example is that the final cause of fire is to spread itself, and this coincides with the formal cause (its fieriness) and the efficient cause (which is that fieriness transmitting to another). Aquinas also talks of incidental and inherent causes. The teacher who drives the car and knocks me down causes me injury. However, her causing me injury is inherently due to being a driver, but only incidentally due to being a teacher. Nevertheless, there is a sense in which the teacher caused me injury, but only incidentally. Causes also operate in chains. The more specified the cause is, the more proximate it is. The less specified, the more remote. What caused the accident? One can reply *this* person, or a human being, or a living creature, or a piece of matter. All of them are correct causal specifications, but characterized with different levels of specificity, in this instance from more to less.

So Aquinas has a set of distinctions available which can be used to explain any phenomenon – an analysis in terms of four causes, a discussion of the relation of those causes to each other, a specification of the priority of causes and of the chain of proximate causes in each kind of cause and also whether the causes coincide or not. This framework will be useful in analysing issues as far apart as the structure of virtue, the nature of human cognition and the nature of the divine essence. With this initial statement of the four causes in place, I shall move on to examine the three crucial distinctions endlessly used by Aquinas, starting with the matter/form distinction.

2.4.2   Matter and form

Matter does not have the same meaning for Aquinas as it does in a modern sense, but it is not entirely different either. Peter Geach notes that it means something like 'stuff' in the modern sense (with the proviso that any stuff always has form as well).[7] The modern sense means something like building blocks, out of which something else is made. With an atomistic scientific world view, this would be fairly readily specifiable – one can discover the ultimate building blocks of the universe. However, with scientific advances, the idea that we find some small particle which explains all the rest is no longer taken seriously. Appeal to string theory or to mathematical formulas specifying kinds of energy have replaced simple corpuscularian theory. This might seem to indicate that 'matter' in Aquinas's understanding is detached from science, being perhaps a kind of metaphysical term of art. Yet Peter Geach has warned against this approach. Aquinas constantly gives examples drawing from common sense or the science of his age, and Aristotle initially developed the theory in the context of his physics, the study of nature. While it does not fit well with contemporary physics, it nevertheless fits with common-sense notions of what something is made from, rather than being a rarefied notion detached from any experience. So while the term does find conceptual use in metaphysics, its roots are in common-sense experience.

Aquinas straightforwardly defines matter in terms of potential – 'we call matter whatever exists potentially' [DPN1]. Potential is left undefined, and is to be understood as a capacity. An egg has the capacity to turn into an omelette, an acorn to be an oak tree, a cub to be a lion. It should be clear that such a potential is something more concrete and real than mere possibility. I might have the possibility of a wide range of things, which, while not impossible, are unlikely – being made president, liking cricket, computing rapidly in my head. A potential on the other hand is a real feature of an individual, such as a frog's innate proclivity to jump or a person's capacity to play music by ear. It is rooted in real features of the individual. Another way of putting that is to say that potential is circumscribed by essence. An essence is connected to the basic notion of kind – frogs have a capacity for jumping, but not for playing piano, this being set by the kind of thing they are. So matter is thought of as capturing this notion of a potential or capacity. Bricks can be assembled to make buildings, flour put together with other things to make bread. In each case the bricks or the flour constitutes matter – something which potentially becomes something else. Becoming something else is the bringing about of a new form, and form is correlated to matter as the actualization of the potential.

However, bricks and flour are also real things themselves, and although they can be thought of as matter relative to houses or bread, they are also in themselves composites of matter and form. So Aquinas uses this idea of a nested hierarchy of matter and form, construed as potential stuff and actualized stuff. The lower-level stuff is matter for the higher-level stuff, which in turn can be matter for a higher level again. Is there a basic level, a kind of brute stuff out of which everything else comes? The ancient philosophers thought so and suggested different physical candidates for this – water, fire, air. Aquinas rejects this approach. He does postulate a bottom level of intellectual analysis, prime matter, but this is a conceptual tool to help make sense of change, rather than something which exists in its own right. Prime matter would be something purely potential, with no actualization, or no form associated with it. Such a thing could not exist in reality. Nevertheless it is useful to think of what is in common between something which changes form from one thing to another – thinking about the matter which loses one form and gains another. This is not to say that there actually exists such a permanent bare potentiality – but one can contemplate the aspect of the thing which is its capacity to change, its matter. Hence everything physical which exists is a composite of matter and form – indicating a potential and actualizing feature of them.

Form is associated with actuality, and is best thought of as something functional and dynamic (like organismic structure), rather than static (like shape). Forms exist in nested hierarchies. The frog has a multiplicity of forms within itself. There is the functional structure of simple properties such as the frog's colour and temperature. There are the structures of its inner organs, the functional systems dealing with respiration, digestion and so forth. There is then the overall organization of the animal into the particular kind of creature it is. Aquinas distinguishes between substantial existence and accidental existence. A substance is characterized by just existing (*simpliciter*), while an accident exists in a certain way (*esse aliquid*). Substances have a priority therefore over accidents – accidents depend on whatever they are in to exist, whereas substances have an independence in this respect. A frog counts as a substance, whereas its greenness is an accidental feature. If it is accidentally bleached (assuming it survives), the greenness goes, but the frog persists. Aquinas says [DPN 1] that strictly speaking one should restrict matter-form composition to substances, while accidents exist in a subject (which is itself something substantial). That is, the distinction of matter/form is most correctly used to specify the metaphysical structure of discrete entities, whereas when speaking of properties, one more properly talks of the subject in which the property inheres.

What sort of reality do forms have? Consider the colour of the frog, the structure of its heart and its overall functional unity. Here are three distinct forms. The first is accidental in nature, the second goes to make up a distinct part of the frog and the third unifies all the subordinate forms into a single unified entity. What is to be said about the kind of existence these forms have? One approach is to give it a reality, to call it a real abstract feature of things, whose reality is independent of those things – a one over many. The greenness of this frog and of that piece of grass is something which they both have in common, and is something over and above either of them. This view has been traditionally associated with Plato, and is one which Aquinas rejects.[8] He thinks that forms do not exist until associated with an actual existent. Wisdom exists, but only as wisdom of Socrates, wisdom of Plato and so on. So to think of the form in itself is a bit like thinking of a mathematical function (e.g. "the square root of....") , which requires an input to become an actual number. A form is therefore always a form of something. We can indeed mentally consider the greenness of the frog and the greenness of the grass independently of the grass and the frog, but this is a mental construct which does not exist in reality apart from the things in which it exists. What exists in reality is grass and frogs – not some abstract entity besides.

2.4.3 Potentiality and actuality

Because of the systematic and interlocking nature of Aquinas's thought, it is not easy to separate out the distinct strands in it and consider them in isolation from the other parts. Matter and form have already been explained in terms of potentiality and actuality. At this point I want to focus more on this latter distinction. While connected to the matter/form distinction, it still marks something different. For a start, it is broader than the matter/form distinction. It can apply to things not containing matter. In Aquinas's world view, influenced by Neoplatonism, the most significant things which exist are not physical – including God, angels, souls. The extent to which these types of thing are viewed with suspicion nowadays is the extent to which a physicalistic metaphysics has come to dominate modern thought.

Potentiality and actuality find their place in a theory of change. Early Greek thought had produced several conundrums about change. Some philosophers championed the priority of change. Nothing is immune to change, and everything is subject to it, a view associated with Heraclitus.[9] Buddhist thought affirms a similar view,[10] as did Nietzsche,[11] the French Existentialists[12] and Alfred North Whitehead[13] in varying ways. This means that there are no stable identities and that everything is in flux. Opposed to that was the view of Parmenides, which argued that change was illusory, the senses did not yield accurate knowledge of reality and the fundamental reality is a unified realm of being with no distinctions within it.[14] This view has resonances with certain kinds of Hindu metaphysics (Advaita Vedanta) which holds to the unity of all things and the ultimate unreality of distinction and change, despite our experience of these.[15] Aristotle found a way through these polarized positions by establishing a more differentiated way of thinking about change.[16] Some changes are minor, and the changing thing retains its identity – for example, I am changing as I type, but am still myself after it. Other changes are major, and the thing does not remain after such a change – the hedgehog flattened on the motorway is a corpse in the process of decomposition and no longer has the identity of a hedgehog. By distinguishing different kinds of change – those which keep the identity of the subject of change and those which do not – the extreme positions of either everything changing or nothing changing can be avoided.

The way to explain how such change is possible is to use the concepts of potentiality and actuality. Aquinas has a sustained discussion of these terms in his commentary on Aristotle's *Metaphysics* and deploys them frequently throughout his work. He notes that the term 'potentiality' is etymologically derived from 'power' [In Sent I d.42 q.1a.1c]. 'Actuality' is etymologically derived from 'action' [De Pot q.1a.1]. The basic meaning of potentiality is a capacity to be realized. Potentiality divides into two main types. Firstly, there is active potentiality, which is an ability to affect change in something else, to act on something (e.g. to kick the cat). Secondly, there is passive potentiality, the capacity to receive something (e.g. to be scratched by the cat).

A potentiality is something real; it is a capacity or power. Therefore, it is something more specific than merely logical possibility, which rests on the notion of non-contradiction. Whatever is possible is whatever does not involve a contradiction and so admits a very wide range. For example, it is not contradictory to imagine that I might yet be a renowned opera singer; it is a logically possible state of affairs. However, potentiality is more specific and depends on the existence of particular powers – so if I were to have the potential to be a great opera singer, it would require very specific capacities such as breathing skills, vocal tone, register, expressiveness, experience and so forth. Alas, I lack this potentiality, although had my life been different, I could have been a contender. I might have developed these skills.

To deny the existence of such real potentiality leads to a form of determinism. Certain ancient Greek thinkers – the Megarics – had precisely denied this, and Aquinas held that it led to seriously counter-intuitive results [In Met 9. 3. 1796–1803]. Anyone displaying a skill would only have it while actually exercising it – so would gain and lose it multiple times (e.g. an opera singer would repeatedly gain and lose his/her skill of singing in a crazily episodic fashion). Properties known to the senses would only exist while being sensed, not existing when not actually sensed. Someone not seeing or hearing would be blind and deaf in the periods when not actually using his/her senses. Anyone who is not currently performing an activity could not begin to perform it, and so will never perform it. To deny potentiality is to embrace such absurdities.

Actuality is correlated to potency, and is construed as a kind of perfection – the bringing to fruition of what had been only potentially in something. One way of thinking of it is as the way form relates to matter, a specific instance of the actualization. While a piece of matter could potentially become a variety of different things, its potentiality is actualized when it receives a specific form. Actuality is frequently connected to movement – whether local movement, or quantitative increase/decrease or an alternation between contraries, but it can also be construed as a perfection – for example, coming to understand something.

Actuality is held to be prior to potentiality. It is prior in definition, in that knowledge of potentiality requires at least a general sense of actuality. It is prior in time; whenever a potential is realized, something actual pre-exists. It is prior in substance, in the way that form is prior to matter and determines what it is. Aquinas also notes its priority in goodness and truth. So in several different ways, actuality is held to be metaphysically superior to potentiality, although they typically coexist and are understood relative to each other. There is one very important exception to this rule, God, in whom there is no potentiality. God is pure actuality, and many of the distinctive features of God are connected to this fact – that God does not change, is not causally impacted upon, does not have parts and so on. While many of these seem counter-intuitive, they can be rendered more comprehensible in a framework with this understanding of actuality.

I spoke earlier of three theories – explanation, change and thinghood – and three distinctions – matter/form, potency/act, essence/existence. It should be clear from discussing the first two theories and the first two distinctions that they are not hermetically sealed off from each other, but interpenetrate. The theory of explanation involves the four causes, so as well as matter and form there is efficiency and finality. Efficiency and finality typically involve change, so potency and act will be involved. Efficient causes have active potentiality to bring about change, and final causes can be thought of as reasons or perfections, final states of actualization towards which changes tend. There was also talk about substances and accidents, roughly speaking, independently existing things and their properties. Such things can be thought about using matter and form, potentiality and actuality. But it is clear that while substances can be thought about in terms of matter/form and potency/act, accidents also can be thought about in these ways. So a further distinction is deployed to make sense of the nature of entities, how they are the kind of thing they are, the range of changes available to them while retaining that identity and the kinds of change which destroys their identity. This is the essence-existence distinction.

2.4.4   Essence and existence

Aquinas has stayed quite close to the Aristotelian world view in his use of matter, form, potency and act. With the essence/existence distinction he moves to a distinctively new position which evolves from the Aristotelian one. He is strongly influenced by Avicenna, who used this distinction as a way of thinking about God's existence. Yet Aquinas's approach is not that of Avicenna, and traditionally scholars of Aquinas have argued that his views on existence constitute the core of his thinking. Critics from Duns Scotus to Anthony Kenny have argued that there is something incoherent in this position on existence. Here I wish to establish the basic features of his view on the relationship of essence to existence.

First off, what is essence and how does it relate to the notion of form? In a section above I said that essence should be thought of as related to the notion of 'kind'. While this is correct, essence is also connected to the notion of 'this individual', and herein lies a tension. The features which make something a member of a particular kind, which it has in common with others, seem to be different to the features which make it an individual. So how is this explained in the term 'essence'? Aquinas devotes his treatise *De Ente et Essentia* to disentangling these issues.

He begins by noting that being can be thought of as real or as something linguistic [DEE ch.1]. In the linguistic sense, anything which can be referred to in a sentence is in some sense real – including lacks or absences. He wants to maintain that essence connects to the more robust sense of being, what exists in reality. It was called the 'what-it-is-to-be-that' by Aristotle, 'nature' by Boethius and 'form' by Avicenna (this latter appellation showing the kinds of confusions which can arise, as it is not simply the formal cause). Essence is primarily applied to substance, to things which exist in their own right, and secondarily to properties.

Aquinas's world has a hierarchical structure, with a chain of distinct kinds of things from inanimate matter, through animate matter, intelligent matter (humans) to spiritual beings and ultimately God. One can think of this as a form of metaphysical pluralism – there are seriously different kinds of things in existence, so he is not an idealist or a materialist, or a dualist – there is a genuine plurality of kinds. The matter-form distinction holds in the realm of matter. The potency-act distinction piggybacks the matter-form distinction for those kinds of things. At a higher level in the hierarchy there is only form (for Aquinas, examples include immaterial beings such as angels or souls separated from the body), and so the potency-act distinction remains, while the matter-form does not pertain. At the highest level, distinctions fall away and God is a purely simple reality. Aquinas notes that essence belongs most properly to simple substances – that is, to substances which do not exhibit a matter-form distinction (the latter called composite substances). However, it is easier to grasp essence in composite substances first and then move on to try to make sense of simple substances (i.e. immaterial pure forms), so that is how he proceeds [DEE ch.1].

While it might seem that essence is to be identified with form, this is not so. Matter serves to individuate physical substances, making them the particular instances they are, so matter cannot be left out of the essence of physical things. Essence in physical substances refers to the composite of both matter and form and not just form alone. Aristotle's taxonomy of kinds of things involves giving a definition in terms of genus and specific difference. The genus is the broader notion of kind, while the specific difference sharpens this to a particular kind. A genus can be thought of as a matter (potential) to the actualization brought by specific form. Everything present in the species is present in the genus in an undifferentiated way. But for physical things, matter must be present in their essence – it is a key part of what they are. Aquinas makes a crucial distinction between whole and part which allows one to distinguish different ways of construing matter. He speaks of the generic notion of 'body'. One way of thinking of this is as naming something which can occupy three dimensions. In a very general way all physical things have this is common, and there are further elaborations of the kind of body which is in question (e.g. inanimate, living, sensate, rational etc.). This is thinking of the notion of body as a whole, which is inclusive and compatible with all the further elaborations. A different way is to think of body as just occupying three dimensions, but exclusively stopping there, over and against any further form or elaboration. This is to think of body as a part, linked to form as a different part. When body is included in the notion of essence, it is as a whole, as something which allows further specification.

Genus and species are relative terms – in that what is generic and specific depends on the place in the hierarchy. Relative to what is above something is more specific, relative to what is below it is generic. Humans are a kind of animal, so humanity is more specific in relation to animality, but more generic in relation to Socrates. Genus and differentiating form are names for an individual, deriving from its material and formal parts respectively. If humans are rational animals, animality is the genus (referring to the material aspect), while rationality is the specific difference (referring to the formal difference among kinds of animals). While indeterminate matter is included in the essence of all physical things, it is determinate matter which makes them to be the numerical individuals they are. Determinate matter is construed as a part (in contrast to indeterminate matter construed as a way of thinking about the whole). Determinate matter contrasts with form (a different part). Socrates is not identical with either his matter or his form – each of these are parts, which together make a whole. 'Essence' refers to this whole, including both the matter and the form. Essences relate to sorting, types and kinds by their fitting into the scheme of genera and species, but relate to individuals by being names of this composite of matter and form. Socrates's essence is an individual, which captures what is distinctive of Socrates. For Aquinas, the only genuine things in existence are individuals. We can mentally abstract and reflect on general, shared features of things, and these are real, not gerrymandered aspects of things. Aquinas thinks that what animals have in common is a real feature of the world (it cuts nature at the joints, as it were), whereas what homeowners have in common is less real, more conventional and open to variation. So the theory of essence is a realist account of kind distinction, which gives an explanation of the key aspects of individuality and kind membership for any substance.

Essences were jettisoned by later scientific thinkers as something irrelevant to genuine inquiry into reality. Rather than speaking of 'dormitive powers', thereby giving a merely verbal definition of what makes people sleepy, a detailed chemical and neurophysiological investigation showing the effects of drugs on the nervous system is what is required. However, to oppose things in this way seems mistaken. The theory of essences does not at all block scientific investigation; rather, it provides a robust philosophical framework for making sense of the orderliness, regularity and amenability to reason of the physical world presupposed by scientific inquiry. To specify this framework abstractly does not do the work of actual empirical inquiry – but that does not invalidate it.

Aquinas thinks of essence as a way of talking about things, but thought of from the perspective of potentiality (given that all essences that exist are actual). An essence is potential in the sense that it need not exist. This is not to say that there is a realm of spooky essences waiting to be actualized into existence (like Avicenna). If there were, what sort of existence would they have? Rather, the thought is that essence is incomplete in metaphysically specifying an entity and requires some further additional specification. For Aquinas, this further element is existence, which is the entity construed from the perspective of actuality. Aquinas uses the Latin term *esse* to refer to existence – this is the infinitive form of the verb 'to be'. Any entity which exists has a real distinction between its essence and its existence (with the unique exception of God, as I shall discuss in Chapter 6). The essence answers the what-it-is question; the existence answers the that-it-is question. Created things do not have to be. There is a radical contingency about everything created, bread and butter, galaxies and universes, quarks and hadrons. This is expressed by saying that for every substance which is not God, its essence is distinct from its existence. In physical things, the matter-form distinction lines up with the potency-act distinction, which now in turn lines up with the essence-existence distinction. This is the most fundamental metaphysical characterization of anything, of any entity. An entity has two distinct metaphysical parts – its essence and its existence. It cannot be without either one. Everything created shares this dichotomy. As noted, there is only one exception – the one uncreated reality, God. But for now, a basic map of the kind of conceptual scheme repeatedly deployed by Aquinas has been given.

3
Reason and Faith

Aquinas believed that human reason and religious faith were not inimical to each other, but by their different methods were in principle capable of reaching some of the same truths. His account of how this is so reaches its most mature statement in ST II-II q.1–7, but it appears in different places in his work. In this chapter I want to examine Aquinas's views on reason, then his views on faith and finally how he considers their relationship. But first I want to stand back from Aquinas's account and examine different possible ways of construing their relationship, creating a spectrum of views on which Aquinas's position can be situated.

3.1 A spectrum of views

At one end of the spectrum is the view that reason is the only appropriate means by which religious belief can be evaluated (Rationalism). This can result in atheism and the rejection of religion, but it can also result in views which defend purely rational religious belief. The Deists of the eighteenth century believed that they had good rational arguments to postulate the existence of a Divine architect for the universe, but that this rational religion was distinct from the superstitions of organized religion with all the paraphernalia of miracles, faith and the supernatural. For them, the existence of God is demonstrable by purely rational means. At the other end is the view holding that reason has no role in relation to religious belief and that instead the appropriate stance one must take is one of faith (Fideism). This too is a complex view, depending on the accounts given of both the nature of reason and faith. Between these poles are positions allowing for both reason and faith, with different degrees of emphasis and differing views of both.

Aquinas's position is in this middle ground, and it is useful to situate his views by first considering the poles he stands between.

3.1.1   Rationalism

Rationalism holds that in human considerations of questions about God, there is nothing other than human reasoning available to adjudicate the issues. Certainly Aristotle believed something akin to this.[1] He affirmed that a God exists, but his God has few features associated with the traditional religious beliefs of the Abrahamic religions. There is no interest in individual fate, no providence, no point to prayer. God operates as a rational posit to explain movement in the universe. Over two thousand years later, despite rejecting Aristotelian views of knowledge and science, Bertrand Russell held essentially the same methodological view. Reason is the sole adjudicator in this matter, and reason shows that God does not exist. Russell thinks the universe itself is the terminus of all explanation, and attempting to go beyond it to talk about spiritual reality is unwarranted.[2] Aristotle and Russell disagree in the details of their metaphysical views, but agree that a purely rationalistic approach is the only appropriate way to deal with the question of God's nature and existence. Richard Dawkins has a similar position, although his account of reason is narrower than that of Aristotle or Russell, being essentially that of the positivists, who accept only scientifically established knowledge as genuine.[3]

So a number of issues emerge from this. What account of reason is the correct one to deal with questions about God? Is reason actually capable of dealing with such an issue? And if not, is there anything else which can? I shall present the kinds of considerations which might lead one to question the appropriateness of reason, when discussing fideism, and shall also discuss there the notion of faith. Here I shall make some comments on different conceptions of reason.

Hilary Putnam has some reflections on the nature of reason pertinent to this discussion.[4] An account of reason such that it renders its own operation impossible, is clearly unacceptable. Views of reason which claim that only scientifically based positions or arguments are acceptable fall into this bracket. The simple problem is what is the status of that very claim? It does not, itself, seem to belong to any of the hard sciences, and when examined in the context of the social sciences, it is hard to see how such a strongly normative view could arise from them. So if the claim itself does not have scientific warrant, it fails by its own lights – which is about as big a failing as a position could conceivably have. So there needs to be space for reasoned reflection which considers the nature of reason, the nature of knowledge, the fundamental struc-tures of reality which can accommodate all the multifaceted dimen-sions of human existence in it – ethics, politics and literature, as well as physics, biology, sociology and psychology. This requirement fits well with William James's observation that a method which rules out the possibility of its objects, from the start, is a flawed method, or one which is skewed.[5] If one adopts a method admitting only entities existing in space and time and detectable by empirical methods, that clearly precludes the possibility of anything outside of that and method-ologically presupposes atheism. So a conception of reason which allows for the possibility of reflection on the nature and existence of God is required – even if ultimately such a conception denies that such exists (the kind of conception held in common by Aristotle and Russell).

Rationalists typically deny that there is any other possible way of dealing with the God question. Faith is regarded as something subjec-tive, unreliable and akin to wishful thinking. Dawkins can be relied upon to sum up this attitude:

> Faith is an evil precisely because it requires no justification and brooks no argument. Teaching children that unquestioned faith is a virtue primes them – given certain other ingredients that are not hard to come by – to grow up into potentially lethal weapons for future jihads or crusades.[6]

Even though Aristotle, Russell and Dawkins have different views of reason and different substantive beliefs about reality, they would all agree that nothing outside the realm of reason can help make sense of reality. This view is challenged by fideism, which maintains the oppo-site – that reason is incapable of dealing with issues about God. Before addressing fideistic worries about rationalism, it is important to note what Aquinas shares with rationalism. Like rationalists, Aquinas holds that reason is in principle capable of addressing many questions about God's existence and nature. However, he is also sensitive to the limita-tions of human knowledge. He notes that such speculative knowledge of God, 'would have appeared only to few, and even so after a long time and mixed with many mistakes' [ST I.1.1]. Thus he believes there is a different way of acquiring information about God through revelation, that is, God's own communication. The appropriate response in humans to this is faith (a view inimical to rationalists), about which more below. But what of the other pole, what kinds of considerations have led fide-ists to reject any role for reason in discussions of God?

3.1.2   Fideism

For fideism, faith does not connect with reason, argument or knowledge, but rests rather on our emotional, passionate and visceral nature – to what is deepest in us. Just as one does not (usually!) get married to someone on the basis of syllogistic reasoning, and even though the phenomenon of getting married is of fundamental importance to those undergoing it, likewise religious commitment comes from levels within us which are beyond the scope of reason. Fideism is defined as the position which separates faith from reason. It comes from the Latin word *fides* (faith) and says that it is legitimate to hold religious beliefs in the absence of any rational basis.

Extreme fideism is a position which actively denigrates reason, holding that it has nothing at all to do with religious belief. It is associated with Tertullian (c. 160–250), one of the Church Fathers, who is reputed to have said of Christ's resurrection, 'I believe it because it is absurd!' He is also credited with the saying 'What has Athens to do with Jerusalem?', meaning that he regarded scriptural belief (Jerusalem) to have been contaminated by pagan Greek rationalistic philosophy (Athens).[7] This view is also associated with the Danish philosopher Søren Kierkegaard (1813–1855), who highlighted the phrase 'the leap of faith', meaning one goes beyond reason. However, the exact interpretation of Kierkegaard is a matter of scholarly controversy, and his work was produced as a corrective reaction to the extreme rationalism of nineteenth-century German Idealism.[8]

Faith necessarily involves an element of belief. This might seem banal or obvious, but in fact it has been a source of controversy in recent years. Some religious thinkers have challenged what they have called a 'propositional model' of faith, one that involves assenting to specific propositions – for example, that God exists, or that God loves us.[9] They hold that this is too intellectualist, too academic and cut-and-dried an account of the richly diverse phenomena of religious faith. It reduces it to a narrow, bloodless assent to a set of beliefs. Now, while it is true that faith involves more than just assent to certain beliefs, it clearly must involve this as well. That is to say, holding some propositionally formed belief is a necessary condition for religious faith. If this were not so, then there would be no content to faith at all – there might be a welter of emotions, impulses, attitudes and desires, but with no focus, nothing on which to hang these. Beliefs are available to us in propositional form – that is, we think in language, at least think consciously and explicitly in language. It is clear that we have much mental activity which is not clear, focused or in our awareness – much of this level we share with prelinguistic beings such as young children and animals. However, much thought is conceptual, and concepts are available to us as language. So when we think consciously about an object in our awareness, we use concepts both to identify it and to have thoughts about it – even something as simple as 'I wonder whether I'll break for coffee now?' Beliefs guide our actions and are connected to our desires and needs (I might put on the kettle and take a cup out). We negotiate our way in the world on the basis of beliefs. Some beliefs are simple perceptual ones – 'the cup is over there'. Others are more complex: 'water boils at 100 degrees centigrade', and others more complex still: 'The democratic mandate is the proper source of political legitimacy'. Such beliefs are formed on the basis of experience – although obviously some are more closely tied to direct perceptual experience (for example, about the cup) and some quite removed (for example, the politics). Religious beliefs are similar to other such beliefs in that they arise from experience, guide our actions and allow us to think about reality in a certain way.

However, belief is not a sufficient feature of faith. That is to say, there may be instances of holding religious beliefs, of entertaining certain propositions as true, but not actually having faith. Traditional Christianity holds that demons are in such a situation. Demons believe that God exists, but their attitude to this belief is hostile and negative (John Milton's marvellous Satan spits venom at heaven). So a further feature of religious faith is having the appropriate attitude to the belief – one of trust, obedience, desire, and so on (although, of course, there are degrees of faith, and sinners can have faith [ST 2–2.7.2]). It is this attitudinal aspect to which the opponents of the propositional view rightly draw attention, but it has to supplement, not replace the propositional content.

A final comment in this initial analysis of the notion of faith is that religious faith is most often thought about in the context of believing in a person. To believe in God is more than just to believe that God exists, but to trust, obey, follow and so forth. It involves a degree of connection. So faith is sometimes presented as relational. To believe in God is to be involved in a relationship with God. Rather than merely entertaining ideas about God in an impersonal, detached way, to have faith in God is to be committed and engaged. Indeed certain accounts of faith, for example, that of Aquinas, discussed below, hold that since faith is a gift from God, to have faith is to share in God's life. This rich view of faith is far removed from a one-dimensional propositionalism – yet it depends on having propositional beliefs. While rationalists reject the view that one is entitled to hold such an attitude in the absence of conclusive reasons, fideists hold that it is proper to have faith in the absence of epistemically justifying reasons.

Extreme fideism is a difficult position to sustain because the severe split it posits between faith and reason makes it implausible, impossible to defend rationally, and probably internally incoherent.[10] It posits the extreme view that faith has nothing to do with reason – reason being flawed, sinful and unredeemed, but faith supplying the cure. Why might one believe in such a fideism? Clearly there cannot be a reason for such a view since it splits faith from reason (even simply claiming that the Bible teaches something involves considerations about whether it really does so or what such teaching might mean – which involves reasoning). So what other source is there for such a view? Other sources for belief include emotion, desire, aversion. However, consider a situation in which one has an aversion to something, say a spider. Such a fear might be based on previous frightening experiences or on carefulness about its potential for being poisonous. But in these cases, both the previous experience and the care serve as a reason for the aversion. An aversion in the absence of such considerations is a phobia, an irrational fear. So even emotional responses, when they are not phobic, pathological or chemically induced, are connected to the reasoning process. There may be ways in which people come to a belief through non-reasoning processes, but usually we think of these as being deficient in some way or other. There is coercion, in which case people are put under duress to think in a certain way, perhaps, for example, the way of a totalitarian state. Or there is wishful thinking, where people want things to be such-and-such a way, and come to believe that they are like that, without good reason for it. Now this is not to say that faith has to be an instance of wishful thinking, but faith so completely divorced from reasoning as the extreme fideist would have it seems problematical.

A further reason why extreme fideism is arguably incoherent as a position involves the nature of belief itself. If faith is thought of as propositional, that it has a content that can be expressed in propositions, then it belongs to what has been called 'the space of reasons'.[11] Any belief, when expressed linguistically, has internal connections to other beliefs. From 'the cat is on the mat', I can logically infer, without any other empirical evidence, the further belief that 'one object is related to another'. There is an internal connection between the former and the latter, such that knowing the former allows me to know the latter. So at this quite abstract level, it seems incoherent to suggest that reason can be completely divorced from faith – the very expression of faith implicates it in the space of reason.

But there are other ways in which faith involves reasoning. One can imagine situations where mistakes are made about the content of a faith-belief, and these mistakes are corrected. There is an old joke about a preacher getting muddled and talking about the twelve commandments, the ten apostles and their wives, the epistles. To sort out stuff like this requires reasoning, appealing to authoritative sources and so forth. It is really difficult to ban reason in the way the hard-line fideist wants.

There is also the problem of conflicting faiths – suppose a fideistic Christian and a fideistic Muslim were to confront each other. How would they meaningfully communicate? They could demonstrate the beauty, depth, compellingness and so on of their views, but to do so would require the use of reason. To communicate their different views of reality, they would need a space in which to hold something in common – a space produced by the universal human faculty of reasoning. Now, to say that reasoning is unavoidable and that the sharp split posited by the fideist is implausible is not to argue for rationalism. To reject extreme fideism is not to say that it makes no sense to speak of faith at all. Rather, there may be a place for faith in an appropriate relation with reason.

3.1.3   A middle view

An issue of terminology emerges here. To what extent is stepping away from extreme fideism still fideism? Is to allow any space for faith a form of fideism? C. Stephen Evans has a useful discussion of the views of Aquinas, Kant and Kierkegaard, showing how they have differing accounts of faith and reason, and in so doing refining different senses of fideism.[12] The important distinction is the one which separates extreme fideism from other positions which allow for faith and reason to coexist.

Not everyone who accepts a notion of faith is one who has to reject reason. It may be that reason is circumscribed in some ways. Perhaps it works well for science and everyday beliefs, but not for religion. In that realm one might have to rely on, for example, tradition, feeling or a kind of sensibility akin to aesthetic experience (e.g. how one reacts to music). The claim would then be that atheists are religiously tone-deaf – they lack the appropriate discriminatory capacities of religious folk. Arguably, Ludwig Wittgenstein and Kant have views like this – and Aquinas can also be situated in this middle space. He accepts the importance of reason and regards the exercise of pure intellectual inquiry as one of the highest operations available to humanity [ST 2–2. 179.1].[13] Nevertheless, reason has its limitations, and there are some religious truths which are not available to pure reason, which are gained in a different manner (by faith, for example, the Trinity and the Incarnation). Faith and reason relate to and interact with each other. But the exact details of this story for Aquinas are complicated. So I shall start with his account of reason, outlining his views of cognition, kinds of knowledge and the place of *scientia*. Then I shall discuss his account of the nature of faith, before addressing how they relate to each other.

3.2   Reason in Aquinas

Making sense of the notion of rationality is a task for the theory of knowledge and, more recently, philosophy of science. Rationality is centrally involved in the job of giving reasons. Evaluating reason-giving, looking at questions about defining knowledge, assessing certitude, analysing the structure of justification is what epistemology does. Given the importance of science in the contemporary world, the philosophy of science connects with this project, whether through clarifying scientific method, establishing different appropriate methodologies for different sciences or indeed seeing whether knowledge is reducible to scientific knowledge.

As noted in Chapter 1, the very idea of rationality is something which is contested by some scholars in current intellectual life. At one extreme is the view which reduces all rationality to one kind, that exhibited in the natural and social sciences, where observation, quantification and testability are privileged. At the other extreme is the view prevalent in the humanities that rationality is fragmented and multiple and there is no possible conception of it which could capture the variegated richness of human reasoning. As I argued above, neither position is attractive, not least because both fail the test of applying their own strictures to themselves. The narrow conception is so narrow that it fails to license itself. The broad conception is too weak to deliver the kind of universal claims it makes.

In the middle ground between these poles are various candidates for a universal account of rationality which allows for intellectual pluralism – that is, an account which gives sufficient content to the idea of being rational, while allowing for diverse ways of exhibiting that feature. Alvin Plantinga offers a survey of such accounts.[14] Aristotle is the starting place, characterizing reason as the feature which distinguishes humanity from other animals. Reasoning is a kind of activity, a way of relating to the world. It involves (tautologously) the giving of reasons for the beliefs one holds.[15] Aristotle's complex story of how this is so, involving an account of belief formation, the relation of thought to language, logical inference and scientific reasoning, the difference between theoretical and practical reason is essentially the one which Aquinas endorses, as I shall explore below. Plantinga notes further developments in the theory of reason, such as the view that connects reason to function:[16] a reasonable belief is one which is arrived at by the proper functioning of one's cognitive apparatus. Specifying exactly what those functions are and what counts as being a proper function is to give a theory of rationality.

Common to all these accounts is the core idea that the possibility of giving good reasons is essential to rationality. This is connected to the idea of epistemic responsibility. One takes on a responsibility in holding a belief, such that one is committed to giving a reason for holding it, for thinking that it is true. Giving a reason means pointing to some factor which serves to support the belief, which a challenger would accept as good grounds for thinking it true. For example, I rummage about in the morning looking for my car keys. I complain (as usual) to my wife that I cannot find them. She says, 'They're on the kitchen table'. I say, 'I can't see them'. She says, 'Look under the papers'. I check and find them. In this humdrum domestic exchange many of the elements of rationality are present. I have a need (the keys) but lack knowledge. I enquire but fail to find them. I check with someone else, who gives me a belief (they are on the table). I challenge this belief (I have a reason not to believe this because I cannot see them). I am given further information as to why I cannot see them (they are obscured by the papers), and then I verify with my own perception that they are where testimony had told me. My wife remembered seeing me absent-mindedly place the papers over them.

Our knowledge has many sources, but standard accounts reduce these to four categories – Perception, Memory, Testimony and Reason.[17] Perception is a fundamental way of relating to the world – using our senses. My wife perceptually forms the belief as to the whereabouts of my keys, I doubt her because I do not perceive them on the table. Memory is also crucial to our knowledge. Most of our perceptual beliefs are lodged in memory. My wife is not currently seeing my keys, but recalls where I left them. Testimony is another important source – many of our beliefs are on the basis of what others tell us. I come to the true belief of where the keys are by virtue of Sue's comment. Reason, in the narrower sense of logical inference or abstract theorizing, is a crucial part of our knowledge. I initially reject her claim about the keys using an implicit logical move: 'If the keys are on the table, I should be able to see them. I cannot see them; therefore, they are not on the table'. She gives further information which rejects the first premise of my inference – even though I cannot see them, the keys are on the table. In this brief early morning exchange, the elements of rationality are evident. A few comments are germane to this. Firstly, acting rationally does not require an ongoing theoretical commentary about the structure of the activity. I seek and find my keys in seconds without a thought about perception, testimony and the rest. That comes in philosophical reflection on what happened. Secondly, rationality finds its roots in commonplace, social activities. The kinds of examples which push one to exotic theories of rationality, for example, the activities of obscure tribes, theoretical physicists tinkering with logical systems, thought experiments about aliens, appear strained when faced with the avalanche of quotidian examples of rationality.

One way of capturing this idea of epistemic responsibility is to speak of the justification of a belief – the reasons for holding it. One approach to rationality privileges the point of view of the reasoner, the subject, and thinks that what is most important is whether the reasoner is justified, or blameless and so forth, and this is called Internalism. This means that one can be rationally justified, but actually hold a false belief. Perhaps it is true that many of our current scientific beliefs will be overturned in the future (by analogy with the past, where we have seen this happen many times). Nevertheless, we are justified in believing in electromagnetic theory, gravitation and so on, as these are the best theories we have, the ones the experts endorse and educational institutions propagate. A different approach holds that having beliefs which are actually true is most important. The value of holding true beliefs is that the world is as we believe it is, and so our goals and actions can be accomplished. This view is called Externalism. One might assimilate rationality to the acquisition of true beliefs – perhaps by the use of methods or processes which yield true beliefs. Examples of such processes include perception, memory and so forth, and we can specify the ways in which these function properly and ways in which they fail. In Aquinas scholarship there is a debate as to whether Aquinas is an internalist or an externalist, which will be discussed below.[18]

Finally, one might note that so far the discussion has been mostly speaking of what has been called theoretical reason – responsibly forming true beliefs about the world. But there are other forms of reasoning. There is the kind of reasoning which concerns the evaluation of action, the setting of goals and determining right and wrong. There is the kind of reasoning involved in means and ends, in producing artefacts or in the creation of works of art. A story about rationality should include these and explain their interrelationships – which is what Aquinas does. Before characterizing more precisely Aquinas's views, let us examine some similarities and differences between his view and more recent accounts.

Epistemology has been viewed as foundational in modern philosophy. From the seventeenth century, it has been held to be intellectually vital to clarify issues about the foundations of knowledge prior to any other endeavour. Everything else depends or rests on the guarantee given by epistemology. From this perspective, scepticism is a crucial issue. The sceptic challenges our entitlement to knowledge and puts in doubt our deepest beliefs. To rebut the sceptic and settle knowledge on a sure foundation was the main task of the epistemologist. This paradigm for epistemology has been challenged in the twentieth century. Wittgenstein in particular has queried the intelligibility of putting everything into doubt.[19] Doubt has presuppositions without which it cannot even be spoken (for example, that meaning is stable). Putnam argues that the conditions of meaning require one to be in contact with the actual world, so the sceptical hypothesis where one might be in an utterly different world to that conceived, is one which severs the link to reality which makes meaning possible.[20] Whatever the argument deployed, it is now commonplace to reject the traditional picture of having to put knowledge on a sceptic-proof foundation. As a result, recent epistemology is more relaxed about seeking inputs from psychology (which have not been sanitized by a prior epistemological process) or with accepting common-sense intuitions as data which have to be accommodated.

Aquinas's approach to reason is out of kilter with the scepticism-dominated approach of early modernity, but fits much more with recent work. He does not discuss the problem of scepticism. Rather, he assumes we do actually have knowledge and seeks to analyse it and find out the means by which we have it. He appeals to psychology, gives an account of cognition and shows how scientific knowledge builds up from rudimentary sensory contact with reality. Another way of expressing his stance is to say there is a basic realism associated with his account. He thinks that the world exists independently of human cognition. Stars, dinosaurs, bacteria, grass and hydrochloric acid do not depend on the human mind to exist and have the structures they do. Knowledge consists in our grasping or latching onto the structures that exist independently of us in the world. We tell the story of that world in more or less competent ways – and about some topics (especially God) we are prone to error and getting it wrong, because our minds are just not geared to the task of articulating truths about such things. Nevertheless, underpinning his whole view of reason is the intuition that human thought is seeking to connect with a world which has an existence and integrity which goes way beyond us. Thus there is a kind of presumption in his approach, which claims we connect with the real world. There is also a humility which admits that we do this to a limited extent and quite poorly in certain domains – 'our cognition is so weak that no philosopher could have ever completely investigated the nature of a single fly' [*In Symbolum Apostolorum*, Proemium].

It is a practice among some philosophers to emphasize the differences between world views and theoretical frameworks across historical epochs and cultures. Granted real differences in substantive knowledge and attitudes between Aquinas's time and ours, there are nevertheless continuities – just as there are differences among our contemporaries, yet also similarities. For example, for people to disagree vehemently over abortion (regarded by many as about as fundamental a clash as one can have given the history of the debates), there is a mass of common and agreed framework to allow the debate to occur. For example, there is agreed medical/physiological data, agreed codes of medical practice (e.g. doctors should not exploit a patient for their own ends), agreed rejection of infanticide in the born and so on. Debates over the status of the embryo, kinds of ethical principle involved, how to apply principles and how to adjudicate conflicting values take place in a meaningful framework, without which there would be no debate, no contact. Likewise, while Aquinas holds many beliefs which differ from contemporary ones, there is nevertheless some structural continuity in questions as to how such beliefs are acquired and legitimized. What might these be?

Using the matter/form tool from his basic conceptual scheme, one might say that his account of reason offers the form which constitutes the matter of our belief system. Aquinas accepts the same kinds of logical inferences as the moderns – the principle of noncontradiction, principles of inference and so forth. True, his formalization of these using Aristotelian syllogistic differs in its technical resources from modern symbolic logic – yet these differences in formalization do not signal a radically alien form of reasoning or logic to ours. The grounds of knowledge are likewise pretty similar. Perception, testimony, memory and reason are all discussed by him. Indeed when discussing faith, rooted in God's communication to humanity, the importance of testimony and the lack of conflict with reason are emphasized. Again, there is not an appeal to some exotic form of 'theological reason' which differs in kind from the kind of reasoning used to tell the weather or plan a journey. The principled appeal to empirical accounts of how (for example) perception occurs compares well with contemporary naturalized or social epistemologies. What I am arguing here is that Aquinas has a conception of reason which is continuous with contemporary accounts, differing certainly in specific details, but not sufficiently different to be something of a different kind. The notion of 'scientific knowledge' (*scientia*) plays an important role in this account, so I shall turn to that now.

Aquinas begins his major work, the *Summa Theologiae*, with a condensed discussion of the nature of Aristotelian science (*scientia*) and its relationship to theology. In an earlier work, his *Commentary on Boethius's De Trinitate*, he had a lengthier exploration of the different kinds of science which exist, how they are to be distinguished and how they relate to each other. A later work – his *Commentary on Aristotle's Posterior Analytics* – gives a detailed account of scientific explanation, its procedures, premises, methods and aims. The basic framework is from Aristotle, and he adapts it to make sense of *sacra doctrina*, which is what he calls theology.

Attention to terminology is important. The meaning of *scientia* for Aquinas is not the same as the meaning of science to the contemporary world. Likewise, the cluster of related terms used to explicate his ideal of science – for example, the verbs *scire* and *cognoscere* and their Greek forebears, *epistarthai* and *gignoskein,* do not exactly match the English 'to know', 'to apprehend'. But then again, depending on one's epistemological theory, 'to know' can have different theoretical significances in contemporary idiom – think of the debates between epistemic internalists and externalists. Aquinas takes Aristotle's distinction between different kinds of intellectual virtue as a basic framework for his discussion of science. Aristotle distinguished between *episteme* (theoretical knowledge) and *phronesis* (practical wisdom), and Aquinas accepts this, calling them *scientia* and *prudentia* respectively. Wisdom (*sophia or sapientia*) is a special kind of *scientia*, and rational intuition (*nous* or *intellectus*) is an operation of mind which grasps first principles and which is a presupposition of *scientia*. Hence *scientia* is knowledge in its fullest sense, which is a virtue – that is a disposition and a form of excellence.

To modern ears, science is a body of knowledge connected to observation and experimental test. There are different sciences with different methodologies – natural, social, cognitive and so on. But despite their differences, a core characteristic is the use of observation and quantitative methods. Aquinas's use of *scientia* includes this, but also expands to include all forms of human knowledge, including purely speculative kinds, for example, philosophy. What marks out a science for Aquinas is not its connection to observation (although for some sciences this is essential), but rather its structure, the systematic logical interrelationship of parts from principles to conclusions. He specifies the features which must be exhibited by principles and exhibited by the inferential relations between such principles and further knowledge derived from them.

The connection between principles and results derived from them is exhibited in syllogistic reasoning. Medieval logic recognized many different forms of inference. The demonstrative syllogism is one in which one gains new knowledge by means of the relationship between the major, minor and middle term presented in three propositions of subject-predicate form. Certain logical structures were codified as valid, others as fallacious. In a valid syllogism, if the premises are true, the conclusion has to follow of necessity. If the premises are certain, then the structure of the valid syllogism guarantees that the conclusion is likewise certain. So one aspect of *scientia* is its internal structure, which provides necessary knowledge.

A different aspect of this account is the starting place of knowledge. These are the premises from which reasoning begins. Some principles are grasped as self-evidently true – for example, the principles of logic, such as the law of noncontradiction. Aquinas introduces an important distinction between what is self-evident to us (*quoad nos*) and what is self-evident in itself (*per se notum*). It may be that some truths, while necessary and in an absolute sense self-evident, are not in fact recognized as such by us. As an analogy, one can think of a mathematical equation containing too many symbols to be taken in without effort and calculation, but which turns out to be true. It is true and necessarily so, but not at first glance obviously so. However, Aquinas thinks there are some truths which are in principle beyond our grasp, such as really understanding God's existence [ST 1.2.1]. This will never be *quoad nos*. The process of inquiry involves the uncovering of such truths as we can know. This is the process of induction, which is not simply the enumeration of individuals to get a probable conclusion, but grasping the universal feature of a group of individuals to express some stable feature of their essence, what they have in common. The principles of scientific reasoning have a number of features which they must exhibit – Truth, Causality, Being Better Known, Being Prior To, Being Immediate and Being Primitive [In PA 1.4 36–37]. Let us take each of these features in turn. Being true is basic for these premises. They are also causes – that is, they involve real features of reality which serve in a causal explanation of reality (understanding here the wider notion of cause discussed above in Section 2.4). They are better known than the conclusions – thus the epistemic warrant they have is transmitted to the conclusions by the demonstrative method. Premises are prior to the conclusions, both in the sense of knowledge (which recapitulates their being better known), but also priority in being. That is, in reality, the causal relationship is such that the premises are more fundamental than the conclusions. The premises are immediate in having no prior demonstrative argument leading to them; they do not rest on syllogistic reasoning (which is mediate reasoning). Primitiveness is a complex feature. For a premise to exhibit primitiveness, the subject is connected to the predicate as a universal truth. It is per se or necessary, and it is distinctive in that it fixes a relationship between subject and predicate which is not exhibited by anything else in the genus. So to say that an isosceles triangle has three angles, while being a universal and necessary truth, is not primitive, since it shares this feature with other triangles [In PA I.9.78]. Primitiveness in this instance is to require the triangle to have at least two equal sides, which is primitive to isosceles triangles.

In discussing the nature of *scientia* in this fashion, the relation of the parts of scientific knowledge mirror the objective features of reality and track the necessary connections which hold there. Thus, *scientia* is an analogical term, having a flexibility of meaning for Aquinas. On the one hand it refers to the virtue or disposition to knowledge of a researcher who grasps the objective features of reality, while on the other hand it refers to the objective nature of reality itself. What these share is form – the existence of structure in the mind and in reality.

This presents a highly idealized picture of knowledge. Indeed it presents a completed science, one which has carved nature at the joints, so to speak. It will be immediately objected that no science actually works like this. However, Aquinas accepts this. He offers remarkably candid admissions of the limited extent of human knowledge.[21] What he is presenting is a framework to make sense of the ontological and epistemological features of inquiry. Scientific inquiry attempts to describe reality as it truly is, capturing what is general and law-like rather than accidental and arbitrary. Our actual achievements may well fall short of this ideal – but it exists as an objective terminus to inquiry, perhaps asymtotically approached. One way in which Aquinas acknowledges this is by distinguishing between a demonstration which runs between causes to effect (*demonstratio propter quid*) and a demonstration which runs from effect to cause (*demonstratio quia*). The latter seeks to show that a cause exists from certain features of reality, rather than explaining those features by virtue of a grasp of the cause. Aquinas's arguments for God's existence are of this second kind – we are not in a position to understand God in the manner required for scientific demonstration of the *propter quid* kind, but we can run the argument to demonstrate that a real cause whose features are largely unavailable to us exists. But furthermore, enquiry might fall short of the full paradigm and involve partial and probable knowledge. Indeed the full articulation of a *scientia* requires a lot of early and provisional work by which one rises slowly to the possibility of something like scientific knowledge. So *scientia* is an ideal, matching the real structure of reality, to which our actual inquiries painfully aspire.

I shall return to further issues about Aquinas's account of reason – specifically questions about where to situate him on the contemporary grid of foundationalist-coherentist or internalist-externalist. However, enough has been said about his account to turn now to his views about faith.

3.3 Faith in Aquinas

Aquinas discusses faith in a number of texts – his *Commentary on Boethius's De Trinitate*, the *Disputed Questions on Truth* – but the central discussion is in the *Summa Theologiae*, where he devotes seven questions directly to analysing it. The context of the discussion is his account of the moral life. The goal of the moral life is to live well, but this can be understood in two ways. Firstly, it can be understood as living a good life in this world, and Aristotle is the main source of Aquinas's reflections on this. However, it also means orienting oneself towards a purpose, end or goal which goes beyond this world. Scripture and the reflections of earlier theological writers, principally Augustine, are the big influences here. These two perspectives are woven together in the discussion of how one should live. In the *Summa Theologiae*, the analysis of human action is followed by a discussion of habits and that by the distinction between good and bad habits, between virtues and vices. After this general outline of the chief elements of moral theory, there is a discussion of law, where his famous reflections on natural law occur, followed by a discussion of grace. There follows his treatment of faith, the first of the three theological virtues, and then he moves on to discuss the cardinal virtues – prudence, justice, temperance and courage. The basic Aristotelian framework he uses in this moral exploration is augmented and shot through with theological considerations about grace and the role of God in helping one lead a good life.[22]

So to get a proper appreciation of Aquinas's views on faith, it is necessary to understand virtue theory, including the inner structure of a virtue, the kinds of virtue, their relationship to human capacities and their relationship to human ends.

3.3.1   The framework of virtue theory

Aquinas moves between two different definitions of virtue in ST I-II q.55. The question addresses whether virtue is a habit, an operative habit, a good habit, and finally seeks to define virtue. In the first three articles he draws mainly on Aristotle. He does not fully cite Aristotle's definition of a virtue – 'virtue is a state concerned with choice, lying in a mean relative to us, this being determined by reason and in the way in which the man of practical wisdom would determine it' [*Nicomachean Ethics*, 2.6, 1106b36–1107a2], but draws on it – saying virtue is a habit, one relating to action, which seeks to perfect action. However, when he comes to establish a definition, he draws on Peter Lombard, who paraphrases Augustine, saying 'Virtue is a good quality of the mind by which we live rightly, of which no-one can make bad use, which God works in us, without us' [Lombard *Sentences* II d.27 Ch.5 citing Augustine *De Libero Arbitrio* II.19].

The tension between the two is between a philosophical and theological conception of virtue. Aristotle's virtue is acquired through training and habituation, relates to one's natural inclinations and dispositions and leads to *eudaimonia*, or living well. Lombard's definition refers to something given by God, which we are not responsible for. The former makes sense of moral theory. To be moral is to live a virtuous life. The second seems to remove virtue from the realm of morality, since it is directly instilled by God and we do not have responsibility for it. How do they coexist? The answer lies in the variegated notion of virtue – there are different kinds, some of which fit Lombard's definition better and some Aristotle's. To clarify this, I need to examine the inner structure of virtue and its different kinds. Aquinas explicitly notes that virtue is an analogous term [ST I–II 61.1], so there are different kinds of it.

Aquinas holds that virtue pertains to the soul. The soul is the source of life and action in humans, and therefore is the ultimate seat of the virtues. More precisely, virtues pertain to the powers of the soul – they are perfections of powers of the soul [ST I–II.55.1]. In Aquinas's terminology, the powers of the soul are the 'subject' of the virtues. Perfection is considered in relation to an end, and the end of a power is action. So virtue pertains to actions in a human being – they are ways of perfecting actions. One way of distinguishing virtues is by noting difference in subject. Insofar as they apply to different powers of the soul, they differ. Aquinas notes that there are two basic principles of human action – reason and appetite [ST I–II.58.3]. Thus, different kinds of virtues apply to these different principles – intellectual and moral virtues (with an important note that Prudence cuts across the intellectual/moral divide). If the subject of a virtue is the power in which it resides, an even more important feature of a virtue is its object. The object of a virtue is what specifies it more precisely; it is what individuates each virtue, what makes it what it is. The object of a virtue is the action, the end, or the perfection towards which the power tends. Just as a natural object gets its identity from its form, an action is specified by its object. [ST I–II 18.2]. So virtue, as the excellence, or perfection, of an action is made to be what it is by the kind of action involved. A multiplicity of different kinds of actions yields many different kinds of virtue. Some actions are transitive, directed to outward entities, for example, making, moving, hitting. Other actions are immanent, in the agent, for example, thinking, wishing, loving, hating. Each of these has an object – that towards which the action is directed. Furthermore, each object can be construed or regarded in varying ways. The distinction between the material and the formal helps clarify this. The material object is the object of the action in a straightforward way – the ball I am going to kick, the page I am going to read. The formal object is the aspect, the element of interest, why I am engaged with it. I can act in relation to the ball by kicking it, painting it, measuring it. The same material object has differing formal objects. Also each of these actions has a different subject – different powers of the soul are in play in kicking, painting and measuring. So, to summarize: a virtue is a perfection of a power of the soul. What makes it the virtue it is partly due to its subject – which power it pertains to, and partly due to its object, what kind of action it involves, determined by the material and formal object of action.

In ST I–II.55.4, Aquinas discusses virtue in relation to the four causes. The formal cause of virtue is gained by noting its genus and difference – virtue is a good quality, or more precisely, a good habit. Its material cause is the 'in which' and 'about which'. The 'in which' is its subject (power of soul), and the 'about which' is the object (action). The end of virtue is an operative habit – but unlike operative habits which refer to evil (vices), virtues help one live rightly. The efficient cause of virtue depends on the kind of virtue involved. God is the efficient cause of some virtues, whereas training, natural inclination and character are the efficient cause of others [ST I–II.63.1]. With this discriminatory machinery, Aquinas can give a comprehensive account of the different kinds of virtue that exist.

There is a basic distinction between the powers of the soul, as noted above. Virtues which pertain to the intellect are intellectual virtues, whereas those pertaining to the appetites are moral virtues. However, intellectual virtues do not, in themselves, make us good persons. I may use my intelligence to bad ends, reason impeccably to an evil act. Thus, intellectual virtues are only partial virtues. The subject of a habit, which is called a virtue absolutely, is the will [ST I–II.56.3]. The four main (cardinal) virtues are justice, prudence, fortitude and temperance. Justice applies to the will, prudence to the practical intellect, fortitude to the irascible passions and temperance to the concupiscable passions. Aquinas's psychology distinguishes the theoretical and practical intellect, the will, the emotions associated with anger and aggression and the emotions associated with desire. All of these issue in actions and the virtues which make these actions good are the chief virtues. Prudence is the key virtue, which unites intellectual with moral virtue and which serves to make the whole person good through individual actions and choices. Aquinas has a positive attitude towards the emotions, or passions, believing that they are good insofar as they are in line with reason, bad when they are disordered. But unlike, say, the Stoics, he thinks emotion is morally neutral in itself [ST I–II 59.2].

This discussion fits the Aristotelian account of virtue well. The nature, subject, object and species of virtue have been discussed and outlined. However, there are two extra kinds of virtue which do not fit with the Aristotelian scheme at all. These are the theological virtues – faith, hope and charity, and what he calls the infused moral virtues – virtues which God causes directly in us. To grasp his account of faith, this extension of the Aristotelian framework needs to be addressed.

Aquinas differs from Aristotle on the virtues in two chief ways. Firstly, he has a role for the will which Aristotle does not have. A virtue in the full sense is one whose subject is the will [ST I–II.56.3], hence the intellectual virtues (except prudence) are not full virtues. Secondly, he has a range of virtues which Aristotle does not countenance, the theological virtues and the infused moral virtues. The theological virtues are faith, hope and charity. The source of these is different to that of the other virtues. The intellectual and moral virtues derive from a mixture of nature and nurture – basic natural dispositions, as well as training and character formation. However, the theological virtues are directly granted by God. Humans have free choice as to whether to accept them and can block them, but cannot acquire them by their own efforts. The reason why such virtues are required is due to the double end of human existence in Aquinas's system. On the one hand, there is the natural end of human life, which is Aristotelian flourishing, while on the other hand, there is the supernatural end of human life that is accessed by means of revelation. Aquinas believes that this latter is essential for human flourishing – but it is not accessible to reason alone. Further assistance to human cognition is required. Hence, the theological virtues are given by God – or 'infused', in Aquinas's terminology. Another way in which they differ from intellectual and moral virtues is that the doctrine of the mean does not apply to them. There is no mean in faith because of its object – God. There can never be enough faith since the object of the virtue so far exceeds human capacities. Thus, in source, object and relation to the mean, theological virtues differ from acquired virtues.

There is a puzzling further element to his full treatment of the virtues, the infused moral virtues. Why duplicate the virtues in this way? Why add the same virtues – say temperance – but this time infused by God and not gained by habit or training? Furthermore, since a virtue is specified by its act – how would infused temperance differ from regular temperance, since they both seem to result in the same actions?

The source of acquired virtue is human nature, which is perfected by that virtue – so there is a structure of natural inclination and then the perfection of a virtue cultivating that inclination. The theological virtues relate to the infused moral virtues in the same structure. Theological virtues operate as a source, and infused moral virtues flow from these as a cultivation and perfection of them. The object of the theological virtues is God – faith, hope and charity all relate to God as their object, but infused moral virtues relate to actions in the world performed in the light of faith, hope and charity. Infused moral virtues are the virtues which govern human life in the light of divine revelation. They differ from acquired virtue in terms of their formal object. Recalling that the formal object is the aspect or interest or intelligible dimension of the act performed – the formal object of acquired temperance and infused temperance differs. Acquired temperance pertains to living well in this life and seeks bodily and mental health. Infused temperance pertains to the specific demands of religious belief – and so fasting for religious purposes would have a place here, whereas it does not in acquired temperance (where fasting for health purposes does).

So Aquinas's treatment of the virtues involves three distinct kinds – intellectual, moral and theological. He also uses the acquired/infused distinction, the sophisticated machinery of subject/object and the four causes, as a way of individuating each virtue into a coherent framework, each related to intellect, will and passions in the human being. This is the framework required for understanding his treatment of faith.

3.3.2 The virtue of faith

Aquinas's discussion of faith in ST II-II 1–7 is structured by the elements of virtue theory. He starts by considering the object of faith, which individuates it as a virtue (q.1), then considers the act of faith, given that an act is the object of a virtue (q.2–3), then considers it as a virtue (q.4) and queries who has faith (q.5) and what are its causes (q.6) and effects (q.7). The discussion is complex and the topics interwoven, so I shall start with the definition of faith.

The definition taken from Hebrews 11.1 is regarded as a canonical statement of faith (4.1): 'Faith is the substance of things hoped for, the evidence of things that appear not'. The limpid Latin says *Fides est substantia sperandarum rerum, argumentum non apparentium*. The first clause indicates that it is somehow incomplete or future oriented, involving hope, and the second that there is argument somehow involved, typically testimony from a reliable source. Faith pertains to the intellect, but is also connected to the will. It entails believing something, not under the conditions governed by reason, but rather under conditions governed by the will. Things believed on faith do not contradict or go against reason, but neither are they established by reason. There is a choice, and the will plays a role in establishing the belief. Why reason does not fix these beliefs, how the will *does* fix them and what legitimacy this process might have are all discussed within the treatment of this virtue, as will be seen. In any individual, faith is akin to opinion in not being fixed by reason, but akin to science in being certain and unwavering.

Belief is a central part of faith. Aquinas discusses the meaning of belief (*credere*) as 'to ponder with assent' (*cum assensione cogitare*) (2.1). He notes that *cogitare* can be understood in three ways. Firstly, in the broadest sense it is any intellectual awareness. Secondly, it is a kind of searching which precedes complete understanding. Finally, it has a technical meaning in Aquinas's account of cognition as a faculty which marshals sensory information in preparation for more general abstract thought. The first is too broad, and the third is to specialized to be relevant to making sense of belief, so the second sense of *cogitare* brings out the proper meaning of belief for Aquinas. Among mental acts, some achieve certainty without a process of cogitation – for example, a grasp of first principles. Others have this process and also have certainty – this is scientific knowledge. Other mental acts have a process of cogitation, but do not produce certainty, hovering between alternatives, such as suspicion or opinion. In any individual person, faith is akin to this latter (opinion), in not being compelled by reason to one of a set of alternatives, but is also akin to knowledge (*scientia*) in firmly fixing to one of the alternatives, but under the impulse of the will.

Having discussed the definition of faith and the meaning of the key term 'belief', let us turn to the framework of virtue theory to make more sense of it. What is the object of faith (which individuates it as a virtue), what sort of act is associated with faith and what is the subject of faith? What faculty of the soul does faith pertain to?

If we recall that the object of a virtue is distinguished into a material object and a formal object, we can analyse faith in this fashion. The material object of faith, for Aquinas, is constituted by the articles of the Creed, these are the central truths about God required for Christian belief (1.1). To believe a proposition is to have cognitive access to some aspect of reality – this is common to scientific knowledge and to faith ('the only reason for formulating a proposition is that we may have knowledge about the real' 1.2.ad2). I shall return to this issue below in discussing the modern debate concerning whether faith should be construed primarily intellectually (or propositionally as it is often labelled) or whether it is something non-cognitive. If the material object of faith is a set of truths, the formal object of faith is called 'the First Truth' (*Veritas Prima*). The formal object is the way, manner or aspect under which the formal object is considered. The beliefs which are proclaimed in the Creed could be subjected to philosophical or linguistic or poetical analysis – in each case this would be a different formal object. Speaking of 'first truth' is a way of referring to God, and what Aquinas means is that the content of faith is mediated by God, not by reason. Faith involves a direct communication by God. So the beliefs which are considered (the material object) are believed because of *who* is presenting them (the formal object). In this sense, faith is a theological virtue – both the material and the formal object are understood to be God. The material object – the creedal statements – are either propositions about God or about other things related to God (e.g. creation), and so are means of being in cognitive contact with God, while the formal object is the direct self-communication by God. For Aquinas, the latter means revelation – the communication by God, which amounts to scripture and the community of believers. Again, what exactly Aquinas understands by revelation will be critically discussed below, but for the moment the discussion of faith in terms of its object serves to specify it as the kind of virtue it is.

What is the subject of this virtue? What power of the soul does it relate to? Aquinas is explicit that its seat is in the speculative intellect: 'the seat of faith is the speculative intellect; this is clearly evident from the object of faith' (4.3 ad3). Yet while faith is an exercise of the speculative intellect, it is unusual in that the intellect is not fixed by reason, as is the case with most other beliefs in the intellect. We do not choose scientific beliefs; rather, they are forced upon us by the evidence. Faith is not forced, but is a choice. The will is the power of the soul which governs beliefs associated with faith, because the will is the power of the soul which desires the good. For the virtue of faith, belief in God is not forced by the intellect, but attracted by the will. Why does not the intellect play a dominant role here?

There are canonical philosophers who theorize about the limits of reason – such as Kant and Wittgenstein. Aquinas is not usually considered with them, insofar as he famously holds that one can argue for God's existence, which is a strong claim for reason. But his position is quite nuanced on this. There are some topics on which reason is capable of making true judgements – metaphysical truths such as knowledge of God's existence.[23] There are other topics on which reason is incapable of forming a true judgement – for example, the eternity of the world. Against his contemporaries he argued that it is impossible to make a reasoned determination on this. We can understand the issue, examine the arguments, but not reach a resolution on them. However, furthermore, there are topics which go right beyond the scope of reason, even in terms of grasping the issues. These are topics which belong specifically to faith and which contain data which is not available to metaphysical or reasoned speculation – God's entering human history in the Incarnation or the inner structure of God as Trinity. Even to grasp the topic, one needs super-rational input, let alone its being possible to give a reasoned demonstration of the truth of such topics. Hence, there are a range of topics which are in principle inaccessible to reason and which are the kinds of topic which are held on faith.

Yet, even for those topics which in principle can be demonstrated by reason, in fact they are held on faith by many people. While Aquinas thinks that one can reasonably demonstrate that God exists, most people do not believe in God on the basis of such demonstrations. For a start, even to attempt such a demonstration requires a high level of sophisticated philosophical training, so most people would not get to belief in God except after graduate training in philosophy. Secondly, only a few people have the requisite natural aptitude, opportunity and drive towards such study, and finally such study is notoriously open to error and dispute (2.4). Hence, if reasoning towards God's existence were the way to believe in God, only a few elderly scholars would be believers. Aquinas himself did not come to believe in God in this way, although by reflecting on the question of God he came to have some kind of reasoned account of God.

On Aquinas's account, faith-based belief and knowledge are incompatible propositional attitudes. If one 'knows' something, then one cannot have faith in it, while if one has faith, this excludes knowledge in the strict sense. Thus, on some topics – the existence and nature of God – it is possible to have reasoned knowledge, although for many this is a matter of faith. On other topics there is no reasoned access in principle (e.g. creation, the Trinity), and so these beliefs can only be held on the basis of faith. Aquinas at times refers to the topics which are in principle accessible to reason as 'preambles' (*praeambula*) to faith, while those topics which are in principle inaccessible are matters of faith proper. Yet it is important to note that for any individual believer, it may well be the case that the *praeambula* topics are also held on faith. If the intellect is limited in this way, why is it not appropriate to be sceptical or agnostic on such issues? Why is it appropriate for the will to play the role it does in determining one's beliefs on these issues?

Aquinas (2.2) draws attention to a distinction made by Augustine – to believe God (*credere Deo*), to believe in God (*credere Deum*) and to believe unto God (*credere in Deum*). The propositions which are believed, the material object of faith, relate to believing in God (*credere Deum*). The formal object, God as teaching truths, is believing God (*credere Deo*). This distinction is one between content and medium, between the 'what' and the 'how' of belief. The content is the information contained in the belief, and the medium is God as presenting, revealing or teaching it. Both of these relate to the intellect – the propositional content which the intellect recognizes and the way in which that propositional content is conveyed to the intellect. However, the third element, believing unto God, (*credere in Deum*) pertains to the will. This speaks of the way the intellect is moved by the will. Notice the close interaction of these, as Herbert McCabe underlines,

> There is an interweaving of understanding and being attracted that cannot be unravelled in practice. We think of what we are *attracted* to thinking of, and we are attracted to what we *think* of.[24]

In the context of faith, the intellect does not have reasons in the way scientific knowledge operates, which impel it to assent. However, the will exerts a force on the intellect and draws it to assent to these beliefs. It is, of course, possible for the will not to exert this force or for the intellect to withhold assent. In this, the assent of the intellect is a free choice, unlike in scientific knowledge. The will operates as a force which desires what it understands as good. In matters of faith, God is conceived as the ultimate good by the will, and this is what draws the will to exert a force on the intellect to assent to the truths proposed. So the basic idea is that the intellect is open with respect to the matters of faith. In these circumstances it is appropriate for the will to direct the intellect to one set of alternatives on the basis of attraction to the good, given that God is the supreme good and the end of all desiring.

Indeed, it is crucial for the virtue of faith that freedom is essential to it. Aquinas has a discussion of the beliefs of devils, which provides some interesting insight into this view (nothing hangs, in the conceptual sphere, on whether devils actually exist or not). He wonders whether the beliefs of devils are the same as the faith of those having faith. The problem is that if they are, how can the devils have a virtue, and if not, how does one makes sense of the kind of knowledge the devils have? He holds that the devils do have faith in some sense, but it differs from the faith of virtuous believers in being unformed; it has no connection to charity. It is not meritorious because it is 'forced from them by evidence of signs' [5.2ad1]; therefore, it lacks the conditions of freedom which makes faith a virtue. Earlier I noted that the form of a virtue derives from its act – what individuates it or makes it to be the virtue it is, is the object to which it is directed. How does this fit with the distinction between formed and unformed faith? The object of faith is the good, and the good is attained by the will, not the intellect (as a voluntary act). Thus, the subject of faith is the intellect, but in this case the intellect is directed by the will. Therefore, it is legitimate to say that the form (understood as a perfection or completion) of the intellect lies in the attractiveness of the good as the desire of will (4.3). Charity (*caritas* – love of God) is what fuels this attraction, and so Aquinas says that charity is what forms faith. The demons have beliefs about God, but lack charity. Hence their faith is unformed – it lacks virtue. In this way Aquinas maintains the essential structure of the virtue of faith, while distinguished the crucial extrinsic link to free will and charity, which marks off meritorious belief from the beliefs of demons.

At this point I shall pause in the presentation of Aquinas's view of faith and return to some of the issues touched upon in the presentation on both reason and faith and their interrelationship. In relation to reason, there is the issue of how to make sense of *scientia* and how to classify it epistemologically. In relation to faith, there is the issue of to what extent Aquinas's view is too propositional or intellectualistic. Finally, there is the fundamental question of whether his view is ultimately plausible as it faces problems including the charge from rationalism of epistemic circularity, from modern Christians of having an outmoded, pre-critical view of scripture and finally from other religious believers, the problem of religious pluralism.

3.4 Assessing Aquinas's position

3.4.1 Reason

As mentioned above, an initial response to Aquinas's account of reason is that it is just too unrealistic. None of our knowledge has the kind of apodictic structure he outlines. He takes the model of something like geometry and then generalizes across all knowledge in an implausible manner. However, against that is that his view is an idealization – an account of the nature of a completed science, which is compatible with our actual knowledge being quite far removed from this. Indeed, despite his optimistic statements about *sacra doctrina*, its firmness and certainty, even theological knowledge can be imperfect. Aquinas's realism allows him to articulate the existence of a science which is not actually in human possession. He distinguishes between certainty as an abstract relation between truths in a completed science and certainty as a psychological state in us (4.8). Absolutely speaking, faith is more certain since it is somehow a sharing in God's own knowledge, but other forms of knowledge are more certain to us. Thus there may be error in our grasp of the truths of scripture or theological principles, just as we may be mistaken in our grasp of first principles, failing to understand them properly or identifying wrong ones.

One of the things this points to is that his account of knowledge acknowledges levels, degrees and kinds of knowledge. It is not univocal. Eleanore Stump convincingly argues that *scientia* cannot be understood simply as 'knowledge', since *scientia* is of universal, certain and immutable truths. Thus, if it were equated with knowledge *simpliciter*, we would have no knowledge of contingent, mutable singular things. It is a particularly high-grade form of knowledge which coexists with knowledge of particulars, probabilistic knowledge and practical wisdom, which work in different ways. *Scientia*, for Aquinas, is dissimilar to modern anti-sceptical foundationalist epistemologies, despite its structural similarities to such. These latter seek a foundation from which one can rebut sceptical assault. What *scientia* offers is a way of deepening our understanding, of knowing the deep causes of things, of limning the structure of reality. Given that, Aquinas distinguishes different kinds of intellectual virtue and says, following Aristotle, that

> the method of manifesting truth in any science ought to be suitable to the subject matter of that science. [Aristotle] shows this from the fact that certitude cannot be found, nor should it be sought, in the same degree in all discussions where we reason about anything. [In NE 1.3.32]

It makes sense to read him as having a diversified and supple account of the different kinds of knowledge. Hence his account of *scientia* serves as an idealized model of a certain kind of cognition, which coexists with a variegated array of different kinds of cognitive activity. Therefore, it seems unfair to accuse him of being procrustean in his account of reason.

3.4.2   Faith and circular reasoning

Here is a response which is often given to Aquinas's account of faith. Granted the subtlety and complexity of the view presented, along with the elaborate discussion of virtue theory and the intricacy of the distinctions made, there still is a sense of its begging the question. When one picks through the details sufficiently to get to the bottom of it, it emerges as somehow free-floating, lacking justification, a castle built in the air. Faith makes sense assuming that there is a God and that God communicates truthfully through revelation, but the story about God and revelation itself rests on faith.

One possible reply to this is to emphasize the independent rational justification for the existence of God – that Aquinas presents a robust natural theology which gives rational assurance of God's existence and that one can then argue for the reasonableness of revelation and other truths on that basis. In such a picture, Aquinas is indeed a kind of foundationalist, providing sound deductive arguments for the claims of his system. Faith can then be reasonable, given the independent justification of God's existence. Certain things are known by reasoning alone (God's existence), while others are communicated directly by God (Incarnation, the Trinity), given we already know God exists. Neo-scholastic apologetics tended to go this route in the face of Enlightenment criticism. However, as I noted above, Aquinas holds that it is appropriate for Christians to believe on faith all the way down, so to speak. There does not have to be a rationalistic foundation (*praeambula*) on which faith-related issues are rooted. But if this is the correct reading of Aquinas, does that not then fall back into the problem of circular reasoning?

Crucial to the intelligibility of Aquinas's position are two related assumptions. Firstly, there is a commitment to the harmony of faith and reason. Whatever is held on faith does not contradict reason. Many atheists will balk at this point, holding that the whole panoply of religious beliefs goes against reason. However, when such arguments are assessed, it emerges that what is usually in question here is a specific conception of reason – typically what is called scientific reason. And here the question is whether beliefs in the existence of God, that Jesus rose from the dead and so on are compatible with that. It turns out to be rather hard to articulate clearly a convincing argument advancing the sceptical view that is not obviously question-begging itself or just wrong. One of the most popular arguments – verificationism – is generally regarded as dead in philosophy, despite having a flourishing half-life in writings of popular science. These are issues which will be examined in more detail in Chapter 5, where I shall examine Aquinas's treatment of what is called the naturalistic challenge. Also Chapters 6 and 7, on the divine attributes, are devoted to Aquinas's sustained attempt to show the reasonableness of what is said about God. But for the moment I shall note that it is by no means obvious that religious beliefs are incompatible with scientific beliefs.

The second assumption is that there are limits to reason. There are some things which are in principle inaccessible to human reasoning. To deny this is to hold that everything is in principle accessible to human cognition. This assumption does not seem very troublesome in itself, and indeed its negation seems to be intellectually hubristic. The tricky element here is to affirm that there is something inaccessible to reason, which nevertheless is accessible in some other way. The 'some other way' – faith – is the troublesome part. Why accept that this is a legitimate source of information?

There seems to be a difference between the epistemological status of those with faith and those without it. Those who have it claim to have a mode of insight into reality which is lacking in those who do not. Contrariwise, those without it argue that the faith claims are mistaken or delusional. For this latter position to work, it would need to be shown that claims to have faith are either impossible or explicable by other means. If it turns out to be hard to show that they are impossible (given the effort to show how they do not contradict reason), much effort goes into giving a naturalistic explanation of them. Freudian or other psychological explanations are advanced as defeaters of religious faith – explaining the sense of conviction or the phenomenology of religious belief in terms of underlying psychological mechanisms. However, it seems that atheism is assumed rather than demonstrated by Freudian psychoanalysis. Sigmund Freud assumes a nineteenth-century scientific world view which renders God redundant, and goes on to theorize about the origins of religious belief in wish fulfilment and delusions. But on his technical account of an illusion, an illusion is a belief that I wish to be true. Hence the truth or falsity of a belief has no bearing on whether it is an illusion or not. For example, whether this book is good or not, it is nevertheless an illusion for me to think of it as being good, since I want it to be so. On such an odd view of an illusion, it seems to say little of importance to call belief in God an illusion. Indeed, Aquinas's view of faith affirms that it is an illusion in precisely this harmless sense – desire is central to holding the belief. One may canvass other kinds of naturalistic explanation of religious belief, but a general observation is that they are compelling only if there is an antecedent assumption that religious belief is not true. On their own they do not serve to defeat the epistemic claims of religious belief. Most sophisticated theists would want to accept whatever is true in such accounts, but nevertheless still maintain the truth of the religious claims. Aquinas's constant refrain on the compatibility of grace and nature allows one to accept natural causes, while still affirming an underlying divine cause. This idea of multiple concurrent causation will be explored in Chapter 4.

What then of this difference between those with faith and those without? Well, at the least it is a phenomenological distinction. That is, those with faith have a certain kind of experience which differs from those without. On Aquinas's account, this difference lies in the experience of the attractiveness or desirability of those beliefs which are held on faith. Reason can have a role in clarifying, removing objections or defending against critique of such beliefs, but does not in itself justify them. However, this phenomenological difference gives a kind of justification to those with the experience which is lacking in those without it. The very having of such a desire (understood in the theoretical context that the object desired is an actual good, indeed the supreme good) is sufficient to make one intellectually virtuous in freely believing such beliefs. However, this epistemic justification is in a certain sense first-personal. It is appropriate for those who have such a phenomenological experience to hold these beliefs – just as it is appropriate for those without it not to. Aquinas tries to show how there is a certain subjectivity or personal responsibility in accepting beliefs on faith, which at the same time is not epistemically blameworthy or deluded. His subtle account has the resources to respond to the charge of crude circularity given his two assumptions of the compatibility of faith and reason and limits to reason. That is, he argues for a space in which the deliverances of faith may be permissible. However, if one accepts this position, there is still a challenge possible about the content of such faith. If one accepts that reason does not tell us everything of importance for humans and that some source of information beyond the merely natural is available to us, what of the problem of the diversity of such accounts? Unlike deliverances of reason, deliverances of faith are notoriously fractious and incompatible with each other. How might Aquinas respond to this problem?

3.4.3 Faith and pluralism

While there has always been diversity of religious belief, the contemporary world acknowledges a bewildering variety of traditions, denominations and belief systems. Furthermore, while such diversity has traditionally led to antagonism and conflict, a new attitude of pluralism exists in relation to such diversity. That is, for the pluralist, no one religion is the sole true belief system, but a variety of incompatible systems may be all appropriate vehicles of salvation for their adherents. So both the extent of religious diversity and attitudes to such diversity are different in the contemporary world from that of Aquinas. This is not to say that sectarianism has been abolished or triumphalism eradicated, but among scholars of religion there has grown a comparatist tendency, a realization that one needs to respond positively in some sense or other to such diversity. While Aquinas acknowledged Jews, Muslims, pagans and Christian heretics as holders of different views to his own (with significantly different attitudes to each of these groups), he was not aware of religious views as radically different to his own as Mahayana Buddhism, Shintoism or Advaita Vedanta. Nor was widespread secularism or atheism part of his world (his example of atheism is taken from Psalm 52). So what could his notion of faith have to offer to the contemporary situation?

Two significant advocates of religious pluralism have argued that Aquinas's work fits well with a pluralistic attitude.[25] John Hick is possibly the best-known advocate of religious pluralism. He argues that the world is religiously ambiguous – one is not rationally compelled to either theism or atheism. Adopting a Kantian epistemology, he distinguishes between the object of religious belief – The Real – and those religious traditions which speak about the real. The Real (analogous to Kant's noumenon) is beyond our grasp, while religious traditions (analogous to Kant's phenomenon) are ways in which the Real is made available. A religious tradition in all its richness (beliefs, rituals, institutions, art, ethics etc.) serves as a cognitive filter by which aspects of the Real are made manifest. Some filters emphasize the more personal aspects of the Real (theistic religions), whilst others emphasize the impersonal (Buddhism, Taoism, Vedanta). Hick's key (and controversial) claim is that each tradition is legitimate in itself and that none has any claim of superiority in relation to the others – which is the religious pluralist position. Hick cites Aquinas in support of his view by focussing on Aquinas's distinction between modes of knowledge and the reality known and his views on the unknowability of God. Aquinas states in many places 'Whatever is known is known according to the mode of the knower'.[26] Given that Aquinas thinks there are different types of cognitive agent (God, angels, humans), each of these may know the same thing but in different manners. For example, human knowledge is temporal, whereas God's knowledge is outside time. Hick, however, links this view to the Kantian distinction between noumenal and phenomenal reality, that Aquinas might agree with his view of The Real as unknown and our knowledge as a filter between us and it – a filter which admits of radically alternative conceptions. And indeed given Aquinas's insistence on the unknowability of God, it might appear that such an assimilation may be plausible. But it is not for the following reasons. While Aquinas thinks that our grasp of God's essence is faint and incomplete, he is certain that one can articulate basic minimal truths about God. A fundamental truth about God is that God is the ultimate cause of creatures and that further negative specifications, such as God is not material, not in time, does not have parts and so forth are all literally true. So these rule out the possibility that views rejecting such claims are valid. Aquinas is committed to the ontological truths of theism. Hence, he cannot endorse a pluralistic approach to non-theistic beliefs. Furthermore, his basic commitment to realism is at odds with Hick's Kantian anti-realism. For Hick, one cannot specify anything about the Real in itself. Aquinas accepts the diversity of modes of cognition, but affirms that they all relate to the same world, of which they give complementary accounts. God knows truths timelessly, while humans know them in time – but the different forms of knowledge are of the same truths. The interpretative point here is that it just seems incorrect to assimilate Aquinas's views to Hick's project, whatever the relative values of their views.

Wilfred Cantwell Smith has devoted sustained attention to Aquinas's views on faith in his book on faith and belief. He distinguishes faith and belief as follows. Belief is narrowly propositional, meaning the set of explicit cognitive claims one is willing to assent to. Faith is wider, an attitude towards reality which includes non-cognitive elements.

[Faith is] deeper, richer, more personal…. It is an orientation of the personality to oneself, to one's neighbour, to the universe; a total response; a way of seeing whatever one sees and of handling whatever one handles; a capacity to live at a more than mundane level; to see to feel, to act in terms of, a transcendent dimension. Belief on the other hand is the holding of certain ideas.[27]

While there may be a great diversity in terms of the kinds of cognitive belief religious believers hold, the structure of faith itself is common to many – an attitude of trust, a quality of human living. Cantwell Smith thereby distinguishes between the propositional and intellectualist notion of belief and the more capacious, attitudinal notion of faith. When people of different belief systems differ in terms of propositional contents assented to, they can come together in terms of the wider attitude towards reality they hold. He holds that this distinction can be found in Aquinas too. His case rests on holding that Aquinas thinks that propositions are a means to an end[28]; they are human constructs which serve as means of accessing reality beyond themselves. What amounts to faith is the total response to such a reality, involving non-cognitive dimensions as well. Hick refers to Cantwell Smith's analysis of Aquinas approvingly as an appropriate way to read him.

Whatever the merits of Cantwell Smith's own position, it seems incorrect to assimilate Aquinas to his project. Firstly, Aquinas thinks that propositions are what we use to express our knowledge of reality. We have no other means available to us. They do not constitute a representational 'third realm' between us and reality. Aquinas's epistemological realism treats them as modifications of our cognitive apparatus by means of which we think about reality. That is, they are not detachable units which can be separated from an overall approach to reality. They make intelligible the notion of reality, presenting it under an aspect to us. While Aquinas certainly thinks there is more to faith than mere propositional belief, it is nevertheless a necessary component of it. As T.C. O'Brien remarked, for Aquinas 'faith is not a contentless existential stance'.[29] Aquinas's discussion of formed versus unformed faith addresses the further elements which should be present with belief to form a full virtue – but crucially he thinks that unformed faith is still the same habit. The bare belief involved in the belief of demons (which is unfree and lacks the appropriate attitude) is the very same as that which the person of faith has, freely chosen and formed by love. Thus there is an intrinsic link for Aquinas between belief and faith, which seems to be extrinsic for Cantwell Smith. Furthermore, there are numerous passages in Aquinas where he affirms the need for explicit propositional assent to the articles of faith, especially in ST II-II q.2 a 5–8 and QDV XIV.11. One has to believe explicitly the primary tenets of faith, namely the articles of the Creed, including the Incarnation and the Trinity. It is not simply a dispositional, or potential assent which is required, but explicit public belief. Hence Aquinas seems very far from accepting anything like religious pluralism and affirms either a robust exclusivism or blind dogmatism, depending on one's attitude to this.

Nevertheless, there are nuances in his position – he acknowledges certain contextual factors – such as historical location, geographical location, social role – which impact on the way one might have a belief. 'The mystery of Christ's Incarnation was to be believed in all ages by all peoples in some fashion, but in ways differing with the differences of times and people' [2.7]. Jews before the coming of Christ believed differently from those after. Those with leadership roles in the community have a greater burden of explicit belief than those without. What of those who live in the forest or are brought up with wolves? Aquinas affirms that if such people follow the good of natural reason, providence will furnish everything necessary for salvation, providing there is no hindrance [QDV 14.11.ad1]. So, in principle, Aquinas allows for the possibility of salvation to those who through no fault of their own have no access to revelation. Nevertheless, he thinks that those who *do* receive revelation, but fail to accept it, are blameworthy. However, it is arguable that, given his allowance of contextual factors, he might think differently in a multicultural context. What exactly counts, in the modern sphere, as 'hearing the Gospel'? With a plethora of competing world views and the disedifying practices of many advancing the views he himself endorses, it is plausible that Aquinas might think that receiving revelation is not quite straightforward.

4
Arguments for God's Existence

4.1 Preliminaries

4.1.1 What is Aquinas doing?

While Aquinas holds that reason is capable of yielding truths about God, he also maintains that it is not necessary that any particular person should acquire such truths by reasoning alone, since faith is sufficient for this, as has been discussed in the previous chapter. What then is the role of reason in dealing with God? Aquinas believes that reason defuses objections to religious belief and clarifies the content of such belief [SCG 1.9]. Yet he also thinks that human reason is capable of attaining some knowledge of God.[1] This is the realm of natural theology, a metaphysical reflection on the world which moves from the obvious to the hidden. Greeks, Jews, Islamic and earlier Christian thinkers had engaged in this intellectual practice, and Aquinas joined them.

His account of *scientia* provided an outline of the nature of such meta-physical explanation. This kind of explanation presented the connections from causes to effects as a comprehensive structural explanation of any phenomenon. However, as one approaches the most fundamental causes, the direction of explanation changes. Instead of demonstrations running from causes to effect (*demonstratio propter quid*), they run from effects to underlying cause (*demonstratio quia*) [ST 1.2.2]. This latter is a weaker form of demonstration than the former (since the former assigns real causes based on the essential structure of whatever is being discussed), and it answers the question *An est?*, whether something exists. This question has a distinctive role in Aristotelian science and is a precon-dition of scientific knowledge – one needs to know that one is talking about something really existent before then moving on to analysing its inner structure. To do this, one has to have some kind of initial nominal definition which picks out the target of discussion. It will turn out that the kinds of characterization of God given in Aquinas's argumentation in the five ways – as first mover, first cause, source of necessity and so on – are all nominal definitions which serve as the basis for the more precise specification of God's nature in subsequent discussions. Aquinas therefore argues from certain observable phenomena in reality to an underlying metaphysical reality which is significantly different from the starting phenomena. Furthermore, one can state some truths about the nature of this underlying reality in clear propositional form.

However, despite the fact that one can rationally state that such a reality exists and can affirm certain truths about its nature, Aquinas contends that reason is nevertheless severely limited in its task. The nature of such a reality and its inner structure are beyond the scope of our mental capacities. Aquinas thinks we can be assured in stating that such a reality exists and that our thinking about it is constrained by certain parameters, but the reality far exceeds our capacity to know it.[2] His realism is thus characterized by a firmness about stating what can be known, but an equal firmness about what cannot.

What then is the purpose of this argumentation about God's existence? One way of thinking about it, natural to modern sensibilities, is to think of it as providing an epistemological justification for one's beliefs. To generate an argument for God's existence is to establish a rational foundation for one's religious belief.[3] However, this is not what Aquinas does. As we have seen in the previous chapter, he does not think that this is psychologically how people acquire religious beliefs, nor is it necessary to justify them in this way. Nevertheless, given the harmony of faith and reason, Aquinas thinks it possible to show that the content of faith is not incompatible with the best of what reason can achieve. One might call this an ontological rather than epistemological construal of these arguments – their purpose is to show how talk about God rationally fits with talk about the rest of reality (our ontology), rather than offering rationalistic justifications of God's existence. In a sense, one might think of this as akin to the way a naturalistic philosopher relates to natural science, not accepting that philosophy provides a justification or foundation for science, but yet believing it has a role in clarifying the logic and structure of scientific talk and its relationships with other forms of discourse.[4] And even accepting this ontological rather than epistemological construal of the arguments, they are not ones which *any* reasonable person would be convinced by straight off. They require knowledge of difficult metaphysical concepts to even make sense of them, let alone be swayed by them. William Rowe has a useful discussion of the relativity of proof in philosophical arguments in general which bears on this.[5] Given that one might think an argument logically valid, one still has to accept the premises, or the interpretation of the terms involved, or the scope of the conclusion. One might think of Aquinas's arguments as rational reconstructions of how one might argue for a basic underlying metaphysical causal explanation of the physical world, given the conceptual scheme he deploys. And of course the conceptual scheme itself along with the rational reconstruction generated from its resources are all vulnerable to challenge and critique.

Indeed, one might observe that Aquinas's arguments for God's existence are among the most anthologized and most criticized passages in all philosophical literature. Objections are regularly marshalled against the concept of causation involved, against his rejection of infinite regress, against the identification of the conclusion of such arguments with God, against the inner structure of the argumentation, against Aquinas's alleged begging of the question, against the use of outdated physics. Given that many philosophers have a glancing familiarity with Aquinas's arguments and probably a greater familiarity with the stock refutations of them, in this chapter I shall focus on the arguments from the *Summa Theologiae* I.2.3 since these are the ones which most English-speaking philosophers know and which face standard objections in the contemporary literature. Nevertheless, I shall draw on his other texts and the wealth of scholarship on this issue to clarify these arguments and present responses to these standard objections. In the remainder of this section I shall survey briefly the variety of texts in which arguments for God's existence occur and note some points which can illuminate the arguments examined below.

4.1.2   Where can Aquinas's arguments be found?

One of the most striking features of Aquinas's work is its interconnectedness, the architectural nature of the interlocking positions which mutually support each other. Hence, the strategy of plucking specific arguments and treating them in isolation from their context (a familiar style in analytical philosophy of religion) has been often criticized by defenders of Aquinas.[6] Nevertheless, Aquinas presented clear arguments, intended to be logically perspicuous and available for rational critique. So while contextualizing those arguments in their larger works is important to get their meaning and purposes right, it is still important to attempt to assess them rationally, rather than merely reverentially repeat them.

As discussed in Chapter 2, Aquinas wrote four theological syntheses – the *Scriptum Super Sententiis*, the *Summa Contra Gentiles*, the *Compendium Theologiae* and the *Summa Theologiae*. In each of them is a treatment of God's existence.[7] Of his commentaries, those on Aristotle's *Physics* and *Metaphysics* have relevant discussions.[8] Two of the scripture commentaries discuss the issue – on John's Gospel and the Letter to the Romans.[9] The disputed questions *De Veritate* and *De Potentia Dei* deal with the issue,[10] as does the opuscule *De Ente et Essentia*.[11]

If we approach these texts chronologically, the earliest writing, Distinction 3 q.1 of the *Scriptum Super Sententiis* (1252–1256) is interesting in that it outlines in a general way Aquinas's subsequent strategy. He appeals to arguments from causation, negation and eminence (following the pattern of Denys the Areopagite) and sets out in a rudimentary way what would later be the third way of the *Summa Theologiae*. What is of particular interest is that he does not cite Aristotle or Avicenna, but rather the central scriptural text Romans 1:20: 'The unseen things of God can be grasped through an understanding of what God has made', along with Ambrose, Augustine and Dionysius. So while the technical hardware of Greek thought came to be deployed by him later, the earliest inspiration for his approach to arguing about God seems to come from Christian sources. In the *De Ente et Essentia*, Avicenna looms larger in his thought, and that work was written while strongly under his influence – a thinker Anthony Kenny referred to as the most important metaphysician in the first millennium.[12] Written towards the end of the 1250s, the discussion of divine providence in *De Veritate* is more detailed than the brief presentation of the fifth way in the *Summa Theologiae*, and is a useful source for interpreting that argument.

The discussion in the *Commentary on Boethius's De Trinitate* (1258–1259) is not directly about arguments for God's existence, but rather about knowledge of God. It anticipates article 1 of ST I.2 in rejecting views which hold that God's existence is self-evident. Aquinas rejects an account of the nature of knowledge, ultimately deriving from Augustine, which holds that there is a special illumination of the mind by God in any act of knowledge. He is an empiricist in holding that all knowledge begins with sensory input. This also fits with his rejection of Anselmian arguments for God's existence based on purely a priori considerations.[13] He never mentions Anselm directly in the ST, but seems to reject Anselm-inspired approaches also linked with Augustinian approaches available in works by his contemporaries, including Bonaventure, Alexander of Hales and William of Auxerre.

The *Summa Contra Gentiles* (1259–1265) is clearly an important source for understanding Aquinas's reasoning, the causal arguments of SCG I 13–15 working out in greater detail the argumentation of the first three ways of the five ways. This is the work which Norman Kretzmann holds up as the paradigm of natural theology.[14] Yet the *Summa Theologiae* (1265–1273) is the most mature statement of Aquinas's views, and the one by which he is best known to the philosophical community. Despite the brevity of the statement of the arguments there, they rest on this hinterland of discussion which evolved through Aquinas's engagement with Aristotle and with Jewish and Islamic commentators on Aristotle. The structure of the discussion is instructive. In the first article he initially discusses whether the existence of God is self-evident and denies that it is. Knowledge of God is not like knowledge of first principles, since no contradiction emerges for us in denying God's existence. Now it may be that if we knew God's essence properly, we would see that God's essence includes his existence – but that knowledge is not directly available to us in any way which would make God's existence an obvious truth. Aquinas therefore holds that arguments have to be made for God's existence, causal arguments running from effects back to their ultimate cause. In the second article he distinguishes the two kinds of demonstration (*demonstratio propter quid* and *demonstratio quia*), holding that the second is relevant to arguments for God. Such arguments are *praeambula fidei* – necessary preconditions of faith, not in an epistemological sense (relative to our knowledge), but in an absolute sense (in principle available to reason and so outside the scope of faith). Aquinas discusses two objections to God's existence, (which are the topic of Chapter 5 below) before going on to present five arguments for God's existence. The first three are variants of cosmological argument, the fourth is a Platonically inspired argument about degrees of perfection and the fifth is a design or teleological argument. I shall discuss the first, third and fifth of these arguments in greater detail in subsequent sections.

Aquinas's *Commentary on Aristotle's Physics* (c. 1268) treats Aristotle's argument for a first mover, and he had summarized much of this material in SCG I.13. While he remains faithful to Aristotle's text, he interpolates some criticisms of Averroes's interpretation and also of Aristotle's views on the eternity of the world. Aristotle had argued for an immanent mover enmeshed in ancient cosmology – the soul of the *primum mobile* which exerts efficient causality on everything physical. In the *Metaphysics*, Aristotle argued for an immaterial first mover who transcended the world. Given the difficulties of interpreting Aristotle's *Metaphysics*, Aquinas's *Commentary* (c. 1272) remains largely faithful to the text of Aristotle, pausing here and there to note disagreements on creation, providence and the knowledge of individuals. The kind of causality exercised by the prime mover in the *Metaphysics* is final causality – and in the five ways Aquinas attributes both efficient (first way) and final causality (fifth way) to God, noting also that all five ways argue to an agent cause.

4.1.3   Reading Aquinas's arguments

A long tradition of scholarship on Aquinas has scrutinized and interpreted these arguments, generally taking them as valid.[15] Likewise, wave after wave of philosophical movement – empiricism, Kantianism, positivism, phenomenology, existentialism, ordinary language philosophy – has treated them as misconceived and erroneous. In the mid-twentieth-century English-speaking world, the discipline of philosophy of religion was strongly influenced by considerations of linguistic philosophy and devoted much time to the defensive task of arguing for the intelligibility of religious discourse, let alone advancing metaphysical arguments for God's existence. One scholar among others has been extremely influential in the reception of Aquinas's views for the anglophone world, and this is Kenny. Kenny considers Aquinas to be one of the dozen greatest philosophers of the Western world,[16] and especially admires his views on mind and action. Kenny believes his metaphysics of being and his philosophical theology are less successful. Kenny's book *The Five Ways* remains a key work in the reception of Aquinas's work, and it is negative in its assessment of the success of Aquinas's arguments. Further important works such as J.L. Mackie's *The Miracle of Theism* reinforce the view that Aquinas's approach has failed.[17] Probably the most significant theistic exponent of natural theology, Richard Swinburne, in his *The Existence of God*, thinks Aquinas's five ways one of his least successful pieces of philosophy, and he refers to Kenny for detailed criticism.[18]

Ranged against this negative assessment are scholars trained in analytical philosophy who believe Aquinas's arguments do still have argumentative strength. Norman Kretzmann has developed Aquinas's arguments from the *Summa Contra Gentiles* into a comprehensive philosophical theism. Brian Davies has defended Aquinas's arguments and conception of God in a series of papers and books, while Scott MacDonald, Eleanore Stump, Gerry Hughes and Chris Hughes have all defended different aspects of Aquinas's philosophical theism.[19] So he has his contemporary defenders.

In the remainder of this chapter I shall deal with three distinct arguments, spending some time on specific arguments rather than attempting an encyclopedic coverage of all Aquinas says. As examples of cosmological arguments I shall deal with the first and third ways of the celebrated five ways (Sections 4.2 and 4.3). I shall discuss his fifth way as an instance of a teleological argument and distinguish it from other, famous, types of design argument (Section 4.4). The terms 'cosmological argument', 'teleological argument' and so on are of course not Aquinas's, but his arguments are classified in this way in contemporary philosophy of religion and my interest in this chapter is to attempt to relate his arguments to contemporary concerns.

4.2   The first way

The first and more manifest way is the argument from motion. It is certain, and evident to our senses, that in the world some things are in motion (*aliqua moveri*). Now whatever is in motion is put in motion by another, for nothing can be in motion except it is in potentiality to that towards which it is in motion; whereas, a thing moves inasmuch as it is in act. For motion is nothing else than the reduction of something from potentiality to actuality. But nothing can be reduced from potentiality to actuality, except by something in a state of actuality. Thus, that which is actually hot, as fire, makes wood, which is potentially hot, to be actually hot, and thereby moves and changes it. Now it is not possible that the same thing should be at once in actuality and potentiality in the same respect, but only in different respects. For what is actually hot cannot simultaneously be potentially hot, but it is simultaneously potentially cold. It is therefore impossible that in the same respect and in the same way a thing should be both mover and moved, that is, that it should move itself. Therefore, whatever is in motion must be put in motion by another. If that by which it is put in motion be itself put in motion, then this also must needs be put in motion by another, and that by another again. But this cannot go on to infinity, because then there would be no first mover, and, consequently, no other mover, seeing that subsequent movers move only inasmuch as they are put in motion by the first mover, as the staff moves only because it is put in motion by the hand. Therefore, it is necessary to arrive at a first mover, put in motion by no other, and this everyone understands to be God.[20]

4.2.1   The analysis of *motus*

Aquinas refers to this argument as *manifestior*, more evident, relative to the other arguments he uses. This seems to relate to what he regards as the obviousness of its starting place, and it certainly is the kind of argument he repeats at various points in his work.[21] In its most mature articulation, in the *Compendium Theologiae*, it is stripped down to its bare parts: (a) everything moved is moved by something else, (b) an infinite series of moved causes of motion is impossible, hence (c) there is a first cause of motion that is supreme over everything and we call this first cause of motion God [Comp 3]. In the *Summa Contra Gentiles*, the argument exists in this form, but with three subsidiary arguments each for premises a and b [SCG 1.13]. In the *Summa Theologiae*, there is a single argument provided to support each of the two premises. The overall argument in the ST can be broken into four distinct steps. Firstly, there is the observational premise that things are in motion. Secondly, there is the claim that things which are in motion are put in motion by another, with a sub-argument defending this claim. Thirdly, there is the denial of an infinite regress of such a system of things in motion and movers. Finally, there is the conclusion that there is an unmoved first mover, which is God. Let us discuss each part of this in turn.

The Latin word translated as 'motion' is *motus*. This has a broader meaning than change of place (the normal modern reading of motion), and can also include change of quality and change of quantity. Thus, *motus* refers to change in three of Aristotle's categories – place, quantity and quality. One might further note that change of place is a form of extrinsic change (e.g. when I sit down I merely change my relation to my surroundings), whereas change of quality or quantity is intrinsic (e.g. I really change as I grow warm, or lose weight). So *motus* is perhaps closer to the meaning of 'change', and from now on I shall use that term. However, *motus* should also be distinguished from *mutatio*, which is a change of substance, where the change is so great that the identity of the thing changed is altered. Hence, *motus* means the kinds of change which can occur in an object without its changing into something else (i.e. change which is not generation or corruption).[22] It is sometimes queried whether this is a genuinely observational premise, since it has been rejected by philosophers such as Parmenides.[23] However, since Parmenides rejects all observational input as erroneous, and it is the analysis of the meaning of *motus* which introduces metaphysical machinery, I think it fair to characterize it as an observational premise which picks out changing things in the world, which is perhaps why Aquinas thinks it *manifestior*. Also it is important to be clear that Aquinas does not include all instances of change within the scope of his starting place. As just noted, he does not include *mutatio* – generation and corruption. Neither will some instances of change in which the change is brought about by something itself unchanged be within the scope of the starting premise – a point relevant below to an important challenge to the argument. He is interested in instances of things being changed – *aliqua moveri*. Thus the starting place is the commonplace observation that change happens in the world, with a note that Aquinas will limit his focus to a subset within all the different kinds of change.

The crucial next phase of the argument is 'whatever is changed is changed by another (*omne autem quod movetur ab alio movetur*). This is not at all obvious, and there seem to be many counterexamples to it. For example, think of your picking up this book. Who or what made you do it? To begin to answer this problem, it is necessary to note a number of issues. Aquinas analyses change using the potency/actuality distinction. And this potency/actuality distinction always involves potency or actuality *in some respect*. Nothing exists in a state of pure potency; otherwise, it would not exist. Hence, things are always a mix of both potency and actuality – existing actually in some respects and potentially in others. The acorn has actuality in respect of its current state and potentiality in respect of its future state, being an oak tree. And this potentiality is a real feature of it, not merely some logical possibility. The future developmental changes of the acorn are shaped by the kind of thing it is, by its essence. Aquinas holds that the transition from potency to actuality is brought about by something in actuality. Why think this? Well, the alternatives are that it is brought about either by something potential or else by nothing at all. Something potential does not as yet exist (the oak tree), while it does exist as something actual (the acorn) – so the change cannot be brought about by something potential in respect to which the change occurs. If the change is brought about by nothing, this is the same as saying it is not brought about, that spontaneous uncaused change occurs. Aquinas does not consider this a genuine possibility. How, then, does this analysis connect to the claim that whatever is moved is moved by another?

Aquinas's example in the text – that fire makes a stick that is potentially hot into something actually hot – misleadingly implies that whatever is moved from being potentially F to being actually F is moved by something which is itself actually F. However, Kenny shows that this cannot be so, as it would preclude thin farmers from fattening cattle, or even more bizarrely live murderers.[24] It is clear that the changing agent has to actually have the capacity or power to move the entity from state A to state B, but does not have to be in state B itself (although it could be, as in the fire example). Could the changer be in state A? That is, could a thin farmer fatten thin cows? Clearly, yes. So how does this apply to Aquinas's argument? The principle employed is that something is brought from being potentially F to actually F by something that is actual. Given that potentiality and actuality have to be specified, we might further say that something is brought from being potentially F to actually F by something actual in respect to the capacity to bring about this change. So the thin cows are made fat by a thin farmer who has the capacity to fatten the cows. That the farmer is in the same kind of state as the cows which change is not relevant. There is no requirement that the agent of change has to be in a different type of state to the one which is being changed. My infant daughter might wake me in the night by crying in her sleep – causing me to move from sleep to wakefulness while still being asleep herself. It seems as if the type/token distinction is useful here. The thin farmer has the same state as the cow qua type, but does not have the same token state – the cow's thinness and the farmer's thinness are two different states. Aquinas needs to claim that any token instance of a state cannot itself bring about a change, but it needs to be changed from without by an agent capable of making that change, which might itself exhibit that very type (e.g. the thin farmer). Thus, the cow's thinness does not itself bring about change; rather, something other than that brings it about. Could some other part of the cow bring it about? Yes, the cow's hunger could lead it to fatten up in the right circumstances (and note that the fattening farmer is part of a chain of circumstances – foodstuff, ingestion, digestion etc.). But this changing aspect of the cow would be some external actual element which brings about the change in relation to the token aspect, which is thin. Thus, on this account, animals are analysed in terms of aspects, or parts, related to each other as potential/actual. And they exhibit the feature that the potential parts are made actual by other parts which are actual, so they observe the premise – whatever is moved is moved by another. But why not just accept that everything exhibits this feature, that the universe constitutes a web of mutually interacting changers? The third phase of Aquinas's argument seeks to block this – the infamous denial of infinite regress.

4.2.2   Infinite regress

Aquinas claims that the chain of things which are changed in this way cannot continue to infinity. Bertrand Russell is famous in responding to such a denial by simply rejecting it. He did not see why the universe might not have always existed.[25] There did not seem to be any incoherence in assuming that the world might have been infinite backwards, that is, that there might have been an infinite past. Why does there have to be a first cause of change? Many have assumed that Aquinas's rejection of infinite regress is simply a form of dogmatism, a blatant begging of the question.[26] To say that a chain of causes must have a first cause seems to be a big assumption. Why must it? Curiously, however, Aquinas also does not see any problem with assuming that the world might have always existed. Indeed he explicitly states (against the majority of his contemporaries) that there are no good philosophical arguments to show that there must have been a beginning to time.[27] He does believe, in fact, that there was such a beginning, but this belief is due to revelation, not to philosophy. So how does this square with his denial of infinite regress in the first way?

It is important to note that he believes two distinct kinds of causal series are in question here. He distinguishes two forms of regress of causes.[28] One kind of regress is called an essentially ordered regress, and the other is an accidentally ordered regress. An example of the latter is human generation. For example, Abraham begets Isaac, who begets Jacob. That Abraham begets Isaac has no bearing on Isaac's begetting Jacob. There is no causal continuity between these; the kind of causation involved in the Isaac-Jacob relation is not dependent on the Abraham-Isaac relation. This is a subtle point. While Isaac's existence may well be due to Abraham, his being a father is not. There is no essential connection between Abraham's bringing Isaac into existence and Isaac's subsequently becoming a father (it is possible for Isaac to father a child even if Abraham is dead). It is called an accidental series because each link of the chain is accidentally related to the next; there is no essential connection. Aquinas's other example is of an imaginary infinite celestial craftsman who wears out hammers for eternity, one following another in an accidentally ordered sequence.[29] Thus, this kind of series does not exhibit transitivity, and there is in principle no problem with such a series continuing forever. However, when my cooking ring heats my saucepan, which boils the water therein, there is causal continuity. The ring heats the pan, which heats the water. Without the ring's heating the saucepan, the water would not have heated. This is an essentially ordered series – the causal powers of later members are dependent on the causal powers of the earlier members. Without the causal activity of the earlier members of the chain, the causal activity of the later members does not operate. Such a series is also instantaneous – the causal interplay from ring to saucepan to water occurs at the same time. Aquinas's claim is that in such an essentially ordered series, there has to be a starting place; otherwise, none of the subsequent activity would be possible. This starting place does not have to be a temporal start – but rather a source or explanation. In contrast, an infinite sequence of things retreating backwards in infinite time is not a conceptual impossibility, as long as they are accidentally related. However, once questions of essential connection are involved, such an infinite chain is impossible, since without a starting place which is not of the same kind, later parts would not occur. To illustrate this, John Haldane has a nice example of a university review in which every lecturer has to be peer reviewed within the university. However, unless there is someone who starts the whole thing off without being him-/herself so reviewed, the subsequent process will not take place.[30]

Opponents of this line of reasoning charge it with exhibiting a number of flaws. Aquinas has argued in a related discussion 'in any ordered series of efficient causes, the first is the cause of the intermediary and the intermediary causes the last, whether the intermediaries are many or only one. But if you take away the cause you take away the effect. Hence if there were not a first efficient cause then there would not be either an intermediate cause or a last cause'.[31] One accusation is that this just begs the question. Aquinas needs to show that there is a first cause, but assumes that here. He is also accused of equivocation about 'taking away'. Certainly removing a link in a causal chain will interrupt the chain. But deniers of the cogency of his argument are not taking anything out of the chain, just denying the special status to one (the supposed first) member. However, one might defend Aquinas by arguing that he does not *assume* the existence of a first cause, but distinguishes between two types of causes – those which depend on an antecedent and those which do not. His claim is that a chain of those which depend on an antecedent only makes sense assuming there is something which does not. But, his opponents argue, why not accept an infinite chain of cause in which each one is caused by the antecedent, the whole chain continuing endlessly? The distinction between essentially and accidentally ordered series is supposed to answer this. Such an infinite series is possible, construed as an accidentally ordered series, but not as an essentially ordered one. As James Sadowsky has argued, in such a series, 'since each condition for the existence of A requires the fulfilment of a prior condition, it follows that none of them can ever be fulfilled'.[32] A further significant consideration is the widespread use of such a principle as the one Sadowksy articulates as a basic philosophical tool. To indict one's opponent of such a regress is typically to show the position untenable. To reject such a principle as a means of blocking the cosmological argument might appear to be too high a price to pay.

One might accept such a regress blocker, but still reject the argument. Notoriously the conclusion – that there is a first cause of change not itself changed by anything and that this is what everybody understands as God seems like a gigantic leap. There could be a multiplicity of such movers. And even if there were one, it does not have to be anything like the classical conception of God, perhaps something like eternal matter, or even Aristotle's unmoved mover, unconcerned with mundane matters. At face value this seems right – the argument reaches a conclusion which seems unwarranted. However, it seems correct to read these arguments in their context, followed by nine densely argued questions on the nature of that which has been identified in these arguments. Whatever has been designated as the conclusion of these arguments is unknown, and to call it God is to situate it in a context. The next questions clarify something of the meaning of this – but even there somewhat minimally. For Aquinas, God is always mysterious, not a mere explanatory posit. Even attributes like oneness need to be argued for – and he supplies such arguments, as we shall see below. Hence, read alone the conclusion is troublesome, but read as part of an extended treatise on God, his strategy is to argue for the existence of something utterly unlike moving, contingent things we are familiar with and to spell out certain features of such a reality. We shall return to this effort to clarify God's nature in Chapters 6 and 7 below. But first, there still remain serious objections to this, 'most manifest', argument.

4.2.3   The counterexample objection

What of the counterexample mentioned above – of your picking up the book – what moved you? For Aquinas, animals (like you, me and the cattle) are self-movers. The analysis of change in such beings carries through in terms of part and whole. An animal moves itself by virtue of one part moving another, consonant with this potency-act distinction. So the premise 'whatever is moved (*movetur*) is moved by another' is not rebutted by the example of self-moving animals, since the part of the animal which is moved (*movetur*) is still indeed moved by another. Aquinas thinks of souls as unmoved movers – a soul is the principle or source of movement in a living organism. Yet does not this pose a problem? As Aquinas is seeking to argue for a single, first, unmoved mover, is not this plethora of unmoved movers (i.e. all living things) a big problem?

One possible response to this comes from specifying clearly what is understood by *motus*. By distinguishing *motus* from *mutatio*, a solution to this problem appears. *Motus* is the kind of change which does not involve generation or corruption, the coming to be or destruction of things. So Aquinas is arguing for a first cause of specific types of change – processes of spatial movement, change in quality and quantity. That a different kind of change is not treated there – *mutatio* (generation/corruption) – does not invalidate this argument. And this is the kind of change involved in the coming to be of living things. It is the kind of change which is the focus of the third way, as will be discussed below. But the relevant point to this response is that the myriad examples of organismic movement (including book reading) therefore do not serve as a counterexample to this argument. The soul is not an instance of 'something which is moved', and so is not an exception to the principle 'whatever is moved is moved by another'.

This raises a problem, however, about the limitation on *motus*. No change due to souls will count as instances of *motus*, which is a severe limitation of the starting place of this argument – which is allegedly *manifestior*. And Aquinas's examples – of the hand moving the stick – seem to count as instances of *motus* for him. So one interpretative issue is whether souls really are unmoved movers? In his argument to show that the soul is not corporeal (ST I.75.1), Aquinas identifies the soul as the first principle of life, a feature which manifests in knowledge and movement (*motus*). As the soul is the first principle of life, it is thereby the ultimate explanation of movement in the organism. Hence it seems that *motus* in an organism is fully explained by the activity of a soul. Now it is clear that the soul itself requires explanation in terms of how it comes about or indeed in terms of its continued existence – but these are not explanations of *motus*, but about *mutatio* or about *esse*.

Yet even though the soul is the principle of life, and hence of motion, in animals, is the soul really unmoved? In the counterexample discussed, your decision to pick up the book is due to the impact of the perceived environment on you, with your cluster of beliefs and desires. Desire is connected to seeing an object as desirable, which moves the will to action. So the soul is changed by perceiving its environment – an account which fits well with a naturalistic story about the relation of the mind/brain to its environment. So it does seem that the soul is indeed something which is moved and belongs to the chain of things which when it changes is changed by something else. So the alleged counterexample to the second premise does not have the force which it might initially seem to have.

4.2.4   Newtonian objections

However, there is another brace of objections to the principle which does highlight a problem with Aquinas's account and which perhaps requires a restriction of the scope of the meaning of *motus*. This is the problem raised by the principle of inertia in Newtonian physics. This holds that the basic state of a body is to be in motion unless acted upon by an external force. Such a principle eradicates the need for an explanation of the cause of motion and thereby the whole thrust of this argument. This is a general objection – that Aquinas's account of motion rests on outmoded and false physics. Furthermore, a more specific objection is that Aquinas's account of local motion seems to be mistaken. He believed that the medium through which a body moves exerts a physical casual influence on it – so that a projectile flying through the air is partly moved by the air, a view which has no place in classical mechanics. It is important to distinguish these two objections – that Aquinas's whole account of change is rendered redundant by Newtonian physics, on the one hand and that his account of projectile motion is incorrect, on the other hand.

How might one handle the general objection? Firstly, it is important to note that the originators of the modern account of motion did not see themselves as being engaged with questions about the source of motion – but nevertheless did consider such a question important and indeed believed that there was a first principle of motion. Newton says

> By this principle [*vis inertiae*] alone there never could have been any motion in the world. Some other principle was necessary for putting bodies into motion; and now they are in motion some other principle is necessary for conserving the motion.[33]

To the extent that the success of modern accounts of motion led physicists and philosophers away from questions about the origin of motion, this is an issue of change of focus, rather than a knock-down argument against such a principle. As for the specific challenge to Aquinas's account of local motion, one could defend his position in two ways. One could concede that his view on the role of the medium is incorrect, but that this does not tell against the basic principle that whatever moves is moved by another – he has just specified the wrong mover. Or alternatively, one could just concede that he is mistaken about local motion and restrict the examples of change to alteration of quality or quantitative change. Scott MacDonald has offered a principled defence of this avenue by pointing out that these two kinds of change (quantitative and qualitative) are intrinsic to an entity, while change of position is extrinsic.[34] So Aquinas can defend his view that intrinsic change requires a first changer, without embroiling himself in controversy about the correct characterization of inertia and local movement.

4.3   The third way

> The third way is taken from possibility and necessity, and runs thus.
> We find in nature things that are possible to be and not to be, since
> they are found to be generated, and to corrupt, and consequently,
> they are possible to be and not to be. But it is impossible for these
> always to exist, for that which is possible not to be at some time is not.
> Therefore, if everything is possible not to be, then at one time there
> could have been nothing in existence. Now if this were true, even now
> there would be nothing in existence, because that which does not
> exist only begins to exist by something already existing. Therefore,
> if at one time nothing was in existence, it would have been impos-
> sible for anything to have begun to exist, and thus even now nothing
> would be in existence – which is absurd. Therefore, not all beings
> are merely possible, but there must exist something the existence of
> which is necessary. But every necessary thing either has its necessity
> caused by another, or not. Now it is impossible to go on to infinity
> in necessary things which have their necessity caused by another, as
> has been already proved in regard to efficient causes. Therefore, we
> cannot but postulate the existence of some being having of itself its
> own necessity, and not receiving it from another, but rather causing in
> others their necessity. This all men speak of as God.[35]

While the first way began from the empirically obvious phenomenon
of change, the third way starts with 'the possible and the necessary',
which seems in contrast more theoretically involved, more philosophical. Indeed, many readers of this argument have connected it to
arguments involving God's unique necessity, such as those of Gottfried
Leibniz, because of this theoretical underpinning. However, Aquinas's
use of modal notions is different to those of others who have generated
such arguments, so one of the crucial interpretative tasks in examining
this argument is to clarify what 'possible' and 'necessary' mean. It is
another curious feature of this argument that most commentators up to
the twentieth century have found it logically unexceptionable, whereas
the majority from the twentieth century on have detected an elemen-
tary logical flaw at its heart.[36]

The key steps in this argument are as follows. Firstly, there is an identification of a phenomenon in the world, things which are possible to
be and not to be – that is, things which come into being and go out
of being, or, using Aristotelian terminology, which are generated and
which corrupt. Secondly, there is an argument that not everything in

the world can be of this kind. There has to be at least one thing which is not of this kind, namely at least one necessary thing. Thirdly, there is an argument for a first source of this necessity, by denial of infinite regress, and fourthly, there is the identification of this first source with God. The third and fourth steps are shared with the first way – denial of infinite regress and postulating that what emerges is to be identified with God. However, the question about modality in step one and the argument that not everything can be merely possible, in step two, are specific to this argument.

In relation to modality, in the aftermath of David Hume and the Logical Positivists a broad swathe of philosophers held that the only acceptable kind of necessity was thought to be logical necessity, and this was typically understood, reductively, to be based on linguistic conventions.[37] W.V. Quine's assault on these conventions led to his general scepticism about modality. Nevertheless, modal notions remain crucial to philosophical discourse, and hence some came to view Quine's sceptical conclusions as an indication that his premises or argument must be faulty.[38] The idea that there might be some robust forms of necessity which are more than merely conventional has gained widespread purchase again in analytic philosophy, through the work of Saul Kripke, David Lewis and Alvin Plantinga, for example.[39] In this context, therefore, it is interesting to make sense of the kind of modal notions used by Aquinas. He clearly accepts a range of modal notions, and he typically does not discuss modality for its own sake, but treats it in contexts such as freedom of the will, or God's knowledge of the future, clarifying the kinds of modality involved to defend human freedom.[40] The question to be addressed here is what kind of necessity is involved in the third way?

Aquinas draws on his Aristotelian conceptual scheme to distinguish different kinds of necessity, linking different kinds to each of the Aristotelian causes. He gives a clear statement of his views in his discussion of the will at ST 1.82.1. There he states that the basic idea in necessity is of something which cannot *not* be. This can be further refined into intrinsic and extrinsic kinds of necessity. As matter and form are intrinsic principles of a thing, and efficient and final causes are extrinsic, Intrinsic Necessity is connected to matter and form, while Extrinsic Necessity is linked to agency and finality. He calls Absolute Necessity the kind associated with form and matter. Formal Necessity captures logical and mathematical truths, his example being the inner angles of a triangle being equal to two right angles. Material Necessity has to do with the constitution of an entity, his example being that something constituted from contrary elements will corrupt. Final Necessity is sometimes called Necessity of Utility. For example, to cross a sea, one has to use a boat. Necessity caused by an external agent is called Coercion, and this is the kind which is incompatible with freedom. From this taxonomy it is clear that in the context of the third way, the kind of necessity involved is Absolute Necessity, and within this the relevant kind is Material Necessity, concerning the physical constitution of things. A contingent thing is something which is generated and which corrupts. A necessary thing does not do this.

Generation entails that the thing had a beginning, and corruption that it ends, or ceases to exist. This coming to be and ceasing to be are due to the kind of thing it is, a composite whose constituents come together and then come apart. Whatever does not exhibit these characteristics is metaphysically constituted such that it cannot do so – it does not have the wherewithal to come together or fall apart. Thus, necessary things, on Aquinas's account, are simple or non-composite relative to contingent things. Yet they are not absolutely simple (examples of such necessary things are angels and human souls), for, recalling Aquinas's conceptual scheme, they still exhibit a distinction between essence and existence. Simple beings, lacking matter and form composition, still exhibit essence and existence composition. They do not cease to exist by corruption, by their contrary parts coming apart, but they can cease to exist by annihilation, by God's ceasing to sustain them in existence. However, at the initial stage of the third way, there is no apparent implication of essence/existence composition in play. The kind of metaphysical composition in question seems to be that of matter and form. Things of that kind come into and go out of existence.

Aquinas discusses the different between possible beings (those which exhibit composition) and necessary beings (those which are simple) in *De Potentia* 5.3. In this question he examines whether God has the power of annihilation. One view, advanced by Avicenna, is that all creatures apart from God are contingent, since their existence comes to them from God (the kind of view many read into the third way). Aquinas rejects this account of possibility and necessity because it treats of the necessity of a being as something extrinsic to its nature. In contrast, he defends the view that what makes something necessary is intrinsic to its nature. It is so constituted that it does not corrupt; it has no possibility in itself for non-being. To have this possibility for non-being is grounded in being materially constituted. Matter is potential to form, and in some beings the matter is open to receiving new forms. Insofar as it does this, the matter-form composite can corrupt. Thus, what makes a being possible is its constitution as something material, which is open to non-being by the loss of a form. This possibility is therefore something which is constituted by the nature of the being. Those things lacking this nature are necessary. Of course, all created things can cease to exist by the direct removal of existence from them, but some things also have the capacity within themselves to cease to exist by corrupting.

Given any contingent being one comes across in the world, it is important to note the modal difference between its generation and corruption. It has actually been generated, but not yet actually corrupted. It is potentially corruptible. Hence, it is *generated* and *corruptible*. Its corruption remains a future possibility. An important question then is do corruptible things have to corrupt? That is, could it be the case that a corruptible thing just happens not to corrupt? Aquinas's answer to this is that corruptible things do have to corrupt (indeed, this is the example he uses of Material Necessity in ST 1.82.1, cited above). His detailed treatment of this is found in his commentary on Aristotle's *De Caelo*. In this he considers the possibility of a corruptible thing's existing forever. For this to happen an infinite amount of time forward has to be postulated. A basic axiom Aquinas accepts is that a thing cannot both be and not be at the same time in the same respect, but can be and not be at different times and in different respects. Thus the possibility of being and not-being is related to different times. Given an infinity of time, could something which is actually in being (and thus also possibly in being, since possibility follows from actuality) have the potency for non-being? That is, is there a time at which it could *not* exist? Since the hypothesis here is that it exists forever and throughout all that time exercises its potency to exist, there is no time at which it could not-exist. Therefore, there cannot be a genuine potentiality for non-existence in it. This means that eternality[41] and contingency are incompatible with each other. Hence, contingent things have to corrupt. Moreover, since it is agreed that they are generated, it is clear that non-being both precedes and follows after their existence – all this deriving from their physical constitution. Therefore, Aquinas states, 'what is possible not to be at some time is not'.

The next phase of the third way is an argument claiming that not everything can be of this kind. The very nature of contingency requires there to be at least one necessary being. It is this section of the argument which attracts the most attention and is suspected of fallacy. Aquinas argues that if everything were contingent, then at one time there would have been nothing, and if there ever had been nothing, there would be nothing now. How does he get from the contingency of all things to nothingness? The tense used is past – so he seems to be referring backwards, to generation, to time before the present, rather than to future corruption. Now, while it is clear that every single contingent thing had not existed at some point in the past, why not think that the chain of contingent things had not stretched eternally backwards? While each individual in the set is limited, why could not the set itself be everlasting, why should the feature applying to each individual (that there is a time before it when there is nothing) apply to the totality (that there was a time before the set of contingent things when there was absolutely nothing)? This seems an instance of the fallacy of composition – attributing to the whole, features which pertain only to the part. This is sometimes called the quantifier-shift fallacy, moving illegitimately from each to all. If each student in the class has a mother, it does not follow that all the students in the class together have the same mother. In this instance, if each entity has a preceding period of non-existence, it does not follow that that all entities together have a preceding period of non-existence. Why does Aquinas make such a move? He is sensitive elsewhere to fallacy of composition. Peter Geach notes that such inferences need to be taken on a case by case basis.[42] While it is true that each child's having a mother does not mean that all of them together have the same mother, a wall made of red bricks is itself red. It has the same colour. So there is something about having a mother which makes it illegitimate to say that the class has a mother, while there is something else about being a wall which allows it to be the same colour as its constituent bricks. Whether the conclusion follows seems to depend on the kind of thing involved.

It is clear that something is missing in the argument, as Aquinas states it. He does not spell out why he thinks that if everything were contingent, then there would have been nothing. And there have been a multitude of strategies suggesting explanations of what the missing story might be. Some think that time is not essential to the argument, and hence discussions about whether Aquinas is thinking of a future or past lack of existence is irrelevant.[43] Others think that time is indeed the crucial issue and that determining whether future or past non-existence is in Aquinas's mind is the key to unlocking the argument.[44] Others again suggest that Aquinas is covertly assuming an infinity of time, which then works as a hidden assumption.[45] The literature on this debate is vast. I shall not attempt to survey it, but will present an account which I think answers the straightforward objection that there is a logical error in the argument.

There are, I believe, three criteria which should govern any attempt to respond to this problem. The first is that it should deal precisely with Aquinas's text. In particular, this has implications for the place of time in the argument, since the adverbs 'sometime' (*aliquando*) and 'at some time' (*quandoque*), as well as the verb 'would have been' (*fuerat*) all implicate time. Secondly, the attempt should cohere with Aquinas's general views, and in this case his views on necessity seem most relevant. Finally, any attempt to rescue this argument from fallacy should not collapse it into one of the other ways, thereby losing its specificity as a distinct argument.

With these criteria in mind, let us look to ways of making sense of it without committing the fallacy of composition. Attempts to say that time is not relevant to the argument have to explain away the use of temporal adverbs, the tenses used in the argument and the fact that incompatibilities in being and non-being are indexed to time and hence temporally sensitive. This seems too far from the text. So, if time is relevant, is it past, or future, or both? The non-existence which threatens possible entities occurs either before they exist or after that. As discussed above, the possibility of non-existence is not compatible with eternality, so possibility here is linked to sometimes existing, sometimes not. Is the relevant sense of non-existence for this argument that which precedes or comes after the existence of a contingent entity? From the text it seems to be that which precedes, since Aquinas refers to the past in countenancing the possibility of there being nothing: 'at one time there could have been nothing in existence'. So what is it about the possibility of preceding non-existence which gives him this result? The contrary supposition is that the chain or several chains of contingent things just stretch back indefinitely. And this supposition is all the more pressing since Aquinas does not think there is a good philosophical argument for the beginning of time – it is conceptually possible and hence non-contradictory to think that the world has always existed.[46] How does the openness to that supposition square with the claim, discussed above, that given an eternality of time, not everything could be possible, or eternality and possibility are incompatible? Well, it could be that a mix of necessary and possible entities have existed from eternity. The supposition that an infinite chain of possible beings could have stretched from eternity only makes sense if one assumes some necessary beings. Thus eternality is not incompatible with the existence of some possible beings, just incompatible with the claim that all things are possible. And indeed the conceptual account of substantial change accepted by Aquinas allows as a possibility some eternal matter which receives different forms. So if eternal backward existence is a genuine conceptual possibility, how does Aquinas reach the conclusion that if everything is possible, then at one time nothing would have existed? The key claim is that the conceptual possibility of backwards eternality requires at least some necessary beings. There being only possible beings precludes this option. Why?

I think the key to understanding Aquinas's thought here lies in the distinction between kinds of things – as seen in the example above of students in a class and bricks in a wall. The kind of thing a class of students is, it does not allow the inference that the class itself has a mother. However, the kind of thing a wall is, allows the inference that it is the same colour as its constituent parts. The kind of thing is captured by the term 'common nature'. Recall that Aquinas adopted an intermediate position on common natures between Platonic universals (one over many) and nominalistic individualism, where such universals are construed as mere similarities psychologically observed. Basic to Aquinas's metaphysics is the thought that only individuals exist, so he rejects real universals. However, the mind grasps real features of reality as it forms universal thoughts – the universal in the mind refers to real formal features of the individuals in reality. Formal features are nested in hierarchies. For example, the form of dog is nested within the genus of animal, which is nested again in the genus of possible beings. Thus, possible being is a very broad genus which picks out real formal features of such beings. The connection or link between the individual and the genus is not a mere enumeration or inductive generalization, but there is an internal formal connection between all instances of the kind. Thus Aquinas's hidden assumption in this argument seems to be that if everything has the common nature of being possible, if there exists nothing with the common nature of necessary being, then absolute non-being would follow. This is because the common nature of such a kind itself conceptually requires an antecedent. Just as each individual first does not exist and comes after a non-existence, the totality, if of this kind, would come after non-existence. The kind in question (like the wall and unlike the class) would exhibit the relevant feature of the individual. Thus, Aquinas gets the conclusion, without a quantifier-shift fallacy, that if everything exhibited the common nature of being possible, then at one time there would have been nothing.

The move from that to the claim that if there ever was nothing, there would be nothing now, and the *modus tollens* rejection of the premise on which this rests (i.e. rejecting the thought that everything is merely possible) are straightforward. One could challenge the axiomatic belief

that nothing comes from nothing, but Aquinas thinks it as secure a principle as one might find.

From the existence of at least one necessary being, Aquinas moves to
a question about the source of this necessity. Does it come from itself
or another? He explicitly appeals to causation, and holds that either its
necessity comes from itself or is caused by another. If the necessity is
caused by another, he invokes the argument rejecting infinite regresses
and says there must be some being which has its necessity of itself. If this
argument works, why might there not be a multiplicity of such beings?
Part of the answer to this comes from subsequent discussions about the
nature of that which is postulated as cause of the effects which begin
each of the five ways. In ST q.11, he discusses the unity of God and
argues that God is one from considerations of simplicity, the infinity
of his perfection and the unity of the world. However, another path to
there being just one God comes from the discussion of necessity. The
necessary beings in question here (souls and angels) are those which
do not exhibit matter/form composition. However, they do exhibit a
different sort of composition, that of essence and existence. Aquinas
argues that in only one instance is there something whose essence and
existence are not really distinct – this is a perfectly simple reality which
has no internal distinctions, no potentiality but pure actuality. If such
arguments work, then there is a principled case to be made for one
fundamental simple, necessary being, which is the source of necessity,
and indeed existence, in everything else. This is a topic to which I shall
return in discussing the divine attribute of simplicity.

While mentioning this, it is worthwhile to note Aquinas's discussion
in *De Ente et Essentia*, which some have regarded as a separate argument for God's existence.[47] He makes the case there that existence is not
contained within the essence of an entity – we can consider the essence
of a phoenix without its actually existing. His distinctive conceptual
claim is that existence is metaphysically distinct from essence. If this
were not so, then the mere essence of something would involve or imply
its existing in reality. Thus, for everything whose essence is distinct from
its existence, it must have been brought into being by something else.
Such a chain ends in that which exists through itself as a first cause.
And such a reality would be a necessary being, one whose essence is to
exist. The relevance of this here is that some wish to link this argument
to the third way – since Aquinas discusses necessary beings in both.
However, as noted above, the kind of necessity involved in the third
way is that of physical constitution – pure forms do not have the wherewithal to corrupt, and there is a potential multiplicity of them. Aquinas

argues then for a first cause of such pure forms. In the *De Ente* argument, it seems as if a different claim is being made for the unique reality whose essence is to exist. It is puzzling why Aquinas did not include this argument along with the five ways as it seems conceptually distinct from them and also central to his metaphysical system. Armand Maurer suggests that it differs from the arguments in ST and SCG because its starting place is not an observation, but rather a metaphysical distinction.[48] Indeed, Aquinas deploys this distinction in ST 1.3.4 and SCG 1.22, but in both cases subsequent to the demonstration of God's existence and in the context of explicating the nature of what had been demonstrated.

An argument linked to the third way also appears in SCG 1.15, where Aquinas argues for God's eternity, drawing on an argument from contingency to necessity and an argument for a source of the necessity of other necessary beings in a first necessary being. Norman Kretzmann has usefully drawn parallels between the five ways of ST and the six arguments of SCG.[49] He notes that in SCG 1.13, where arguments for God's existence are advanced, there is no parallel to the third way present. The argument closest to the third way comes in SCG 1.15, but the point of this argument is to show that God is eternal. The relevance of this seems to be that interpreting the third way as involving the incompatibility of contingency with eternality is supported by the method of SCG and offers a clue as to what the hidden reasoning is behind the enthymemic presentation of the third way.

4.4   The fifth way

> The fifth way is taken from the governance of the world. We see that things which lack intelligence, such as natural bodies, act for an end, and this is evident from their acting always, or nearly always, in the same way, so as to obtain the best result. Hence, it is plain that not fortuitously, but designedly, do they achieve their end. Now whatever lacks intelligence cannot move towards an end, unless it be directed by some being endowed with knowledge and intelligence, just as the arrow is shot to its mark by the archer. Therefore, some intelligent being exists by whom all natural things are directed to their end, and this being we call God.[50]

4.4.1   Design arguments

It is clear that Aquinas's fifth way bears some resemblance to the plethora of arguments seeking to establish the existence of God on the basis of order in the world. As noted by many authors, there is an infelicity in the naming of such arguments.[51] They are not arguments *from* design, but rather are arguments *to* design, seeking to establish design on the basis of observed order in the world. Probably the most famous of such arguments comes from William Paley.[52] There, the argument is by analogy. He distinguishes between coming across a stone and a watch while walking over a field. One might be tempted to assume that the stone had always been there, or was a particular form of matter, or had been generated by some impersonal force. But with a watch, on account of its complexity, the way its parts come together in a purposeful way, such explanations seem plainly false. We rationally accept that it had a maker. Paley then moves to say that given the greater complexity of the universe, surely all the more so must it not have a designer? Brian Davies calls this kind of design argument a purpose-based argument.[53] It argues to purpose behind specific phenomena in the world.

Classical objections to this form of reasoning were, ironically, stated before Paley published his work. Hume deployed a series of challenges to such arguments to a designer.[54] He argues that the analogy between the watch and the universe is spurious. A watch is clearly an artefact requiring a maker, but the universe is not obviously so. Indeed, this would be the conclusion of a successful argument, but it cannot be assumed at the start, which is what the argument by analogy does. Furthermore, our epistemological position in relation to watches and to the universe is significantly different. We have come across things like watches and can reason about their production on the basis of experience, but we have no such relevant experience in the case of the universe. And perhaps most devastatingly, even if one accepted the analogy, accepted the epistemological situation, allowed the argument some validity, it still would not add up to a theistic conclusion. All it would yield is a designer who might be defunct, or be a committee or be otherwise non-divine.

The specific features of nature beloved by proponents of design arguments tended to be things like the eye of an eagle. They would point to its complexity, how well designed it is to catch prey and so forth, and how unlikely it is to have come about by mere chance. However, since the advent of evolutionary theory and genetics, such arguments have been undermined. The processes of evolution, involving random mutation, natural selection and long periods of time, suffice to explain how adaptive features such as the eye of the eagle came about – without design. Long series of brute mechanistic changes can explain complex end products. Therefore, the order evident in nature does not seem to require a designer.

Nevertheless, there is a different kind of design argument which Davies has labelled a regularity-based argument.[55] This does not pick out a specific phenomenon as a candidate for design, but rather points to the pervasive regularities in the natural realm as the phenomenon needing explanation. Swinburne has developed such an argument.[56] He argues that the basic scientific laws which govern the universe constitute a set of regularities which are not self-explanatory and which require a further kind of explanation. He distinguishes two models of explanation – scientific and personal – and argues that the former is ultimately explicable in terms of the latter. Explaining the existence of basic particles and basic laws in terms of the intentions of an agent with considerable powers is, according to Swinburne, a simpler, more elegant and more consistent form of explanation. I shall not enter the details of the debates about Swinburne's position, but I believe it is useful to consider the differences between his kind of argument and that of Paley to clarify what Aquinas proposes.

Swinburne's is not an argument from analogy, but rather an argument about what is the most appropriate form of explanation. Thus, Humean challenges to the analogy between artefacts and the universe do not impact on it. Likewise, it looks for an explanation of natural processes which are more fundamental than the biological functions governing evolution and which are presupposed by evolutionary theory. Therefore, it is not explainable away in an evolutionary fashion. Furthermore, the kind of epistemological scruples stated by Hume about the origins of the universe do not seem to inhibit physical cosmologists, so perhaps they should not inhibit philosophers reasoning about explanations for the kinds of structures inherent in that universe. If it turns out that Aquinas's argument is closer to that of Swinburne than that of Paley, then several of the standard objections to design arguments do not seem to be relevant to it. And indeed Aquinas's argument does seem of that kind. He refers to natural bodies acting in the same way to achieve the best result – which seems a fair enough description of basic physical processes. Is it legitimate to argue from this phenomenon to an intelligent explanation of it? To try to answer this, it is important to get clear about the explanatory framework employed by Aquinas, particularly his employment of the notion of a final cause, alien to the kind of position defended by Swinburne. So in the remainder of this section I shall explore Aquinas's case by comparing the fifth way to other similar arguments in his work and bringing out the teleological dimension to his explanatory framework. That done, I shall query the viability of the use of such a framework.

4.4.2 Aquinas's version

The fifth way is a shortened version of an argument which appears in its longer form in *De Veritate* q.5 a.2 on whether the world is ruled by providence. The two essential claims of the argument are

(1) things in the world, lacking intelligence, act for an end,
(2) working for an end requires the input of intelligence.

The reason stated for accepting the first claim is observational – that one can see in nature things acting in the same way to achieve an end. The kind of observations are ones of functional processes – so, for example, in the animal realm one can see reproductive and nutritive processes which operate to serve the flourishing of the individual. That these processes sometimes break down is not itself problematical. Occasional glitches serve to highlight the basic orderliness of the world. Also, it is assumed that purposefulness is evident in rational conscious beings – human action is purposeful. However, the kind of acting for an end seen in human actions involves conscious awareness of that end. The acting for an end seen in non-conscious entities in the world does not require that they themselves are conscious of such ends – so there is no need for anthropomorphism or suggesting that non-intelligent things have strange 'purposes'. What seems to be in focus here is the thought that orderly functional processes pervade the natural realm. The second claim – that such orderly functioning requires intelligence – is much more controversial. Indeed, one might think that evolutionary explanation is a wide and systematic refutation of such a claim – showing again and again how random mutation and adaptation can lead to complex orderly processes and functions without the input of intelligence. No one would challenge Aquinas's example that an arrow directed by an archer is dependent on the intention of the archer for its goal. But many would challenge the appropriateness of this metaphor when applied to the natural realm. The pumping of my heart, the evaporation of water, the cycle of seasons, while all exhibiting order and function, do not at all obviously rely on some intelligence directing them in the manner of the arrow.

The parallel discussion of this kind of argument in *De Veritate* contains references to Boethius, and it seems clear that his views influenced Aquinas.[57] A feature of Boethius's discussion in the *Consolation of Philosophy* is his sense of the obviousness of the need for intelligence to guide the order evident in the world. Such intelligence is called God's providence. Boethius says

> I could never believe that events of such regularity are due to the haphazards of chance. In fact I know that God the Creator watches over his creation. The day will never come that sees me abandon the truth of this belief.[58]

Despite agreeing with Boethius's conclusion, Aquinas does see the need for argumentation about this, and in *De Veritate* engages with the opposing views. He discusses the views of ancient Greek thinkers who understood natural processes to be explicable in terms of either chance or necessity, which in either case rules out providence. Some allowed only material causes in their explanatory schemes, while others allowed both material and efficient causes, but all ruled out final causes. His argument against this view is that the lack of a final cause removes the possibility of explaining why things work in a regular and orderly way. It leaves such orderliness to chance – and Aquinas argues elsewhere that chance is always derived from pre-existing orderly causal chains.[59] He then repeats the claim that things lacking intelligence cannot act for an end themselves, but must be directed by intelligence. Modern philosophical sensibilities find both of Aquinas's key claims counter-intuitive: i) things in nature act for the sake of an end and ii) acting for an end requires intellect. So let us see what kind of case can be made for them.

4.4.3   Teleology in nature

The first thing to note in discussing whether any purpose can be found inbuilt in nature, is that Aquinas's account of causation differs significantly from later, early modern accounts. Hume's influential model of causation was of a cue hitting a billiard ball and it moving off. This was construed as two separate events connected together by constant conjunction in experience – this moving off always happens when cues hit balls. One attraction of such a model was that it postulated little beyond the realm of observable experience, whereas Aquinas's account is more complex and embedded in the metaphysics of substance and essence. Depending on one's attitude to the possibility of metaphysics, one will respond differently to the accounts. Hume's account generates puzzles about induction and the difference between accidental generalizations versus laws – but does not commit itself to metaphysical machinery. Aquinas's account allows for systematic treatment of a wide variety of phenomena, but is committed to realism, essentialism and the potency-act distinction. Aquinas gives a detailed presentation of his views on causation in *De Principiis Naturae* and in the *Commentary on Aristotle's Metaphysics* Bk.5, ch2. In that account, what most closely connects to the Humean notion of cause is the notion of efficient cause – the agent or maker which produces an effect. However, an efficient cause is unintelligible apart from the notion of final cause. Efficient causes have determinate ways of acting. For example, fire always heats, and water cools. The regularity in such processes is connected to the notion of finality. Such finality is not some kind of unconscious purpose, but rather a way of accounting for the regularity observed in causal processes, as he says 'tending towards is simply having a natural bias towards something' [DPN 3]. Finality explains the otherwise odd tendency of things to act with regularity. Finality is also connected to the notion of formal cause. A formal cause is the structure, type or kind of an entity. By virtue of the kind of thing it is, it has a range of causal powers. Ice can cool water, but it cannot ignite firewood. Aquinas's metaphysics is one of entities (substances) which have a distinct identity as individuals organized in kinds which can be classified. His view is realist in that these are not conventional, but cut nature at the joints (and it is of course possible to have taxonomies also of conventionally constituted entities). With this in mind, an important distinction for Aquinas is that between priority in nature and priority in time. Something might be prior in the sense of being more fundamental in reality (an adult is a more 'realized' than a child), whereas a child precedes an adult in the process of growth. He also notes that further distinctions are possible in relation to all the causes. There are primary and secondary causes, inherent and coincidental causes, simple and composite causes, actual and potential causes. With this systematic array of different kinds of causes linked together, and different modes in which causes can operate, Aquinas has a rich explanatory schema. And a further difference from the Humean model is that causation is not construed as a two-stage process with a temporal gap between them. The billiard cue striking the ball is a single event, viewed actively on the side of the cue and passively on the side of the ball. This single event can be construed under two descriptions – as agent and recipient. So the conceptual possibility for a Humean, that a different second event might follow the first, it being only habituation which leads us to expect it, does not have the space to arise on this model.

4.4.4   Rejecting teleology

This framework of different kinds of cause was decisively rejected with the rise of modern science. A mechanistic and quantitative framework replaced the Aristotelian scheme of causes. In part, this was due to the inhibitory role played by scholastic concepts – they did not give adequate explanations of physical phenomena. To explain the mechanics of vision, or heat transfer, by appeal to formal causes seemed empty and unresponsive to the genuine puzzles posed by natural phenomena. As Derek Gjertsen put it, 'by providing an explanatory form capable of handling virtually all interactions, differences are ignored, problems obscured and very little actually explained'.[60] The subtle framework of explanatory structures proved useless for detailed empirical observation, and worse than that, seemed to block or prevent the progress of the investigation of nature. Thus the chemist Robert Boyle says of Aristotelian forms 'whatever we cannot explicate without them, we cannot neither intelligibly explicate by them'.[61] As is well known, René Descartes rejects the framework of scholastic thought and seeks to establish a new philosophy. However, the exact connection of this thought to his medieval forebears is subtle and complicated, and many elements carry over.[62] He does say 'I consider the customary search for final causes to be totally useless in physics; there is considerable rashness in thinking myself capable of investigating the purposes of God'.[63] In this passage, Descartes construes finality as involving a search of God's mind – an impossible task. The list of figures involved in the overthrow of the Aristotelian framework reads as an impressive showcase of the leading lights of the new scientific approach – Tycho Brahe, Galileo, Francis Bacon and so forth. The situation became such that Molière could crack a joke at the Aristotelians' expense in *Le Malade Imaginaire* – the doctor, when asked why opium sends one asleep, replies that it is because it has dormitive powers.[64] This was to illustrate the empty tautological nature of the Aristotelian approach and contrast it with the rise of chemistry and the other natural sciences which could give illuminating answers to such questions.

One way of attempting to salvage the Aristotelian framework is to distinguish between science and philosophy, or physics and metaphysics. It could be argued that the Aristotelian framework continues to have use in relation to philosophical questions, while it is indeed redundant in relation to scientific issues. Now, whatever its continuing philosophical validity, it is not immediately clear that such a decoupling of physics and metaphysics is possible. For Aristotle, as for Aquinas, there is a continuity in the concepts deployed in physics and metaphysics – matter/form, potency/act and so on are operative in both. The scope of metaphysics is wider than physics, treating things beyond space, time and change, but it still deals in causation, potency and act, and so forth. And Aristotle intended his view as responding to genuine scientific questions, in astronomy, for example, views accepted as true by Aquinas. To separate the philosophical conceptual scheme from scientific practice is false to the origins of that scheme – the two were construed as fitting together.

However, a further suggestion is that the very practice of science as understood by Aristotle differs significantly from that of the early moderns. The latter were seeking technological control of nature, using increasingly sophisticated quantified methods. Aristotle on the other hand was engaged in a search for first principles, for understanding. Putting it another way, using Aristotle's taxonomy of different kinds of knowledge, Aristotle was seeking *episteme*, a theoretical account of basic principles, while the moderns were more concerned with *techne*, the ability to manipulate and predict. This is not quite true, in that modern science did construe itself as seeking to find the disinterested truth about nature – but it seems right to think that there was some significant difference in the goals and not only the methods of Aristotelian physicists and early modern empirical physicists. The former were much closer to what we might call philosophers of science, while the latter were closer to scientists. Returning to Molière's joke – the appeal to dormitive powers is obtuse as a scientific response, but not obviously so as a philosophical response. In the latter idiom, it is not an empty tautology but a substantive statement about explanation, committed to powers, tendencies, essences and so forth. And pitting such an essentialist account of natural phenomena against empiricist regularity theories is by no means a dead debate. Kripke, Putnam and Lewis are not read by scientists wanting to learn about water, but are read by those wanting to clarify modal properties and the nature of natural laws.

So if we suppose that the framework of natural teleology has not been completely discredited by the seventeenth-century scientific revolution, that in principle some sense might be made of it, what sort of support could be found for Aquinas's assumption that teleological structures are pervasive in the natural world?

Biology is an obvious place to look for purposefulness – most animal organs are characterized functionally in terms of their goals, whether for pumping blood, sensing the environment or conducting neural information. At a deeper level, the language associated with DNA is awash with purposeful idiom – encoding, planning, directing, information, data, controlling. David Oderberg has made a good case that for inorganic physical processes such as the water cycle, it makes sense to describe

them in a robustly teleological fashion which does not smack of anthropomorphism or panpsychism, speaking of roles, functions, contribu-
tions.[65] And Geach argued that basic physical properties are identifiable
as 'tendencies', associated with exactly the kind of functional regularities which final causality highlights.[66] Kenny agrees with much of
this, holding that there is much more teleology evident in nature than
early modern science allowed. Yet there is not the universal presence
of teleology insisted on by Aquinas, and neither is it clear how non-
conscious teleology relies on conscious teleology in the way Aquinas
finds so obvious.[67]

Aquinas's argument for conscious teleology grounding non-conscious teleology is an exclusion argument. He thinks that three options
exhaustively cover the possible explanation of teleology in natural
things – chance, necessity or conscious choice. Chance is ruled out
as being dependent on explanatory prior causal chains. That a farmer
comes across gold while digging in his field is a matter of chance –
but this depends on the coincidence of two prior causal chains – the
farmer digging and the person depositing the gold in the field. Chance
is always dependent on the coincidence of a confluence of prior causal
chains – and these prior causal chains cannot themselves be ultimately
explained by chance without a vicious explanatory regress. What then
of necessity? Aquinas thinks of necessity as the presence of material and
efficient causes without final causation (otherwise it would be teleological). Aquinas holds that the regularity and purposeful action of efficient
causes lacking awareness cannot be explained without invoking a final
agent cause which governs things by mind. Such causes would produce
effects, but not good or beneficial effects. Again, this discussion depends
on an Aristotelian conception of causation and the interdependence
of efficient causation with final causation. Yet could there not be final
causation without intellect? That is, could one not construe a teleological
natural process – say the pumping function of the heart – as teleological,
but having come about by natural selection? That is, one can give an
explanation of the reason why beneficial effects arise without appealing
to mind. And indeed evolution seems to give precisely such an account.
To insist that random mutation and natural selection are directed by
mind seems hardly less controversial than just asserting God's existence.
And if one's argument for God's existence rests on such an assertion, it
would seem thereby weakened.

But perhaps Aquinas's style of argument could be adapted by restricting
the scope of both elements. Rather than claiming universal teleology in
nature, he can point to a range of teleological phenomena. And rather

than claiming that all of these require intention to be intelligible, his claim can be that some of them, or indeed the more fundamental of them, do. For example, there's Geach's claim that basic dispositional properties require teleological explanation. These are more explanatorily fundamental than the kind of teleological explanations seen in evolutionary theory. So it could be that the sort of non-conscious teleological explanation seen in nature rests on more fundamental teleologies which do require intellect. To make such a claim is to follow Swinburne in his contention that scientific explanation is insufficient and needs further support from personal explanation – invoking the agency of a being with certain powers and intentions.

It is clear that Aquinas's explanatory framework is different to that of Swinburne. The latter uses cumulative inductive arguments to support the probability of theism over its rival, naturalism, on the model of a scientific hypothesis. Aquinas uses deductive reasoning to try to demonstrate conclusively a necessary truth about reality. Their views on causation differ, and their views on God's nature differ greatly. Despite these important differences, I think Aquinas's case for God's existence based on teleology has significant structural affinities with Swinburne's argument about design. The phenomena which are the focus of the argument are fundamental physical processes, and the claim that is the best explanation for their orderliness and structure is to invoke the mind of an agent outside the realm of natural phenomena.

5
Objections to God's Existence

Objections to God's existence come in two kinds. Firstly, there are the types of argument which seek to undermine positive arguments for God's existence, the kind of dialectic seen in the previous chapter. Secondly, there are arguments which seek to independently show that the existence of such a thing as the God of classical theism is impossible or irrational to believe. Of this latter kind the two most powerful in contemporary discussions are the problem of evil and the arguments in favour of naturalism. The problem of evil arises in different forms, but basically seeks to argue the incompatibility of a good and all-powerful God with the manifest evil and suffering present in the world. Naturalism, on the other hand, argues for the explanatory redundancy of God. Defenders of naturalism hold that God is an outmoded concept, deriving from a prescientific age, used to conceal our ignorance of the workings of reality. As we grow in knowledge, the vacuity of the notion of God emerges – explaining the rise of atheism among intellectuals and the more highly educated.

Aquinas discusses both of these topics as objections to God's existence in ST I.2.3. In summary form he presents the problem and then articulates a rejoinder to it. However, he also has discussions in other texts which provide greater insight into his approach to these significant problems for classical theism. In this chapter, I shall begin with the problem of evil and then move on to naturalism.

5.1   The problem of evil

5.1.1   Introductory distinctions

Aquinas presents the problem of evil in the context of the five ways discussion as an incompatibility problem. If one of two contraries were infinite, then the other could not exist. God is supposed to be infinitely good, and so that would rule out any evil. Since there obviously is evil, then there cannot be a God. His response to this recapitulates a response made by Augustine, in that God allows evil to exist in order to produce good. By his power and goodness, God can bring good out of evil. Aquinas has more detailed discussions of evil in ST 1.48–49, QDM q.1 and SCG 3.1–10, and there are associated discussions of goodness, human action and free choice which feed into his account. Before exploring Aquinas's views in detail, I would like to discuss the general ways in which this issue has been addressed by philosophers of religion.

Aquinas's brief statement at ST 1.2.3 belongs to a long line of reflection on the problem, which has produced many different formulations of what the problem actually is, what solutions, if any, are available and what assumptions are being made by protagonists in these debates. Epicurus is credited with one of the earliest formulations of the problem, famously reiterated by David Hume:

> Epicurus's old questions are as yet unanswered. Is he willing to prevent evil, but not able? Then he is impotent. Is he able, but not willing? Then he is malevolent. Is he both able and willing? Whence then is evil?[1]

A multitude of questions underlie this. What exactly is evil? Dualists of different kinds, for example, Gnostics and Zoroastrians, have argued for a battle of polarized cosmic forces.[2] Others, for example, certain classical Indian philosophical systems which reject dualism, have denied that evil is a reality.[3] Others again have agreed that evil's metaphysical constitution is such that it is not a positive reality, but that does not mean it is illusory (e.g. Augustine and Aquinas). Perhaps one of the best formulations of the notion is evil is given by R.M. Adams and M.M. Adams who say that 'philosophers and theologians have for centuries lumped all of life's "minuses" together under that rubric, giving "evil" a very wide signification'.[4]

While clarifying the nature of evil is one issue, a different one is the nature of the alleged incompatibility. Epicurus holds that the existence of an all-good and all-powerful God rules out the possibility of evil. Aquinas holds that it does not. So what is the force of this argument? John Mackie produced a strong, clear version of the incompatibility argument, holding that it was a positive case for the irrationality of classical theistic belief. And he was careful to rule out inadequate responses which sought to change the goalposts of classical theism, watering down God's power.[5] However, Alvin Plantinga's robust defence against what has come to be known as the Logical Problem of Evil, has persuaded many, even atheistic, philosophers that the strong incompatibility case is too hard to achieve.[6] Any logically possible scenario in which God might have a reason to allow some evil will defeat the Logical Problem of Evil. As a result, recent debates have shifted to the Evidential Problem of Evil, arguing that while evil does not provide a logically compelling refutation of God's existence, it swings the balance decisively against the rationality of belief in God. Such debates are sometimes conducted using confirmation theory and probability theory, and have given rise to debates about the extent to which we are capable of weighing counter-vailing intuitions of what is good or what is evil for human beings.[7]

All of these considerations are theoretical, and concern attempts to judge the truth or falsity of theistic belief. Clearly, these are distinct from practical issues about what to do in the face of evil or indeed more general issues about how to make sense of evil if one is a non-theist (for example, Buddhist discussions of suffering). So 'the problem of evil' in this context is explicitly a theoretical problem about the rationality of belief in the God of classical theism confronted with the extent of evil in the world. However, a further distinction can be made even about these theoretical discussions. Religious believers have wrestled with the problem of evil independently of trying to argue with atheists. It is a problem which arises for any reflective theistic believer. We might call this problem an Aporetic Problem, since the context of the discussion is belief in God and then a puzzle or an aporia which arises for such belief. In contrast, the Polemical Problem is between theists and non-theists, with the latter challenging the former. Aporetic and Polemical debates differ in the range of assumptions underlying each. One might think of the Book of Job as an instance of the problem of evil as an aporia. At no point does Job doubt God's existence, but nevertheless Job seeks an answer to the evils which afflict him. This scenario differs from the case of someone whose belief in God is antecedently low or non-existent who will weigh the force of the problem of evil differently. Hence we see the bewildering variety of approaches and discussions of the problem.

Next I want to discuss a number of the crucial distinctions operative in these debates and some of the main assumptions underlying different approaches. Then I shall chart some of the main strategies used by theists to defend the compatibility of God and theism before sketching what is distinctive about Aquinas's contribution.

A basic distinction generally agreed on all sides is the difference between moral and natural evil. Moral evil, on the one hand, is the kind which results from free choice – for example, murder, theft, geno-cide and so forth. Natural evil, on the other hand, is not due to human agency, but comes from the nature of the physical world – for example, illness, death, disaster, earthquakes and so forth. Both kinds need to be squared with God's goodness, and it may be that certain theistic strategies of one kind, but not the other make sense (and both kinds may overlap, e.g. I can choose to smoke, leading to disease). Also the question of the enormity of these evils is relevant to the debate – why does there seem to be so much needless suffering in the world?

A long-standing strategy in defending classical theism is the Free Will Defence,[8] which argues that God has a morally sufficient reason to allow evil to occur in the world. A world without free creatures who always do good is clearly good, but creatures who are free to make moral choices, to do good or evil, it is argued, is a higher kind of good. The existence of free creatures makes possible the presence of evil in the world; hence, this explains why God allows evil. Many rejoinders have been made to this, including querying why God, if all powerful, could not have made creatures who, although free, always do good? A further problem with this approach is that it leaves natural evil untouched. It only explains the kind of evil deriving from moral agents, not illnesses and natural disasters. Richard Swinburne has an ingenious response to this, arguing that natural evil is a precondition of moral evil and certain ways of being morally good. One has to have observed accidental suffering and death before one is in a position to knowingly inflict this on others; otherwise, it would just be a further set of accidents.[9] The question of the extent of natural evil then becomes relevant in challenging Swinburne's account. A small amount of natural evil would have sufficed to teach this lesson – so how come there is so much of it and it is repeated ad nauseam?

A different kind of response is to appeal to mystery. This response claims that we are not in a position to know the mind of God and are not in an appropriate epistemic state to judge whether the evil in the world does or does not count as evidence against God. Essentially this is the case made in the biblical Book of Job – where, after being challenged by Job, God appears in a whirlwind and questions Job about the making of the world – effectively silencing him in a display of might. Depending on one's antecedent commitments, different responses to this may arise. A theist might well take this in an apophatic manner as an acceptance that the mystery of suffering is beyond us. An atheist or agnostic on the other hand might wonder why the mystery stops short at the existence of God. If the theistic defence is one from ignorance, why not push this further, into God himself? We are not in a position to know whether such a reality exists.

A related approach derives from Ludwig Wittgenstein, but was developed by the group known as Wittgensteinian fideists, as exemplified by D.Z. Phillips.[10] They argued that terms such as 'divine omnipotence' or 'divine goodness' only make sense in a religious context. Hence, to consider the problem of evil as a philosophical issue about whether God exists or not is to wrest these terms from their proper context and treat them as quasi-scientific or technical terms, generating the kind of dialectical arguments seen above. To think about evil and God is appropriate in the context of the language of redemption, covenant, sin, atonement and so forth, but not in the irreligious technical idioms of secular philosophers.

There is a sense in which Aquinas uses elements from all of these approaches in his response to the problem of evil, but he does so with assumptions and a conceptual scheme which make his position distinctively different from many of the antagonists in these debates – both theists and atheists.

One of the most fundamental features of Aquinas's position is his integration of questions about evil with his general metaphysical conceptual scheme. He characterizes evil in such a way that it is not a positive reality in itself, while still being real. In this way he makes a case for the inevitability of what we call natural evil in a physical universe such as ours. Thus, the viability of his metaphysics has an important bearing on his treatment of evil. In relation to moral evil, Aquinas thinks this is due to human free choice. However, his account of this is subtle and argues that human freedom is compatible with God's causal action, while he nevertheless denies that God is responsible for moral evil. So how can Aquinas hold together the prima facie incompatible theses that God causes all things, humans are free and God is not responsible for moral evil? Finally, his views on human happiness and what constitutes living a good life have a direct impact on his evaluation of evil. Natural evil proves less significant than moral evil, and our limited perspective makes it hard for us to adjudicate in any particular case the eternal perspective on cases of suffering – what the ultimate meaning of apparently meaningless suffering might be. In the following sections I shall treat each of these in turn – the metaphysics of evil, human freedom and human destiny. In giving a full account of Aquinas's views on evil, one needs to note how he brings God and moral and natural evil together in his discussions of the passion of Christ. But since these are theological issues, I shall not address them in this philosophical discussion.[11]

5.1.2   The metaphysics of evil

If one were to make an inventory of all the phenomena in the world – classifying them into their various kinds – how would one treat evil? Is it a thing, a force, a power, an action, a property, a universal? Listing such labels takes us obviously into the fundamental realm of general metaphysics – beyond the higher level classifications of, for instance, biology, economics, psychology, physics. Metaphysics asks what are the fundamental intelligible structures of reality. It seems clear that evil has some relationship to goodness; hence, a way of making sense of the nature of evil is to get some clarity on the nature of goodness. Aquinas says 'One opposite is known through the other, as darkness is known through light. Hence also what evil is must be known from the notion of good' [ST1.48.1].

A significant tradition in English-speaking philosophy accepts a sharp distinction between facts and values. Hume famously states that one can never derive an 'ought' from an 'is'. Facts about the world are morally neutral, and value comes from somewhere else (for Hume, from the emotions).[12] G.E. Moore made canonical the 'naturalistic fallacy' – that the moral realm and the realm of facts about the world are quite distinct, and it is a mistake to attempt to analyse goodness drawing on any facts or features of the world.[13]

Aquinas's account of goodness does precisely what Moore thought impossible. Aquinas thinks that goodness can be explicated by its relationship to being. That is, goodness is indeed connected to facts about reality. Being is divided into different kinds, captured in the classifications of the categories with different genera and species of substance and their properties. This sort of division emphasizes the differences between things, the plurality of differences in being. However, there are also distinctions to be made in being which are general – which apply to every existent thing no matter how different in kind it is. These differences transcend the categories, and they came to be known as 'the transcendentals'. Avicenna discusses five such transcendentals, which numbering Aquinas sometimes follows [QDV 1.1], while sometimes they are abbreviated to three [ST1.16.4].

Being, because it is such a primitive concept and has nothing excluded from itself, cannot have anything added to itself from without. However, the transcendentals illuminate *modes* of being. That is, they focus on different aspects of it. Considering any being, one can take it in relation to itself (*per se*) or in relation to another (*per aliud*). Considered in itself, there is one thing which can be predicated affirmatively of any being. This is its essence, by which it has existence, and Aquinas uses the term 'thing' (*Res*) to express this universal affirmation. Likewise, if a negation were predicated of every being considered absolutely, this would bring out the undivided nature of each thing, and the term 'one'

(*Unum*) captures this. Thus, two transcendental terms – *Res* and *Unum* – are shown to be intrinsically connected to being.

The remaining transcendentals relate to a being considered in relation to something else. When thinking about the difference between one being and another, that one thing differs from another, the term 'something' (*Aliquid*) applies, which is another transcendental. Correlatively to difference, there is the correspondence which a thing might have with another. To capture this correspondence (*convenientia*), there must be something which can relate to all beings. Aquinas, following Aristotle, thinks that only one thing has this capacity – and that is the soul (as expressed in *De Anima* III, 'the soul is in some sense all things'). The two powers of the soul are appetite and knowledge. As a thing is an object of the appetitive power of the soul, it is good (*Bonum*). As a thing is an object of the intellectual power of the soul, it is true (*Verum*). Thus the list of five transcendentals is achieved – *Res, Unum, Aliquid, Bonum, Verum*. This is sometimes abbreviated to Being, Truth, Goodness. There is a difference, however, between goodness and truth as transcendentals. While the primary location of goodness is in the object desired by the will (external to the will), the primary location of truth is in the intellect rather than in the object known (internal to the intellect) [ST 1.16.1]. While being, goodness and truth are the same in reality, in that they have the same reference (*Suppositio*), they differ in terms of what is meant, the aspect drawn attention to (*Ratio*). Of these transcendentals, Being is the most fundamental, but everything insofar as it exists is also good [ST 1.5.3].

Goodness, on this account, is formally or internally related to desire. It is the object of the appetite, or the will. Furthermore, this account does not restrict goodness simply to the appetites of beings with souls. Aquinas also extends the notion of desire to natural tendencies, such as stones tending towards the centre of the earth. While this could be easily dismissed as simplistic anthropomorphism or animism, the more fundamental reasoning working here is that desire is connected to perfection – what is desired is seen as a way of perfecting a thing, and perfection is related to actuality. A thing is perfect insofar as it has achieved its actuality. So as an object tends to achieve actualization, whether by natural processes, or rational choice, it exhibits 'desire' in this sense. As noted, a thing is good insofar as it exists, since existence is the precondition of actuality. Of course, there will be levels of actualization and therefore levels of goodness, so that the goodness associated with mere existence is just a basic level [ST 1.48.4]. But, nevertheless, existence itself brings in its train, as a transcendental accompaniment, goodness. So goodness follows upon being.

To grasp Aquinas's treatment of the problem of evil, one has to grasp this metaphysical context. Evil is a privation of being [ST 1.48.1]. This means it is parasitic. It has no positive reality in itself, but presupposes some other existent, good, thing. It is important to note that a privation is different to an absence. For example, my friend Ciaran may lack wings, but since as a human it is not part of his make-up to have wings, this is an absence and has no actual impact on him. However, were he to lose a limb, this would be a privation. In normal circumstances (based on our knowledge of physiology), humans possess four limbs. To lack one of these results in limitations and difficulties of various kinds. So lacking a limb would be a privation for Ciaran, and Aquinas would reckon this an evil. In contemporary linguistic usage, we tend to restrict the term 'evil' to more extreme phenomena – perhaps serial killers or genocide. On Aquinas's view there are levels of evil ranking from minor physical discomforts such a headache through loss of limb to the full panoply of horrors we encounter in the daily news. All of these can be construed as kinds of privation. Evil, therefore, is understood by him to be a lack, gap or malfunction in something which is good. Aquinas distinguishes evils into two kinds – evil suffered (*Malum Poenae* – literally the evil of punishment) and evil done (*Malum Culpae* – literally the evil of blame, so called, for Aquinas, after the sin of Adam) [I.48.5], which readily map on to natural evil and moral evil, as discussed above. I shall discuss moral evil in the next section, but will focus on natural evil in the remainder of this section.[14]

A basic feature of Aquinas's understanding of evil suffered – of illness, disease, disaster and all the other misfortunes not caused by moral agents – is that it is a necessary feature of the kind of world we live in.[15] A physical world with creatures liable to corruption – creatures which are metaphysically constituted such that their form and matter come apart, creatures as diverse as humans, fawns, mountains, galaxies – will necessarily entail suffering for those creatures which are sentient (that is, for the humans and fawns, not mountains and galaxies). The kind of world we inhabit, with the great diversity of kinds of things and with change as a basic phenomenon, brings with it evil suffered. Aquinas analyses the metaphysical underpinning of such a world. First of all, the diversity of the world is due to God [ST 1.47.1]. Beings are brought into existence to communicate his goodness to them, and this requires a diversity of beings. A background to this treatment is his discussion of Parmenides on being, whom he interprets as denying change and diversity in being [In Met 1.9.138; In Met 12.10.2651]. Parmenides holds that being cannot be divided since there is nothing outside being.

But in doing this, Parmenides treats being like a genus, where it is the same in all instances (it has a univocal meaning). Aquinas counters this by noting that being exists differently in different things. Parmenides fails to distinguish between absolute non-being and relative non-being. While absolute non-being is opposed to being, relative non-being exists internally within the realm of being. The very notion of plurality depends on this relative non-being. Aquinas says 'this particular being is only divided from that particular being because this being includes the negation of that being' [In BDT 4.1resp]. This connects to the transcendental term *'Aliquid'*, discussed above – the meaning of which arises from considering things in relation to each other based on difference.

For Aquinas, diversity is present both at the level of species or kinds and also within the numerical individuals of those kinds. It is the totality of creation which reflects God's goodness, not each individual. Each individual must be considered in relation to the totality. Hence the lion and the lamb together reflect God's goodness, and part of this is the tendency of lions to devour lambs. The nature or form of the lion includes its predatory capacities. Were it not to have these, it would be a deficient lion and would die. So in such a world, the natural tendency to flourishing of some creatures entails the corruption of others. Likewise, this is so with the lion and the microbes which will devour it in turn when it dies. Aquinas discusses such natural processes using the pre-scientific examples of fire, air and water, noting how the presence of fire brings about corruption to water [ST 1.49.1]. The examples of the lion and of fire represent fully functioning processes. There are also processes which do not function well, due to faulty forms or faulty matter – he gives the example of animal movement which might not be well developed in young animals (weakness in the power of movement), or else impaired by lameness (weakness in the bones) [ibid].

Two problems are often posed in relation such natural evil. The first is its extent – how come there is so much of it? Frequently this is voiced after a conspicuous disaster, for example, the Lisbon earthquake in which thousands died. Secondly, why does God allow it to happen? Why does God not intervene?

On Aquinas's account, the extent of natural evil is what one would expect – it extends as far as the natural realm does. A world such as ours exhibits death, illness, suffering, disease as part of its fabric. One which did not would be either not physical at all, or else physical in a very different sense. To this can be countered why did God create such a world at all? Would it not be better not to exist than to endure the suffering of such a world? Certainly some people experience this keenly and take their own lives in response. However, for Aquinas, goodness is the overriding principle – the evils of the world are parasitic on goodness and can ultimately be brought to achieve goodness. This last point is important for Aquinas – 'this is part of the infinite goodness of God, that he should allow evil to exist and out of it produce good' [ST 1.2.3 ad1]. How this might happen is not obvious. It raises questions about human destiny, human happiness, whether death is the terminus of life and God's providence, which I shall postpone until section four below. But such considerations are relevant to answering the question why God does allow such natural evils and shed light on the name Aquinas gives to them, '*Malum Poenae*' – the evil of punishment. This also clearly relates to the question of divine intervention: why does God not intervene? It can seem that the metaphysical account of plurality and corruption is rather callous and unfeeling in relation to individuals. An account of the metaphysical implications of plurality is of little comfort to someone dying of a painful disease, and seems incompatible with the idea of a personal God. So this must be considered below. In the meantime I shall turn to moral evil, where similar problems about God's inaction in the face of evil arise.

5.1.3   Human freedom

Aquinas makes the natural/moral evil distinction in terms of *Malum Poenae* (evil suffered) and *Malum Culpae* (evil done) [ST 1.48.5]. As noted earlier, evil is understood as a privation of goodness. Goodness has two aspects in any entity [ST 1.48.5]. The first is the form, structure or configuration of any thing (the species structure), and the second is the operation of that thing – the actions characteristic of the kind in question (natural inclinations or tendencies). Whatever defect impacts on the first kind of act – the form or structure – is evil suffered. Aquinas's example is blindness – there is a defect in the visual system of an organism. Clearly some structural flaws will also impact on the operation (e.g. a person with faulty visual apparatus cannot see). A distinguishing mark of this kind of evil is that it is involuntary – the subject suffering it is not responsible for the flaw. However, there are defects in the operation for which the subject *is* responsible, and these occur only in voluntary agents. The kind of evil which results from these defects has the character of a fault – these are actions for which the agent is culpable. Furthermore, being subject to evil suffered does not actually make one evil. There is no blame in disease or disaster (although it is possible that the two kinds of evil are mixed in a single situation – in one respect, I may not be responsible for an illness, but in another respect, I may be by virtue of choices I have made, e.g. smoking). But while being subject to evil done doesn't make one evil, it lessens the quality of goodness in one and serves to impact on one's character and the disposition to do further blameworthy actions [ST 1.48.6]. So experiencing moral evil, for Aquinas, is worse than experiencing natural evil. To grasp his account of moral evil, some background on his view of human action is required.

Aquinas's account of human action is complex, but it derives fairly directly from his basic conceptual scheme of essential natures with the associated structure of causal explanations.[16] To explain human action is to use the full variety of kinds of cause and to distinguish the respective roles of intellect and will in humans. He offers a dynamic, multi-layered analysis of the reciprocal relations between will and intellect. From his general view that nature is constituted of entities with distinctive natures, he articulates a view of the world in which things act in distinctive ways, according to their nature. For example, sulphuric acid dissolves gold, water evaporates at a certain temperature, plants grow towards the light, animals seek food. The inclinations exhibited by these beings can be classified into a hierarchy displaying levels of sophistication – basic physical processes, levels of sensory interaction, levels of intellectual interaction with the world. Beings who are capable of reasoning about the world have an inclination, a desire of the good [ST 1.19.1]. This is the will, defined as a rational appetite. As an appetite, it is an inclination, but it is also guided by the intellect (which is not to say that it always works well or identifies an actual as distinct from an apparent good). Aquinas holds that the will can be analysed using the four causes [ST 1.82.1]. The matter of the will is the living nature of human beings, which is given the formal characteristic of desire or tends towards what is desired. What is desired is an end, presented to the will by the intellect. The will can also be coerced or made to do something by an efficient cause outside itself. The material, formal and final causes of the will operate with necessity, constituting the will as a rational appetite. However, this necessary structure is a precondition of choice. It sets up the scene within which one can choose freely. Only coercion, the causation due to an external efficient cause, is incompatible with the will's moving freely.

Given that the will is moved to its desired end by the intellect, does that put the intellect in charge? Is the intellect superior to the will? Aquinas distinguishes two ways in which one thing can be superior to another – absolutely or under a certain aspect [ST 1.82.3]. In absolute terms, the intellect is held to be higher than the will since its object is simpler, more abstract and therefore metaphysically superior (e.g. the ideal of good rather than a particular instance of it). Now the object of the intellect is contained in the intellect, whereas the object of the will is external to it. When considering the relation of intellect to will relative to the object thought about or desired, the superiority changes depending on the nature of the object. If the object desired by the will is itself superior to the intellect, then the will is the superior power in that respect. Hence, love of God (in the will) is better than knowledge of God (in the intellect). Also, given that the intellect can move the will by presenting it with its object (exercising final causality), the will causally impacts on the intellect by, for example, directing its attention (exercising efficient causality). Given this complex pattern of causal interactions, Aquinas further distinguishes different stages in human action.

He gives a brief account of human action at I–II.15.3. 'Now the order of action is this: First there is the apprehension of the end; then the desire of the end; then the counsel about the means; then the desire of the means'. This statement shows that a basic distinction in his action theory is that of means and ends. He holds that happiness is the end all people desire (discussed in the next section) and that this is an automatic process, without deliberation involved. For all other lesser goals and means to those goals, deliberation is involved. Thus, in human action there is a complex interplay of intellect and will, ends and means. Aquinas makes the following analytical distinctions about the parts of human action, meaning that they are not necessarily phenomenologically available to the agent, but can be distinguished in rational reconstruction. Intention (*Intentio* I–II q.12) is the act of will which selects an end and determines a means to achieve it. Choice (*Electio* I–II q.13) is the selection of a specific action as means to the end. Counsel (*Consilio* I–II q.14) is the deliberative process which precedes the choice of means. Consent (*Consensus* I–II q.15) is the assent to various appropriate means, which choice picks (identical to choice when only one option is available, but distinct otherwise). Use (*Usus* I–II q.16) is the act of the will which operates on whatever is within the immediate control of the will – for example, the body, intellect or even the will itself – setting a chain in motion. Finally, Command (*Imperium* I–II q.17) is the imperative to perform an action by the intellect, presupposing the operation of the other acts of the will. Human action, therefore, is a dynamic and complex process – in which actions are closely interconnected with each other, each one potentially describable as means and ends in a nested hierarchy. While Aquinas thinks we have no choice about the ultimate end of action – we are hardwired to seek happiness – we have free choice about how we construe the end and how we go about seeking it. And free choice (*liberum arbitrium*) is not the same as free will. As we have seen, human action exhibits a complex interrelationship of intellect and will. Hence, free choice is a system-level capacity of the human being, one essential component of which is will. Freedom pertains primarily to the agent who chooses freely by virtue of the choices the intellect presents to the will and by the process of deliberation on ends and means. Where does moral evil fit into this picture?

Functioning properly, the intellect apprehends the good and also apprehends the means to achieve it. It selects means and subsidiary ends to achieve this overall end. However, the process is liable to malfunction either in terms of an incorrect apprehension of good (mistaking an apparent for a real good) and by weakness of the will, where it is turned from the path of right reason by other appetites which fuel incorrect apprehensions of the good. This process happens over a person's lifetime, and is embedded in an account of virtue and vice, how a person has been morally educated, how choices impact on character traits, how internal physical or psychological dispositions impact on one's operation of intellect and will. So when someone performs an evil action, it is part of a dynamic web in which the person's moral fabric is altered incrementally for the worse (and mutatis mutandis for a good action). From the perspective of the philosophical problem of evil, two puzzles arise about Aquinas's account. Firstly, how is free human choice compatible with God's universal causal power and providence? Secondly, why does God allow appalling moral actions to happen – is not this lack of intervention a moral defect in God?

God's causal interaction with the world is through creation, not construed as a temporally distant starting point, but as an ongoing sustaining in existence. Thus, God's causation manifests not *in* the world, but rather as constituting the world within which causal forces compete. Aquinas holds that God is causally responsible for the world and all the entities in it. God is also responsible for the natural events and natural evils of such a world. However, free creatures are responsible for moral evil by virtue of their free choices, and his claim is that God is not responsible for these. But how can God causally sustain someone like Adolf Hitler and not be responsible for the evils he commits? Aquinas answers this with a subtle distinction between logical contradictions and logical contraries [ST 1.19.9 ad3]. If one rejects one of a pair of logical contradictions, one is forced to accept the other ('This is not white, hence it is not-white' is logically binding). However if one rejects one of a pair of logical contraries, one is not forced to accept the opposite contrary ('This is not white, hence it is black' is not logically binding, since it may be grey). How is this relevant? Aquinas holds that with moral evils, God does not will moral evils not to be. That is, he allows them. But this does not mean that in consequence he wills moral evils to be. He neither wills them to be nor wills them not to be. He allows free choice. The free choice of an agent committing an evil act is sustained by God's creative causality, but the evil manifested in such an act is a deficiency in what should be there in a good act, so while God is causally active in the act, God is not the cause of the evil. And God's allowing of free choice is analogous to his allowing of necessary and contingent creatures [In PH 1.14]. God causes both necessary and contingent creatures and processes in the world. The necessary ones have certain features, and the contingent ones have different features, but both are causally dependent on God. Likewise, God causally sustains beings who cannot act voluntarily and causally sustains beings who do so act. Therefore, God's causal power does not hinder freedom, but is a condition of its operation. This position is possible because causation is not understood in a univocal, Hume-style analysis,[17] but as an analogous concept with different but related aspects to it. God is causally operative in evil acts (sustaining the agent), but does not cause the evil in those acts, which is understood as a gap or a lack, a falling away from the goodness which ought to be there.

As to whether God's permitting of such actions to happen is a moral defect in God, Aquinas's conception of God differs from much contemporary discussion of this issue.[18] Simply put, God is not a moral agent. Aquinas is unwilling to place God along a continuum where he exhibits maximal moral features, say, while we have less. If he were to do this, then there would indeed be a problem about God's permitting lesser beings to act the way they do. We would hold him to the same standards. But Aquinas holds that the transcendence of God entails that he is not along this continuum. He is not a moral agent; rather, he is goodness itself. He is not a mere being; rather, he is being itself. In response to critics (such as J.L. Austin, who dismissed the metaphysical notion of existence as being a kind of metaphysical ticking over, like breathing, only quieter)[19] who would challenge the intelligibility of such statements, Aquinas would be likely to agree, but with an important proviso. They do not (and cannot) make sense to us (*quoad nos*), but they do make sense. His earlier arguments about God's existence are arguments designed to point to the existence of something which transcends our intellectual capacities. Yet we are capable of making some claims about the grammar or logic of our talk about this mystery – that it makes sense to think of God as a source or font of goodness, and it does not make sense to think of God as a super being. Whether such a position is tenable touches the core of Aquinas's project. Timothy McDermott nicely sums this up by saying that agnostics typically are sure of what God is like, but are unsure whether one exists. In contrast, Aquinas is sure that a mysterious reality exists, but is in principle unsure as to many specifics on what it is really like.[20]

Still, a number of unanswered questions remain. Why did God create a world in which physical suffering occurs? Why does God permit horrendous moral evil? To get a fully rounded sense of how Aquinas thinks about these issues, we need to turn to his views about human happiness, human purpose and divine providence.

5.1.4   Human destiny

The axiom that grace builds on nature is important in grasping Aquinas's account of human happiness.[21] While he follows Aristotle in presenting an account of human happiness as flourishing by means of living according to the virtues, there is also an essential dimension which goes well beyond Aristotle. Flourishing in this life is always incomplete and imperfect. Aquinas holds that true happiness can only be found after death, in union with God. This presents a way of looking at evil which is significantly different to that of those who believe that life ceases with death. While this belief is obviously theological in character, Aquinas nevertheless presents a significant number of rational arguments about the different kinds of human happiness.

The second part of the *Summa Theologiae* deals with the return of humanity to God, which is another way of characterizing Aquinas's views on morality. Given his views on the metaphysical constitution of reality – that reality is structured hierarchically with different kinds of substances displaying different kinds of potency-actuality composition in a teleologically ordered dynamic system – he begins his discussion of morality with an account of human purpose embedded in such a picture. Many human actions are incidental and not deliberate (e.g. absent-mindedly scratching one's chin – what he calls 'acts of humans'). However, actions arising from free choice, those involving intellect and will ('human actions'), are constituted by having an end or purpose [ST I–II 1.1]. Hence to desire, choose and act requires an end – this is an analytical constituent of what it is to act.

A more controversial claim is that there is an ultimate goal of human life. Given that each deliberate act has a goal, this claim means the whole ensemble of any given person's acts also has a goal. This is not obvious. It may be that we have different goals at different times, or indeed different goals at the same time. Why not a plurality of goals? For example, I may want a career, a happy family life, wealth, health and so on. In what way are all these subordinated to one goal? To grasp Aquinas's answer, it is important to note that Aquinas is arguing formally at this point [ST I–II.1]. Before putting content into the claim about what is the end of human life, he wants to establish that such a thing exists. And he is not arguing from an empirical or sociological description about what many people do – it is rather a theoretical argument based on the nature of action. The crucial text is ST I–II 1.4, where he considers whether one might have a multiplicity of ends, stretching out infinitely, multiplying endlessly. There are parallels in his discussion here to the arguments in ST I.2.3 about God's existence. He denies the possibility of an infinite regress – in this case of final causes. Final causes are purposes or ends. If such causes were merely incidentally related to each other, there could indeed be an infinity of them. However, they are not incidentally related, but essentially related. The operation of a higher-level cause governs lower-level causes. Thus, there is a hierarchy of ends, each one modified by a more ultimate one, until a final end is reached. So, in the objection cited above, it turns out that career, family, wealth and health are all intermediate elements in a more ultimate picture. In ST I–II 1.5 Aquinas argues that there is a parallel between the metaphysical structure of reality and the hierarchy of ends. Each species in each genus has a determinate structure which establishes an appropriate end for that species. The total structure has an end in its efficient cause, which is also the final cause, and this is God.

But what then of the obvious diversity in action and ends exhibited by people? Aquinas holds that this exhibits the formal structure he has outlined – except that there may be mistaken final ends. People arrange their lives to maximize wealth or fame or pleasure. Even though such an end is mistaken, on Aquinas's view, it still confirms the formal structure – our deliberations and actions are end oriented. ST I–II q.2 is devoted to exploring why goals such as honour, fame, power, wealth and so forth are not appropriate final goals.

These are external factors, and Aquinas offers four general arguments as to why they cannot constitute happiness [q.2.4]. Firstly, they can be present with both good and bad people, while happiness is associated with well-being and hence not with evil. Secondly, happiness involves a kind of self-sufficiency, and even with all these things one might still need wisdom, health, and so on. Thirdly, no misfortune arises from happiness, but it might arise from these. Finally, happiness comes from human nature itself, but these are external things which are often conferred by luck. So in light of these negative arguments, one can see that happiness positively involves goodness and self-sufficiency arising from human nature. Why not this then (a life lived according to the virtues), as a characterization of happiness, a view which appears to be Aristotle's? The final four articles of q. 2 turn to internal or intrinsic factors of human existence, such as body and soul, arguing that none of the goods pertaining to these suffice for true happiness. He rejects the Epicurean view that pleasure is the good [2.6] but also the Stoic view that self-perfection in some form is happiness [2.7]. While it is true that one way of thinking about happiness involves a state of human existence, in another sense it is not. Happiness is the grasp of unrestricted good. Such a goal exists outside of (and above) human existence. It is God who is the object of desire. God cannot be grasped in corporeal human existence, and so the happiness we experience on earth is incomplete. Complete happiness is only possible after death, when union with God is possible in the beatific vision [2.8]. Aquinas here distinguishes between the objective content of happiness, which is God, and the subjective acquisition of the vision of God by the individual [3.1]. Thus, happiness is a state of the individual, but intrinsically connected to the nature of reality.

This clearly goes beyond Aristotle's conception of happiness as a life lived in accord with the virtues. For Aquinas, Aristotle's picture is of incomplete happiness (sometimes termed *Felicitas*), in contrast to complete happiness (*Beatitudo*). While this is theologically distinct from Aristotle's vision, it is still possible to construe Aquinas's position as a distinct philosophical option, based on the general metaphysical considerations which make belief in God rational and consequently such an account of human happiness as rational. One might also notice Aquinas's agreement with Albert Camus on the infinity of human longing, which is why Aquinas thinks we cannot be truly happy in this world.[22] For Camus, this is the source of absurdity in human existence, since there is no God. For Aquinas, it is the key to understanding genuine happiness as something which can only come after life on earth is ended. Thus, his attitude to the vicissitudes we suffer during this life is strongly influenced by his view of human destiny.

How does this help make sense of his views on evil? Aquinas holds that God exerts provident care over the world. In ST 1.22, he articulates his view that God's creation involves placing everything into a system in which they are ordained to an end, endorsing Boethius's view that 'Providence is the divine reason itself established in the supreme principle of all things and disposing them all' [ST I.22.1; Boethius (1973) 4.6,

p. 358]. God is the source of the entire causal structure of the world, so nothing escapes his causal power. This is nevertheless compatible with human freedom,

> Intelligent creatures because they have control over their actions through free judgement come under Providence in a special manner. Blame or merit is imputed to them and is requited with punishment or reward. [ST I.22.2ad5]

How does this bear on the problem that dreadful things happen to people during their lives? Providence causes defects to happen in the natural world and causes free agents to commit evil acts (while still being free – see above). In the natural realm, the claim is that the suffering of an individual is part of the whole in which the overall plurality of being reflects God's goodness. In the moral realm, suffering evil is regarded as less bad than perpetrating evil. Therefore, suffering both forms of evil is compatible with God's providence. Were life to finish with death, there would certainly be a problem about the raw deal for the individual of a short, unhappy life. But for Aquinas, death is a transition to eternity and adds a further essential element to the understanding of evil. This points to the fact that his approach to evil, while involving philosophical reflection on its nature, kinds, causes and outcomes, is ultimately theological. He thinks that specific Christian beliefs about the death and resurrection of Christ are vital for a full response to the phenomenon of evil. But furthermore, the existence of evil is deeply mysterious. As Brian Davies notes, 'On his account, there being a world with evil when there might have been no evil at all is thoroughly mysterious (as is God)'.[23]

Aquinas's discussion of the immortality of the soul at ST 1.75.1 relies essentially on intellectual cognition's being incompatible with materiality. It is a subtle issue – since matter in the modern sense and Aquinas's matter differ in meaning. Nevertheless, the capacity of the soul to receive into itself all other forms in intellectual cognition is regarded as a mark of the fact that it is not itself a material entity. Whether contemporary cognitive science disproves this or not is a moot point. At the very least, Kenny points out that abstract human reasoning, and indeed the rule-governed activity of language use, is not easily reducible to physical mechanism.[24] Whether such activity could happen in the absence of *any* physical substratum is of course the key concern here. There is a sense in which Aquinas acknowledges the importance of such a physical substratum. The soul (which is the substantial form of the body) is in an unnatural state separated from the body. And in his account it is the resurrection of the body which provides the ultimate terminus for the separated soul. Herbert McCabe sums this up nicely when he says

> Aquinas speculates bravely on how a separated soul, at least in heaven, could somehow think as well as have the understanding which is the beatific vision ... it is all rather an uphill struggle and it is with a sort of relief that Aquinas reminds us that in the Scriptures it is not immortality of soul we are promised but the resurrection of the body.[25]

It would be easy to dismiss the appeal to the afterlife as a solution to the problem of evil as explaining the implausible by the even more implausible. However, Aquinas's account is multifaceted and not a simple kind of dualism. As Thomas Gilby says, discussing Aquinas's attitude to the radical Aristotelianism at Paris which was the backdrop to his discussion of happiness in 1269, 'with much of the contemporary movement he was in agreement, especially as regards the recovery of profane values, the hard-headed rationalism, and the appeal to earthy evidences'.[26] His discussion of incomplete happiness is not to dismiss such a state – he devotes many articles to explicating such a state in the *Secunda Secundae*. Rather it is provisional and relative, and needs to be understood in light of a larger context. This larger context, while the object of faith, is also susceptible to rational defence, which he provides.

5.1.5 Conclusion

An important issue in contemporary philosophy is the place of history. Are philosophical positions to be evaluated *sub specie aeternitatis*, or have they to be seen as contingent, historically conditioned developments? There is a sense in which analytical philosophy tends towards the former, while continental the latter. Aquinas's own approach is closer that of the analytic – yet he is also conscious of historical development and of the evolution of ideas. He discusses the evolution of concepts through Presocratic thought and understands Aristotle as reconciling opposing earlier views.

Aquinas's treatment of the problem of evil has many facets – a metaphysical discussion of the nature and place of evil in the world, an account of human action and freedom, an account of human happiness and destiny. It is historically rooted in both the Aristotelian framework he adopts and the Christian tradition which is his milieu. To what extent it is successful depends on the attitude one takes to the component elements within it. What is clear is that it is a sophisticated and thoughtful response to this problem, offering penetrating analyses of important aspects of human life.

5.2   Naturalism

5.2.1   The straight response to naturalism

The problem of naturalism, as Aquinas states it in the second objection of ST I.2.3, sounds like an application of Ockham's razor, that is, a principle of intellectual parsimony. When causes fully account for something, we do not need to postulate more. But the natural world has natural causes and human intervention to explain all the phenomena contained in it, so no further cause is required. Aquinas's response is to argue that natural and human causation do not exhaust the causal story and that one is led to a first cause which is unchanging and which of itself must be. The response connects directly to the corpus of the article, with its arguments for a first cause and with associated texts in the *Summa Contra Gentiles* and the *Commentary on Aristotle's Metaphysics*. But modern naturalists would not be moved by this dialectical strategy, since basic to their position is a methodological objection to the possibility of making such a move as Aquinas's. There is not a possibility of appeal to a higher science than those exhibited in the natural sciences, and various arguments are presented to make this case. Simply asserting that there is such a science would be met with disbelief. Michael Rea in a recent book on naturalism notes that the majority of contemporary philosophers (at least in the English-speaking world) are naturalists, although exhibiting a high degree of variegation in how they construe it.[27]

Aquinas's views on the methods and nature of the sciences are contained in summary in ST question 1, in greater detail in his commentary on Boethius's *De Trinitate* and in the commentary on Aristotle's *Posterior Analytics*. He endorses Aristotle's deductive method, defends a form of foundationalism, argues dialectically for the necessity of intellectual first principles, has a hierarchical conception of the sciences, distinguishes practical and speculative science, uses the idea of subalternated science, distinguishes the formal and material aspects of scientific inquiry. Among the features I would like to note is the systematicity of his views. His account of cognition in the individual, the relation of sense to intellect and the different workings of the intellect dovetail with the account of the differences between disciplines, but also with the way intellectual disciplines constitute habits of mind directed to the goals of human existence. Typically these issues are treated as distinct in subsequent discussions – indeed, philosophy of science, epistemology, moral psychology and issues about human destiny are rarely considered together in contemporary academia.

The contemporary intellectual world is therefore less integrated than the one presented by Aquinas. But it also poses important challenges to the methodology used by him. Naturalism as a recognizable phenomenon clearly was a possibility considered by Aquinas, but it was in the nineteenth century that it became a genuine contender as a world view. The kind of scepticism about speculative reason exhibited by Hume, the advances in the physical sciences and the kind of ideology shown by Auguste Comte all generated a momentum which flourished in the ideals of scientific philosophy expressed by Gottlob Frege and Bertrand Russell, which were deepened and refined by Rudolf Carnap and W.V. Quine. Quine stands as a watershed. The development of cognitive science, the work of naturalists such as Daniel Dennett, Patricia and Paul Churchland, Patricia and Philip Kitcher and Michael Devitt all flow from his conception of the lack of principled distinction between natural science and philosophical reason. This is a powerful current in contemporary philosophy, and reverberates more broadly in the popular works of Richard Dawkins and Dennett. So is Aquinas's work merely a chapter in the history of ideas, or can it engage with contemporary naturalism? It seems to me that Aquinas has the resources to challenge some of the arguments of the naturalists, and indeed various contemporary anti-naturalistic philosophers are developing positions which look curiously familiar to those who know Aquinas. In the following sections I shall discuss the naturalism of Carnap and Quine, especially in relation to the notion of analyticity, examine some responses to Quinean naturalism and then compare these to Aquinas's account of mind and language. Aquinas's position is robust enough to work as a viable alternative to naturalism, and is not at all dissimilar to contemporary anti-naturalistic positions.

5.2.2   Carnap and Quine on naturalism

If Quine is the most influential theorist of naturalism in the latter part of the twentieth century, Carnap is the most important influence on him. Recent studies of Carnap emphasize the neo-Kantian constitutive aspect of his work and play down the simple-minded verificationist caricature popularized by A.J. Ayer.[28] One can think of his work as a continuation of the neo-Kantian project to clarify the a priori aspects of inquiry in a linguistic register. He was influenced by Frege to value formal language and the need for a perspicuous system of representation, believing that many problems of philosophy are spuriously generated by the illusions of language. Russell supplied him with the model of scientific philosophy, Wittgenstein with a linguistic account of logical truth and logical consequence. He was reacting against nineteenth century German Idealism, despairing that sentences such as 'The Absolute is identical with itself' could be clarified, argued about or given truth values. His early work was on the idea of space, making sense of the developments of relativity theory, followed by an attempt to work out rigorously, using the logic of *Principia Mathematica*, an account of sense knowledge on the model of Russell's *Our Knowledge of the External World* – this was The *Logical Structure of the World* (1927). Following this, was a turn to the nature of logical and mathematical truth in *The Logical Syntax of Language* (1934). Carnap defended the use of linguistic rules to constitute logical calculi, developing notions of truth, consequence and proof relative to these languages. The task of the philosopher is to develop this formal apparatus, which first-order workers in mathematics, applied logic, philosophy of science and the sciences in general would use. Central to this project is the idea of analyticity. An analytic proposition is one made true by the rules of the linguistic framework, while a synthetic one is made true by the world. Philosophy has a clear method – using linguistic frameworks, translating and analysing unclear natural language notions into highly tooled artificial concepts which can be applied scientifically. Philosophy does not articulate truths about the world, but aids science in doing that. The constraints on the use of formal languages are pragmatic – what the working scientist finds congenial and helpful to use. A clear statement of this can be found in 'Empiricism, Semantics and Ontology' (1950). Carnap's work has strands of empiricism, pragmatism and neo-Kantianism woven together within the guiding principle of the linguistic turn in philosophy. Unlike Wittgenstein's approach to language, Carnap was a technician, avoiding natural languages and seeing the core role of philosophy as the production of carefully honed linguistic frameworks which would facilitate the answering of those questions which can be answered, and the avoidance of those which cannot. But, like Wittgenstein, he thought that language leads one astray and that metaphysics is a linguistic fiction, mistaking the form of representation for the matter conveyed by that form.

Quine was an early advocate of Carnap's approach to philosophy, which seemed to fit well with American pragmatism. He gave lectures at Harvard in the mid-1930s defending the approach which took analyticity as central. His 'Truth by Convention' of 1936 is typically read in light of his subsequent repudiation of analyticity, but is better seen as still internal to the analyticity project, dealing with internal tensions in it. Particularly that paper probes the problem of how a notion of analyticity might ground logical truth without presupposing it. However, the main break comes with 'Two Dogmas of Empiricism' (1950). There, Quine examines the different possible ways in which analyticity might be explicated and finds them all wanting. He is dubious about the notion of meaning, construed as sense. One can work with an idea of reference, or extension, but intensions are opaque. Ideas of conceptual containment are merely metaphorical. Carnap's use of linguistic rules is rejected as ad hoc. Definitions rely on pre-existing linguistic practice and do not explain that practice.

There is much interpretative debate about Quine's exact target and his purpose in this celebrated paper. It seems important to distinguish the semantic question about how to make the analytic/synthetic distinction, from the epistemological question of the a priori/a posteriori distinction, from the metaphysical question of the necessary/contingent distinction. These are often elided, but they are distinct. Quine attacks the semantic distinction between analytic and synthetic, but as a way of challenging the epistemological distinction between a priori and a posteriori. Analyticity seems the only way to explicate the a priori. An a priori proposition is one justified independently of the senses – analyticity explains how this is so using linguistic rules. Hence, by attacking the analytic-synthetic distinction, Quine also attacked the a priori/a posteriori distinction. Indeed the necessary-contingent distinction also fell, since logical necessity rested also on analyticity.

By attacking the sharp analytic/synthetic distinction and replacing it with the idea of a continuum – sentences which are very closely linked to observation and sentences far removed from observation – Quine presented a different conception of philosophy to what had gone before. There are no neutral pure observation sentences; there are no pure theoretical observation-free sentences. By being linguistic, observation sentences are contaminated by theory. By being part of our web of belief, logical, mathematical and general scientific beliefs are connected to observation. We are reluctant to alter logical and mathematical beliefs because of the knock-on effect, but this is in principle possible (for example, dropping some of the classical logical laws in discussing quantum phenomena might make for more elegant theories). Quine has articulated a picture of knowledge which is empiricist, coherentist, pragmatist and most importantly naturalist. There is no first philosophy which either gives a foundation to science or clarifies it from without. Philosophy is part of the ongoing quest for truth, but has no special method which distinguishes it from other parts of that question – it is self-reflective science (including the humanities and social sciences in this characterization of science). He repeats Otto Neurath's image of the human quest for knowledge as akin to sailors on a ship who are forced continuously to use the ship to stay afloat, but who can replace broken bits one at a time. For Quine, everything is revisable, but only against a critical mass of stability.

This kind of naturalism is primarily methodological. The methods by which truth is acquired are those of science broadly construed. There is no pure a priori method which rivals that of science. Quine is a physicalist rather than a materialist. Physicalists accept the ultimate theory of the world to be that delivered by physics – so it is revisable and ongoing. Quine's actual ultimate ontology is something like a neo-Pythagorean picture, in which mathematical sets provide the most tractable account of the world. But if science licenced clairvoyance or immortal souls, then these would be incorporated into the ontology. To look for a grounding for science is to seek what cannot be given, there is no Cartesian bedrock. While there are many debates about the details of Quine's views, this picture has proved enormously influential – pragmatic, fallibilist, fruitful in terms of the interactions of philosophers with psychologists, linguists, neurologists, biologists, and so on. The contemporary explorations of consciousness which are multidisciplinary are the fruit of such a view.

However, not everyone is sanguine about this development. Some worry about the further developments of Quine's work. For example, there is the doctrine of the indeterminacy of translation, which holds that they are no facts of the matter about meaning. There is Quine's famous dismissal of modal notions. His account of the mental is famously austere and behaviourist. Dennett mischievously defines the verb 'to quine' in his dictionary as to deny the existence of something obvious and important (self-consciously ironically, given Dennett's Quinean view of consciousness). I want to discuss two critical reactions to Quine's work. The first, from Laurence BonJour, worries that Quine presents a corrosive scepticism about reason, and the second, from Paul Boghossian, worries that Quine presents an incoherent scepticism about meaning. Both suggest correctives to Quine. My argument is that there are problems with both of their positions, but adjusted and amalgamated they make an attractive response to Quine. However, this amalgam turns out to exist already, and it is the position defended by Aquinas.

5.2.3   Reactions to Quine

BonJour defended a robust conception of the a priori rooted in rational intuition against moderate and extreme empiricists in his *In Defence of*

Pure Reason (1997). Carnap counts as a moderate empiricist and Quine as an extreme one. Moderate empiricists have an attenuated account of the a priori and modal knowledge by their doctrines of analyticity and conventionalism, while extreme ones reject any a priori. BonJour challenges various accounts of analyticity. His fundamental problem is that the notion does not do the epistemological or metaphysical work required of it. Certain versions of it straightforwardly rely on a pre-existing account of logical truth (what he calls reductive accounts). Therefore, these cannot serve as explanations of logical truth. Other versions obfuscate and disguise their question begging, relying on hidden appeals to the a priori or to necessity. He notes that conventionalism cannot explain logical truth (conventions are freely chosen, while logic is not), and wonders about the very status of the moderate empiricist claim – is it analytic and conventional? What then is its dialectical force? He turns then to the Quinean position.

It seems to him that Quine's rejection of analyticity is rooted in epistemology. Quine really wants to jettison the a priori, which he understands as unrevisable truth. But BonJour wonders, why not allow for a fallible conception of the a priori? Consider complicated calculations. Anomalies occur, checking is carried out and the calculation is amended. It is canonically a priori but also corrigible. Given that Quine devotes much effort to attacking unrevisability, BonJour seeks to separate the issue of the a priori (beliefs not justified by experience) from revisability. A different argument is to query the very status of the naturalistic claim. It cannot be based on a priori reasoning, on pain of contradiction, but if it rests solely on assuming that reason consists in adjusting one's beliefs to experience, it assumes its conclusion illegitimately.

In opposing Quine, BonJour defends the Aristotelian notion of *nous*, rational intuition (also defended by Russell). Part of his dialectical strategy is to dismiss alternative accounts. His positive account relies on the phenomenology of cases in which one considers a fundamental logical or conceptual truth, and 'sees' its validity. This is direct, immediate, non-discursive. It can be assimilated to the idea of 'true-in-virtue-of-meaning' – except here the epistemological work is being done by appeal to a faculty of reason rather than the conventionalism of the logical empiricists. BonJour argues that rational intuition of this kind yields insight into the nature of reality – the modal structure of the world. He explicitly acknowledges that this will require some account of intentionality in which concepts reflect the metaphysical structure of the world, and appeals to Aquinas as a model for such an account. I shall return to this below.

Boghossian challenges Quine on different grounds, fearing that Quine's view results in a corrosive form of scepticism about meaning. Opposing Quine, he defends a form of analyticity, articulating this position in his 1999 paper 'Analyticity'. Boghossian distinguishes kinds of analyticity. Frege analyticity is that which assumes pre-existing logical truth (like BonJour's reductive account). Carnap analyticity, on the other hand, grounds logical truth itself. Quine's arguments are effective against Frege analyticity, but not Carnap analyticity. Carnap analyticity is a form of implicit definition, where the meanings of the terms are defined in use. But what of the conventionalism and anti-realism associated with such views? Boghossian denies that implicit definition has to be committed to such views. Against conventionalism is the view that certain inferences are found to be primitively compelling, for example, *modus ponens*. There is not a conventional free-for-all, but our practices are rationally constrained. Against anti-realism is his claim that what grounds these implicit definitions is reference to the logical objects which make such inferences valid. So, for example, the negation sign refers to a certain kind of logical object, which governs the inferences we use. Whatever the details of Boghossian's exegesis of Quine and others, the position he defends is one which appeals to metaphysical objects to ground logical inference and to the reference relation as the link between mind and world. There is genuine a priori knowledge available through reflection on the conditions of meaning. He dismisses rational intuition as mystificatory and 'flash-grasping'.

BonJour and Boghossian have a number of things in common. They think that Quine's position ends up in scepticism (about reason and about meaning, respectively). They believe that genuine substantive a priori knowledge is possible. A priori knowledge is realist, in that it connects up with the deep metaphysical structure of reality. They differ in their accounts of that deep metaphysical nature – BonJour being broadly Aristotelian, and Boghossian being Platonist. They also differ in the mode of access to this reality. BonJour relies on rational intuition. Boghossian relies on basic inferential practices which confer meaning on the syncategorematic terms of our sentences. Boghossian is dismissive of rational intuition, relying on the Wittgensteinian notion of practice and the un-Wittgensteinian notion of logical object. The weak element of BonJour's case is the raw appeal to rational intuition, which seems prelinguistic and mystificatory. The weak element in Boghossian's is the ad hoc nature of his Platonism (and the standard objections to metaphysical Platonism). So, perhaps a response to Quine is possible in which a) rational intuition is drawn closer to language and practice, and b) the account of reference of basic logical terms is not platonized. It seems that Aquinas's account of meaning supplies exactly this.

5.2.4 Aquinas on meaning

In this section I wish to outline the elements of Aquinas's account of meaning, discuss how synonymy and analyticity can be accommodated within it, show how the basic explanatory work about conceptual connection is being done by real natures with their modal properties, and draw comparisons with the views of BonJour and Boghossian.

Aquinas inherits the Aristotelian account of the relationship of language, mind and reality. A significant feature of this account is the linking together of semantics and cognition – the story about meaning is internally connected to the story about knowing, and they cannot be treated independently of each other. It is also a realist account, in that mind and world are closely connected, and problems about piercing the veil of appearance, knowing other minds and scepticism about the external world do not arise. As in Hilary Putnam's brain in the vat challenge to scepticism, the conditions of meaning are intrinsically connected to the way the world is, such that scepticism cannot even be clearly articulated. Thus, a root assumption is that things in the environment of the thinker are capable of being known by her. Aquinas has a detailed account of how this happens, the details of which I shall pass over here. However, a key element in this account is that there is a metaphysical link between the structures which exist in the world and the person who knows them. That is, the forms which exist in the world come to exist in the soul of the person thinking about them. The same form exists in the world and in the thinker. Aquinas needs a psychological account of how this is possible and speaks of the capacities in the soul and the process it undergoes which allows for this kind of cognition. The process by which the soul grasps intelligible content from its environment is *intellectus*, a precondition for the further process of making propositions (compounding or dividing) called *ratiocinatio*.

The relationship between mental content and the forms in objects is natural and universal. This relationship is a basic recognitional capacity which allows us identify and individuate objects in our environment. But the use of names is conventional. Natural languages associate labels with mental content, by the process of imposition. So in any situation in which I recognize, say, a cat, there is a natural psychological process by which I recognize the kind of thing it is and a simultaneous conventional element by which I have been trained to associate a word with that recognition. The temptation here is to think of this as a three-part process. The thing in the world causes a concept, which is then labelled by the word. Classical empiricism had such an account in the theory of ideas, which existed as a representational third realm between mind and world. Such ideas seem to be in a realm of natural private language, which is then translated into communicable public languages. Aquinas is not committed to either a third realm or to private language. He says 'words refer to the things they signify through the mediation of a conception in the intellect' [ST 1.13.1]. The crucial word here is *'ratio'* – conception. This is the intelligible content of the thought held by the thinker. It is the means by which the object in the world is thought by her. There are two terms in cognition – the object cognized and the cognizer. The alteration to the cognizer caused by the apprehension of the object has a kind of character, a way of being thought about. This is the *ratio* – so it is not a third thing itself, but rather is the way by which the cognizer grasps the thing known. The way in which a knower develops in cognition can parallel the grasp of natural language in the way in which developmental psychologists tell us. Knowledge is socially inculcated, involving training in recognizing and naming, with no need to postulate a private language. So knowing the meaning of a term is linked to our capacity to recognize things in the world, does not entail the existence of mysterious mental items as a third realm between entities and minds, and does not require a private language.

A key concept in explicating the notion of meaning for Aquinas is *significatio*. As P.V. Spade says, this notion is a causal psychological term of art.[29] Signification relates to the way in which things in the environment are knowable to the cognizer. Things in the environment exert a causal influence on the knower, which leads to psychological change. Of course, 'causal' here has multiple meanings. There is an element of efficient causation in terms of Quinean impingements on our sensory surfaces. But even that basic level is shot through with through with notions of formal causation, for example the transfer of formal structure from object to medium to sense to intellect. The signification of a term is expressed in the *ratio*. Signification therefore has to do with the realm of form, essence and intelligible content. Clearly this has some similarities with Fregean sense.

A further term is *suppositio*, which is typically translated as 'reference'. Standard accounts in the thirteenth century distinguished various kinds of supposition a term might have. Aquinas does not engage with this detailed kind of distinction making, but does note an important way in which the supposition of subject and predicate terms differ from each other [ST 1.13.12]. A noun in a subject place typically supposits, or stands for, an individual, and so is concrete in its supposition. The predicate is held to operate more like a verb, and so supposits some abstract quality which is applied to the subject. Thus the predicate typically supposits in an abstract way, requiring that there be a subject in which the quality inheres. By distinguishing the different modes of signification of subjects and predicates, Aquinas can avoid the danger of Platonism, the hypostasizing of abstract qualities as concrete individuals – good conceptual therapy in the manner of Carnap or Wittgenstein.

The distinction between *res significata* and *modus significandi* does a lot of work for Aquinas.[30] The *res significata* is typically the extra-mental object. The *modus significandi* is the way in which this is referred to in language. The same *res* may have different *modi significandi*, which includes both the conventional linguistic term and the universal *ratio* associated with it. This distinction allows him to make intelligible, for example, the doctrine of divine simplicity – in which a metaphysically simple reality is referred to using different *modi significandi*, yielding genuine, contentful, non-synonymous information about it. With this sketch of Aquinas's views on the conditions of meaning in place, let us now turn to questions about analyticity, modality and the a priori.

Quine makes a significant statement in 'Two Dogmas of Empiricism', when he asserts that meanings are what essences became when wedded to the word.[31] This is to dismiss meanings, since essences were clearly outré for him. However, after Putnam and Saul Kripke, it is once again respectable to allow real natural kinds with their own metaphysical natures which exert a causal influence on meaning. And meanings, rather than being free-floating conventions constituted by linguistic fiat, are shaped and governed by the deep structures of the things to which they are connected. The conventional element is there in natural languages, but also non-conventional elements in our thinking about them, fixed by the real features of objects.

Aquinas discusses the ways in which subjects and predicates relate to each other in sentences. In some sentences, there is an internal connection between subject and predicate, such that the *ratio* of the subject involves the *ratio* of the predicate. Recall that the *ratio* is the intelligible content of the term and that this is fixed by the real nature referred to. So whether the subject and predicate are linked is fixed by the world. Subjects may necessarily involve the predicate – if they are involved in their definition. Scott MacDonald usefully points out that definitions are not primarily linguistic, but are real structures in reality which get expressed linguistically.[32] Thus *scientia*, or knowledge, is both a propositional attitude of individuals and an objective set of propositions matching the real structure of the world. When a subject includes its predicate, this is a necessary feature determined by the nature of the entity. If it excludes it, this is also a necessary feature. Otherwise, there is a contingent connection between subject and predicate. (This is not simply the distinction between substantial and accidental prediction, since there can be necessary accidents.)

Also, there is a strong distinction drawn between the order of knowledge and the order of being. Whether or not subjects are necessarily connected to predicates is the case whether or not this is known to us. So some propositions may be self-evident in themselves, in that the predicate is objectively included in the subject, but unknown to us. Aquinas believes that God's existence is of this kind. God's existence is necessary, and if we knew God's essence, we would see this, but God's essence is in principle inaccessible to us. Knowledge of some necessary connections is yielded by empirical research into the real features of things – for example, that water is H_2O. Other necessary connections are revealed by reflection and dialectic, and so are gained in an a priori fashion, but always rooted in a connection to real kinds.

Logical and mathematical knowledge is also necessary, but traces the connections between mental conceptions, or second intentions. But even these are rooted in the real metaphysical features of reality. The principle of non-contradiction, which is fundamental to our reasoning, relies on the non-compossibility of contradictories. This rests on the impossibility of being and not-being in the same respect at the same time. This principle cannot be argued for demonstratively on pain of circularity, but can be defended by showing the absurdity of denying it. So necessary connections exist as a real feature of the concrete individuals of distinct kinds in the world. Necessary connections also exist in our thought about them, insofar as our thought faithfully mirrors those real features, and in the structural features of our thought, logic and mathematics. Thus the explanatory bedrock for Aquinas is his account of real kinds in reality which exhibit modal properties of themselves. Thought tracks these structures to the extent it can, and the language we use reflects these structures. Analytic propositions are those whose subjects and predicates are connected by virtue of second intention – logical and mathematical relations. Synthetic propositions are those whose subject and predicate are connected by real kinds. Knowledge of the former is always by reflection. The latter may be by reflection or by empirical inquiry.

Aquinas gives a way of making the analytic-synthetic distinction, explains conceptual containment by reduction to real definitions and gives an account of intentionality based on formal identity. He avoids conventionalism and gives a realist grounding to definition, synonymy and linguistic usage. Like BonJour, he appeals to rational intuition and defends it both through appeal to phenomenology and dialectically. But he also connects the cognitive grasp of logic primitives with their linguistic usage. Thus, the direction of explanation is from intellect to behaviour. Our primitive logical apparatus tracks genuine truth-preserving features exhibited by the formal aspects of thought. He is akin to Boghossian in treating language as important, but connecting it to cognition and avoiding Platonistic metaphysics.

Opposition to this approach comes by claiming it is mystificatory – indeed critics of BonJour's position label it neo-Thomist as a pejorative description. Without the background conceptual scheme of a metaphysics using form and formal causation, the story does not make a lot of sense, and such a conceptual scheme is not very prevalent in contemporary discussions. However, recent work by John O'Callaghan and Jonathan Jacobs serves to make one reconsider the theoretical resources of such a position. O'Callaghan analyses and defends Thomas's semantic triangle and argues for its strength.[33] Jacobs argues that Aquinas's concept-externalism has the resources for a non-sceptical solution to such issues as Quine's thesis of the indeterminacy of translation, Nelson Goodman's grue paradox and Kripke's plus-quus paradox. In each case the puzzle arises as to how to explain normativity about concept use.[34] Such engagements seem fruitful, particularly in light of how philosophers are independently adopting positions akin to Aquinas's.

5.2.5   Conclusion

I began by saying that Aquinas's response to the problem of naturalism is to restate his account of the hierarchy of sciences and the need for metaphysics. What I hope to have shown is that contemporary naturalism grew out of a debate about conceptual relations and a cluster of debates about linguistic rules, the foundations of logic and the relationship of language to the world. Aquinas's views on these issues seem germane to contemporary debates and provide an indirect, but ultimately more compelling, way of defusing the naturalistic objection.

6
God's Nature: The Way of Negation

6.1 Disputes about God's nature

6.1.1 Divine attributes

The task of making sense of God's nature is of interest to both theists and atheists alike. Theists obviously have an interest in trying to establish whatever can be known about God through the resources of human reason. The medieval period was the golden age of this kind of project, drawing on patristic authors such as Augustine, with major figures such as Boethius, Anselm and Aquinas contributing to the discussion.[1] However, atheists also have a stake in this project, albeit a negative one. They want to argue for the incoherence of the supposed set of attributes predicated of God, whether taken individually or collectively. For example, some might want to reject the attribute of eternity itself as unintelligible, or else deny that omnipotence and omnibenevolence are compatible with each other, given that there is evil.

As has been discussed, a standard objection to Aquinas's arguments for God's existence in ST I.2.3 is that even if successful, they do not yield the classical conception of God – but merely a first mover, or designer, or some such less-than-divine entity.[2] Such an objection is unfair since the arguments were not meant to stand alone, but were the first stage in a process which would build up a complex picture of a simple God. Yet whatever about the hermeneutical problem of reading Aquinas in this way, it still might be the case that his account of what the first mover must be like may not stand up even when read charitably. David Hume had famously argued that the design argument is compatible with an infant or a defunct god, or even a committee.[3] So, understanding Aquinas's arguments about the nature of God is an essential part of adjudicating the cogency of objections like those of Hume. Aquinas's elaboration of

God's nature is lengthy and complex, but an essential companion to the existence arguments. John Mackie has argued influentially that God's omnipotence (coupled with omniscience and goodness) is not compatible with the existence of evil and that many attempts to answer this problem merely appear to do so by changing the goalposts, by reinterpreting what is meant by God's power.[4] To adjudicate such powerful objections, a clear sense of Aquinas's overall position is required.

The full list of divine attributes is controversial, however, and varies from theorist to theorist. Traditionally, such a list draws on revelation to get a sense of what people mean when they use the term 'God'. Yet it also draws on philosophical concepts deriving ultimately from Greek metaphysics. These two sources are frequently thought to be in tension with each other. For example, Blaise Pascal had opposed the God of the philosophers to the God of Abraham, Isaac and Jacob.[5] The former relies on Greek metaphysical modes of reasoning, while the latter is the true object of the religious attitude. The former is frequently construed as a deistic postulate, a requirement of some sort of ancient physics, while the latter is the genuine source of spiritual nourishment for generations of religious believers. The God of metaphysics has alleged properties such as immutability, eternality, simplicity, and impassibility, which seem to make it impossible for such a thing to be a person or have any personal characteristics. For example, if God cannot change, exist in time, be acted upon or interact with beings in time, then this bears no relation to the biblical data which refers to God's doing precisely such things. To take one instance, what is the point of praying to a being who will not change, will not be affected by that prayer, does not have emotions and does not react?

This has led many contemporary philosophers of religion to reject this more traditional conception of God – which is often labelled 'classical theism'. While God is construed as having maximal power, maximal knowledge, maximal goodness, God is not construed as being outside time, as unchanging or as impassible, since it is held that these properties cannot cohere with personhood. And such contemporary philosophers therefore eschew both the conceptual scheme of Aquinas and the account of the divine nature he presents.[6] Richard Swinburne, probably the leading contemporary practitioner of philosophical theology, rejects divine eternity (construed as timelessness) and simplicity.[7] Alvin Plantinga, a leading contemporary analytical philosopher of religion, rejects divine simplicity, and various other examples can be adduced.[8] Brian Davies notes that 'If there is anything characteristic of modern American philosophy of religion, it is the view that God is temporal'[9].

Davies supplies a useful list of the kind of contrast between a lot of contemporary theistic philosophers of religion and those supporting classical theism. A fundamental claim in the classical tradition is that God's existence is not distinct from God's nature. This is an extremely difficult doctrine to elucidate, but one way of attempting it is to say that God is pure existence, or, there is nothing to God other than his own existence (this will be discussed in the next section). A multiplicity of objections attend this claim, ranging from Plantinga's observation that this makes God into a property, and a bare property could not be a person[10], to Anthony Kenny's worry that existence is too thin a predicate to ascribe to anything as its nature.[11] The classical theist's insistence on this peculiar doctrine leads to a variety of other claims. As a key one, God is not classifiable as relevantly similar to anything creaturely (although analogical predication allows some comparisons). However, contemporary philosophers are happy to compare God to us in respect of knowledge, power, emotion, activity. God is a person who wrestles with the problem of evil, who may have limits, who may suffer. To distinguish God from creatures is a matter of degree, therefore, not of kind. God is moral in the sense that we are. We are on the same evaluative continuum. By characterizing God in this way, some contemporary theistic philosophers argue that they are closer to the Christian tradition, closer to the biblical conception of God. Bracketing for the moment whether this is true or not, it is clear that they diverge sharply from the classical conception. On that account, God is simple, perfect, unchanging, eternal, not moral in the same sense as a human is, not a person in the same sense, indeed not a being in the same sense as we are. Whether such classical theism is coherent or even intelligible is a disputed point in contemporary discussions.

6.1.2 Aquinas's account of divine attributes

Even though Aquinas can be classified as a classical theist, there are still interpretative debates about the precise nature of his work.[12] A more traditional style of interpreting him is to think of his work as expressing a unified system, from which can be extracted clear metaphysical or epistemological or semantic positions, which might be called the systematic reading. The century from the inception of the Leonine edition of his works (1879) witnessed a proliferation of studies of his work, many of which can be understood as interpreting his work in this way. However, there was also the development of approaches which situated the work in its historical, philosophical and cultural context, examining the developments, changes and nuances across the chronological progression of this text. Let us call this the historical reading. Fergus Kerr has presented a good analysis of the debates between these groups.[13] The more traditional systemic approach resisted what was seen as the historicizing and relativizing of Aquinas's work. The scholars who advocated the historical approach argued that the traditionalists were misinterpreting Aquinas and, unknown to themselves, importing concerns actually foreign to him. This is still a live debate, for example, the discussion of whether analytic readings are a form of procrustean forcing of Aquinas into debates alien to his work.[14]

One particular problem for the systemic reading is the obvious changes he makes in his discussion of the divine attributes. In the *Summa Contra Gentiles*, Aquinas presents the argument from motion (similar to the first way, but more developed and closer to the text of Aristotle's *Physics*) in chapter 13 and begins the discussion of God's attributes in chapter 15 (although strictly speaking, under divine simplicity, there are no distinct attributes in God, see below pp. 161ff). Norman Kretzmann[15] reads chapter 15 as articulating a distinct and powerful argument for God's existence as a first necessary being, having its necessity of itself. With this starting place, Kretzmann points out that Aquinas uses the eliminative method, deploying 80 distinct arguments to exclude some 19 predicates from God. Having established that there is a first necessary being, that fact by itself can lead one to deduce what features such a being must have (or indeed not have). In chapter 15 Aquinas begins with the eternity of such a being and works through various other features to end with perfection in chapter 28. In contrast, treating the same topic in the *Summa Theologiae* qq.3–11, Aquinas starts with simplicity in q.3, followed by perfection in q.4, and only reaches eternity in q.10. Why do the texts differ in this way? What is the respective logic of development in each one, and what is the significance of the difference?

A major methodological distinction between SCG and ST is that the former follows a philosophical methodology on this topic, while the latter is theological. However, it does not seem as if there is some essential difference in logic or derivation between the earlier and later treatment. It is not as if philosophy essentially requires one to start with eternity, while theology requires simplicity. Rather, the difference seems one of structure, organization and mode of presentation of the text. Note that the style of the ST, divided into articles and questions, differs from that of the chapter sequence in SCG, representing a pedagogical development.[16]

To deal more fully with the difference between SCG and ST on the divine attributes, it is necessary first to be clear on Aquinas's underlying strategy, which is his adoption of the Dionysian *triplex via*. Aquinas deploys causal arguments in ST q.2 to affirm the existence of something which is the source and origin of motion, causation, necessity, and so forth. Having performed that task, he then goes on to characterize what this reality must be like. His method is negative. We cannot say what God is, but can characterize what God is not, that is, specify what is inappropriate to attribute to him. But this negative approach must itself be tempered, by attributing perfections to God. This threefold dialectic of causation, negation and eminence (called the *triplex via*) is borrowed from Denys the Areopagite and governs Aquinas's discussion of God's nature.

Fran O'Rourke, in his illuminating study of Aquinas's use of Denys the Areopagite, points out that the latter uses a basic distinction of kataphatic (positive) and apophatic (negative) modes of talking about God.[17] Underlying both of these is an assumption of God as the cause of all things. Thus, Aquinas refers to the *triplex via* of causation, negation and eminence, discussing this in, for example, DDN 7.3, InBDT 6.2, ST I.12.12 and ST I.13.8. However, the order of this triple way is not always fixed. For example, in ST 1.13.8, eminence comes first. And furthermore, the process could be construed as fundamentally one of causation and negation, since both eminence and negation can be subsumed under a higher form of negation, namely, denying any purely creaturely predications of God. Eminence holds that God is greater than the creaturely version of the attribute (e.g. goodness), while negation denies any applicability of a creaturely predication to God (e.g. matter). The point of all this is that Aquinas does not have a simple formula which he applies in an algorithmic fashion, but varies his manner of presentation depending on context and the specific argumentative context. As Brian Shanley remarks, Aquinas is not wedded to a single schema in his discussion of the divine nature.[18]

Given we have seen that the SCG employs a philosophical mode of exposition, while the ST a theological one, how might this alter the ordering of the divine attributes? Aquinas frequently contrasts the mode of being with the mode of knowing.[19] Presenting and elaborating how we come to know something requires a different approach to the actual intrinsic structure of the thing itself. For example, if I give an overview of the streetscape of Dublin, this is a different task to giving you directions of how to go from A to B in the city. In the latter case, starting with where you are and what you know, I give you directions to get to where you need to go. In the former I can abstract from your actual situation. This distinction is all the more pressing when dealing with aspects of reality which do not readily lend themselves to our intellects. Our mode of knowledge starts with the senses and deals in structures which have distinct parts. When dealing with realities not grasped by the senses and not consisting of parts, the articulation of the overview is quite different to the articulation of the finding out.

The discussion of eternity in SCG 1.15 arises quite naturally from the causal arguments deployed there. A necessary being whose necessity derives from itself is one which will not be in time, and so the order of the attributes arises logically from the previous step. 'God therefore is eternal, since whatever is necessary through itself is eternal'. Such an eternal reality does not begin or end, and hence is immutable. So the argument for an independent reality, one exhibiting the characteristic of aseity (absolute independence), leads also to predicating immutability and timelessness of this reality – all discussed in chapter 15. There is no connection to matter of such a reality (17), and neither does it have any passive potency (16). It is not composite (18) or subject to external influence (19). It is not anything corporeal (20). A discussion of the lack of composition into essence and existence ensues in 21–22, while a range of more or less technical Aristotelian issues are covered in 23–27 – it has no accidents, is not specified by difference, not in a genus, not definable and not a universal formal cause. Finally, imperfection is denied of it in chapter 28.

The order of the attributes in the *Summa Theologiae* is different. Q. 3 deals with simplicity, but under this heading denies corporeality of God (a.1), form and matter (a.2), essence (a.3), the essence and existence distinction (a.4), genus and difference (a.5), substance and accident (a.6), internal composition (a.7) and external composition (a.8). The arguments for God's existence are more variegated in ST 1.2.3 than in SCG 13 and 15. There is less of an emphasis on the argument from motion, and so there seems less of a need to derive rigorously the divine attributes from this, as is the case in SCG. The view that God has no potential is highlighted in q.3 a.1, and this seems to dominate Aquinas's thinking in detailing the divine attributes in the *Summa Theologiae*. The denial of distinction between essence and existence is also emphasized early on there, appearing at q.3a4. This raises the interesting developmental question whether Aquinas's views had matured on the nature of the distinction between essence and existence. Even though it appears early on in *De Ente et Essentia* (written in 1256), there Aquinas is still influenced significantly by Avicenna, and it is possible that he did not realize the deeper significance of this distinction in developing a metaphysical account of participation in being (which I shall examine in the next section).

Given the multiplicity of attributes discussed by Aquinas, I shall be selective in dealing with them. An analysis of the structure of the *Summa Theologiae* shows that the attributes discussed in qq.3–11 deal with God's being (q.12 and q.13 deal with our representations of God), while qq.14–26 deal with operations of which God is capable. So a natural textual approach is to carve them up that way. However, some of the attributes can be construed negatively, some positively. After God's simplicity (negative) comes perfection (positive) and then goodness (positive). Eternity comes later (negative), while knowledge and will are later again (positive). In line with the underlying Dionysian dialectic of treating negation first, then eminence, I shall begin with the fundamental attribute of Simplicity. This establishes how one must think about the kind of existence God has (or better, *is*) and also governs how the other attributes must be understood, so I shall treat this in Section 6.2.

In Section 6.3, I shall examine God's relationship to time, which will also require a discussion of immutability. In the next chapter, I shall begin with Goodness, and move then to Knowledge and Will. The inter-relationship between these attributes will be clearer there – for example, showing that God's knowledge of future contingent events does not entail determinism requires some support from God's eternity. One final, but very important, note must now be made of Aquinas's views on language and God. How is reference to God possible in his system?

6.1.3   Linguistic issues

Talk about God differs in important ways from talk about ordinary things in our experience. Aquinas is acutely conscious of this and develops an account of God-talk which seeks to find a middle way between crude anthropomorphism, on the one hand, and simple agnosticism, on the other hand. He does this by developing an analogical account of language which cuts between univocal and equivocal accounts, as I shall explain below. So before examining his views, it is useful to query what are the issues with God-talk? Frequently, we hear claims such as 'God is good'. What does this mean? It seems we are attributing a property to God, in a manner similar to the way we might say 'this steak is good' or 'my daughter is good'. Yet when we speak of moral goodness, we mean things like having morally desirable tendencies, having good character, overcoming difficulties, fortitude in adversity and so on. Yet these do not apply to God, at least on Aquinas's account, for being non-spatiotemporal, immutable and simple, God has no attributes at all, let alone those which involve growth, development or overcoming difficulties. Neither is God succulent, tasty and goes well with Bordeaux, as with the steak. So it seems that whatever God's goodness is, it is different to the kinds of feature which constitute goodness in people or things in our experience. But if it is completely different, we have no grasp of what God's goodness means. It is something hopelessly other, and agnosticism ensues. The issue is made all the more pressing by the challenge advanced by logical positivists. Rather than denying the truth of religious utterances, logical positivists tended to deny that it was the kind of thing which was truth-apt – it did not even make enough sense to be rejected as false. So an account of religious utterance is required which is robust enough to bear truth, but sensitive enough to cope with the differences between our ordinary talk and talk about God.

Much talk about God is metaphorical. 'God is a rock, a mighty fortress'. What makes it a metaphor is that it is literally false – God is not a kind of geological feature, nor has God any castellations. A metaphor takes something which is true in one realm and applies it to something else where it is literally false, but carries some useful or informative associations which illuminate what is being discussed. So while God is not made of granite, rocky features such as strength and immutability do apply to God. One of the benefits of metaphors is that we tend not to be misled by them. We know that God is not geological, and are not tempted to think so when we hear 'God is a rock'. When we move to try to say things which purport to be literally true (such as 'God is good'), it is much harder to make sense of what is being said, and there is real danger of applying terrestrial terms and criteria directly to God.

Aquinas makes a number of basic distinctions in his approach to explaining how we can talk about God [ST 1.13.5, SCG 1.32–34]. A word is univocal when it means the same in each instance of its use. Words used of humans and of God are therefore not univocal, as the examples above suggest. Aquinas's reason for this is that in creatures, words pick out a quality in things distinct from their being (for example, the wisdom of Socrates), while in God such words pick out God's being itself (there is no distinction between God's wisdom and God's being). This issue will be discussed below in connection with divine simplicity. Equivocal words have different meanings, but are lexically similar – a stock example being 'bat' as applied to Dracula and to baseball. If goodness as used of humans and God were equivocal in this way, we would have no idea of what God's goodness might mean, and agnosticism would follow. Aquinas therefore defends the use of analogical language about God – which allows for similarity and difference. Analogy is an enormous topic in Aquinas scholarship, quite disproportionate to what and how much he actually says about it.[20] One train of thought makes the analogy of being fundamental to his metaphysics, an elaborate synthesis of Aristotle and Neoplatonism, which deploys participation in existence in a hierarchical structure of all existing things. While much of this picture is indeed there in Aquinas, what is questionable is linking this to the rather sparse comments he makes on the use of analogical language. A further complication is the account of analogy given by the major sixteenth-century Thomistic commentator Cajetan, taken as canonical for centuries, but now generally regarded as mistaken and distorting of Aquinas's actual views.[21] So in the remainder of this section, I shall look at some of the textual basis of his views on analogy and see how to present his views so as to make sense of the divine nature.

The central place for Aquinas's views on analogy is his discussion of the use of language in relation to God in ST 1.13. There is also a discussion in SCG 1.31–34, QDP 7.7 and SS 1.35.1.4. In this last text, a metaphysical argument is given as to why univocity cannot occur between God and creatures. There he says that the sort of commonality which links univocal things is to be found in their natures, not in their individual existences (Aquinas here deploys his metaphysical distinction between essence and existence in any existing entity). Common features belong in the essence. However, God's nature is self-subsistent existence; therefore, there is no distinction in God between essence and existence. Thus, there is no possibility of commonality between God's nature and any other nature. Hence, nothing applies univocally to God and creatures. A different argument is used in ST 1.13.5, in which he argues that cause and effect cannot have the same property univocally if the cause is superior to the effect. If a cause is simple and perfect, but the effects are multiple and divided, properties do not exist in the same way in the cause and effect. Hence, God as a single, simple cause has whatever properties he has in a way different to the way his effects have them.

A useful distinction in making sense of this view is that of the mode of signification (*modus significandi*) and the reality signified (*res significata*), for example in ST1.13.3 and SCG 1.30. Modes of signification pertain to human knowledge. They are multiple and interrelated, and our web of knowledge comprises a network of such conceptual representations. Yet what is signified is distinct from them, and what exhibits being in a different way to the modes of creaturely existence can nevertheless be referred to by such creaturely representations. We know the meaning of 'goodness' or 'wisdom' from its paradigm instances in the world. Yet when we refer to God's goodness or God's wisdom, this refers to the cause, source and ultimate paradigm of such qualities, which exist in

God in an eternal, undifferentiated, primal unity. The target of such talk is therefore not fully captured in the linguistic conceptualization. Nevertheless, such language does manage to articulate truths, albeit imperfectly and with limitations.

To affirm that we are capable of such talk, Aquinas appeals to both philosophy and scripture. He holds at ST 1.13.5 that Aristotle proves many things about God (a hard text to explain away by those who think Aquinas has no connection to philosophy) and also cites Romans 1.20 'The invisible things of God are clearly seen being understood by the things that are made'.

Aquinas distinguishes two kinds of analogical predication (ST 1.13.5). In one way there are many things proportioned to one (*multa habent proportionem ad unum*). There is a primary thing which is the focus of the predication, and other things are said to have it by virtue of some relation to the primary thing. For example, health applies primarily to an organism, but secondarily to urine as a sign, or medicine as a cause of health in the organism. This is problematical for thinking about the relationship of God to creatures. If what is in some analogical sense common to God and human beings is understood by virtue of its relationship to some further ulterior reality, then God is subservient in some sense to that reality. So it cannot be understood in that way. The other mode of analogy is where one thing had a proportion to another (*unum habet proportionem ad alterum*), and Aquinas affirms that this is the way in which an analogy occurs between creatures and God. There is some kind of relationship between the two terms. One aspect of this relationship is causal. When we say that God is good and humans are good, it is because God causes goodness in humans. But this is not sufficient, since God also causes things (such as mud and squirrels) which we would not want to predicate analogically of God (I.13.2). Thus, as well as causing analogical properties, the properties also pre-exist in God in a different way. As God's mode of being is different and superior to that of creation, so God's goodness is also different and superior to creaturely goodness. In fact, we do not understand or grasp it, but only imperfectly approach it through our knowledge of human goodness.

In the process of discussing issues about language, Aquinas articulates a subtle doctrine of relations which serves to clarify some of the paradoxes which arise about predicating properties of God (1.13.7). For example, if God only becomes creator after the world is created, how does this square with his alleged eternity and immutability? Aquinas distinguishes three sorts of relation. In the first, the relation is purely intellectual, a product of reason. Examples of this include self-identity (where something relates to itself), or where it relates to nothing, or when it is classified into genus and species, which are construed not as real things, but as mental constructs. In the second kind of relation, there is real extra-mental relation on both sides. Examples of this include quantity and causation. However, a third form of relation involves reality on one side, but is merely intellectual on the other side. Aquinas's examples are intentional relations, between sensation and the object sensed, or knowledge and the object known. There is no change in the object known, but there is a change in the knower. These latter kinds of relation occasion what have been called merely Cambridge changes. As I move about my desk, a real change occurs in me, but a merely Cambridge change occurs in the desk, in terms of its relationship to me. This third kind of relation holds between God and the world. In causing the world, a real effect occurs in the world, but a merely Cambridge change occurs in God. God's creation of the world is a free, eternal, unchanging feature of God, but is constitutive of the being of the world. As we shall see, this approach will be used by Aquinas to dissolve supposed problems about simplicity, eternity, knowledge and freedom.

6.2 Divine simplicity

6.2.1 Introduction

Aquinas discusses simplicity immediately after demonstrating God's existence (ST 1.3). It has a key role in the elaboration of the rest of the divine attributes, insofar as it governs the way these attributes exist in God, and how they must be thought about by us. It is also one of the most controversial elements of Aquinas's account, and is widely rejected by contemporary philosophers of religion.[22] In this section, I wish to discuss the sources of Aquinas's views, the exact nature of the doctrine of Divine Simplicity and then treat three significant objections to it: firstly, that the account of existence involved in Divine Simplicity is implausible, secondly, that Divine Simplicity is incompatible with God's having personal characteristics, and thirdly, that it makes God into an abstract entity.

Divine Simplicity has religious and philosophical roots. The three major Abrahamic religions affirm that God is one, is the cause of all else and is not under the power of anything else. While this does not automatically convert into claims about Divine Simplicity, a tradition of philosophical reflection came to view simplicity as the best way of capturing and expressing these religious beliefs. Plotinus (205–270) had synthesized the thought of Plato and Aristotle and developed an account of reality which is hierarchical, with the One at the apex of reality. Plotinus's account was in competition with religious views – it was a pure philosophical account of reality which dispensed with the need of prayer or ritual, but which required both moral and intellectual purification to see the world aright. As Plotinus characterized the One, it was beyond the limitations of anything below it in the scale of being. This meant that it was beyond being and utterly simple. Any distinction within it would be a form of imperfection. It was not amenable to conceptual thought (which operates using distinctions), although rigorous conceptual thought was the only way to approach it.[23] Augustine used the thought of the Platonists in order to conceptualize the God of Christianity, having vanquished scepticism and converted to Christianity. His famous exegesis of Ex 3.14 established a link between the God of Abraham, Isaac and Jacob and the treatment of being in Greek metaphysics. Drawing on Neoplatonic metaphysics, Augustine was to claim that whatever a simple being has, it just is. That is, there are no distinctions of property or subject in such a being. Hence, God's wisdom, goodness, power and so forth are not distinct attributes within God, but are God's being itself.[24] Anselm reiterated this claim in his *Monologion*. In God, it is the same thing to be as to be x.[25] Thus, by the time Aquinas discusses God's nature, there is a well-entrenched religious and philosophical tradition which asserts the simplicity of God. Yet, as Aquinas spells out what this means in ST, he does so within the conceptual framework he inherits from Aristotle.

Aquinas denies that God is a body (3.1). Furthermore, in God there is no composition of matter and form (3.2). There is no distinction between nature or kind and subject. That is, God is not an individual of a kind; rather, he is outside the schema of types and tokens as an utterly unique reality (3.3). The fundamental feature of Divine Simplicity is that there is no distinction between God's existence and essence. Everything else receives its existence from without, is caused by something else. God, as uncaused, has his existence in a way unlike anything else. That is, he does not *have* existence, but is his own existence (3.4). God does not belong in the schema of genus and difference (3.5) or of subject and accident (3.6). Summing up in 3.7, Aquinas says there is no composition of any kind in God, and in 3.8 he says that God does not enter into composition with anything else.

This means that God's existence is a metaphysical singularity, utterly unlike the existence of anything else. God does not fit into the Aristotelian scheme of being, with the range of distinctions including matter and form, potentiality and actuality, essence and existence. God's existence is analogously linked to the existence of other things as their cause, but God's existence exceeds the existence of all else in reality and in thought. How this might be so is highly controversial. But before engaging directly with the metaphysics of existence, it is important to draw out some of the implications of Divine Simplicity.

God has no spatial parts – which is a fairly uncontroversial idea. However, he also has no temporal parts; he does not exist in time (which will be discussed in the next section on eternity). But here, note that eternity is an entailment of simplicity, via immutability. God has no accidental properties; hence, nothing changes in God. All God's properties are essential, which means that if anyone denies one of the classical theistic properties, he/she is seriously mistaken about God. But furthermore, there are not really distinct essential properties in God. If there were, there would be distinction. So God's goodness is the same thing as God's knowledge. All of this is rooted in the key claim that God's essence is not different to God's existence. And while this claim can be made propositionally and affirmed as being true, the reality it refers to is not thinkable. We are not in a position to realize that 'God exists' is an analytical proposition – even though it is.

It is worth noting the Platonic strain in Aquinas's thought at this juncture. Kenny has remarked that while he is an Aristotelian about earth, Aquinas is a Platonist about heaven.[26] An older school of Aquinas scholarship tended to emphasize the Aristotelian aspects of his thought, especially his endorsement of Aristotle's criticisms of Plato's forms. He summarizes standard objections to separated universals, both in the Aristotelian commentaries and in the *Summa Theologiae*,[27] and diagnoses the basic problem as that of hypostasizing features of the mode of being of universals in the mind onto alleged abstract entities. And as Aristotle is dismissive of the mystificatory nature of talk about participation, Aquinas scholars shied clear of this too. Hence, in such a classic work of scholarship as Étienne Gilson's *The Christian Philosophy of Thomas Aquinas*, there is no index entry on participation.[28] In the mid-twentieth century, two important works, by Cornelio Fabro and Louis Bertrand Geiger, corrected this tendency by noting the importance of Platonic themes, especially participation, in Aquinas's work, and since then a number of works have further explored this Platonic strain in his work.[29]

It is clear that Aquinas has a nuanced approach to Platonic themes, and so it is useful to examine what he accepts and rejects from Plato's work (bearing in mind that his view of Plato is mediated mainly by Aristotle and Proclus). In his *Commentary on Aristotle's Metaphysics*,

Aquinas goes through the various arguments against separated universals, or the forms. He summarizes the crucial points, saying of Aristotle:

> He argues first that they are useless in explaining motion; second that they are useless in explaining our knowledge of sensible things; third that they are of no value as exemplars; fourth that they have no value as the substances of things; and fifth that they are of no value as causes of generation. [In Met 1.15.226]

In his discussion of Divine Goodness in ST 1.6.4, Aquinas rejects the idea of the species of natural things subsisting separately in themselves. In different places he gives a general diagnosis of the basic flaw in Platonic reasoning. Plato takes features which concepts have – generality and universality – and holds that entities with these characteristics actually exist in reality, whereas these are actually features pertaining to the mode of being in the mind. [In Met 1.10.158] Thus Aquinas's basic objection to Plato on the postulation of Forms, construed as One-over-Many abstract entities, is that this illicitly hypostasizes in reality what really exists only in the mind. But there are other aspects of Plato's thought which Aquinas endorses. In the passage on Divine Goodness cited above, where he rejects separated forms, he says Plato is correct in establishing that there is something which is first in goodness and first in being. He also accepts a resolutely hierarchical conception of reality, for example:

> The established order of things is for higher beings to be more perfect than lower, and for whatever is contained deficiently, partially, and in a manifold manner in the lower beings, to be contained in the higher eminently, and in a certain degree of fullness and simplicity. [ST 1.57.2]

Aristotle had cast doubt on the usefulness of the notion of participation, rejecting it as a mere change of name from the notion of 'imitation' used by the Pythagoreans and noting that both the Pythagoreans and Plato left unclear what it meant by 'participation' [*Metaphysics* 987b14]. Aquinas, however, does not reject participation at all, but gives a detailed account of the different ways in which participation might occur and crucially, for current purposes, connects it to the exploration of the meaning of existence, especially the kind of existence which is distinctive of God. As Gregory Rocca notes,

[Aquinas's] thought fuses the Platonic/Neoplatonic and Aristotelian streams that had remained independent for centuries, combines and changes what it extracts from these sources, disengaging participation from its matrices in the Platonic Forms and Neoplatonic One, and radicating [*sic*] act and potency – beyond every imagining of Aristotle – in being as the act of essence.[30]

To understand what Aquinas has to say about existence – distinguishing the act of existing from essence, characterizing God as self-subsistent being, arguing for the ontological dependence of every other being on God – it is important to get clear on what he means by participation and in what way it is altered from its Platonist origins. A useful place to start is with Aquinas's *Commentary on Boethius's De Hebdomadibus*.

Boethius had written a theological tractate, *De Hebdomadibus*, in which he discussed dialectical problems arising from the general ideas of goodness and being. Aquinas commented on this, probably in the late 1250s. In this work Boethius drew a distinction between the act of being (*esse*) and that which exists (*id quod est*). What exactly Boethius's distinction was and how it relates to Aquinas's metaphysics is a tangled scholarly question,[31] but what is relevant here is that in explicating Boethius, Aquinas distinguished between three different kinds of participation. The fundamental idea in participation 'is as it were to take a part, and therefore when something receives in a particular way what pertains to another, it is generally said to participate in it' [In Heb 2].

An example of the first version of this is when humanity participates in animal, or when Socrates participates in humanity. Thus species participate in their genus, or individuals participate in their species. The elements involved in this kind of participation are second intentions, or purely conceptual. Aquinas does not think of species and genera as real things, but as conceptual classifications of real individuals. So this first kind of participation is purely conceptual, the narrower concept taking part in the broader.

The second kind of participation follows the pattern of something narrower being received in something broader, but this time the elements involved are real. Aquinas's examples are matter being received in form, or subject in accident. Matter relates to form as a specific bundle of matter's being informed in a particular way. The matter is said to participate in the form (the form being more extensive than the matter). Likewise, when a subject takes on an accidental alteration, the subject participates in the accident. For example, when we say Socrates is white, the whiteness that is instantiated in Socrates is not the same as the totality of whiteness. This does not require one to postulate an abstract whiteness is general, but just to recognize that there is more to whiteness than what is instantiated in this specific instance. In this way one can make sense of the notion of a part participating in a whole without needing abstract Forms.

A third kind of participation is where an effect is said to participate in its cause, especially when it is not equal to the power of the cause. This seems to require the notion of exemplar cause, which is not contained in the Aristotelian four causes. An exemplar cause is a formal cause, but considered by an agent as a model or plan for making something. The basic notion is of an architect using a model to make a building. Such exemplars exist in the mind of God, both as models for what is created and also as speculative ideas of even possible beings which are never instantiated in space and time.

> As an exemplar therefore, it has respect to everything made by God in any period of time; but as a knowing principle it has respect to all things known by God, even though they never came to be in time, and to all things that he knows according to their proper type, in so far as they are known by him in a speculative manner. [ST 1.15.3]

God is the cause of existence of all things, and things participate in God's existence on this third model of participation, but how exactly does this work? Does it lead to pantheism, where everything shares the same existence, or does it commit one to the paradoxical notion of things receiving their existence from without, but somehow or other having a shadowy possible being to which existence is added?

6.2.2 Simplicity and existence

Traditional Thomists have regarded Aquinas's account of being as the pinnacle of his metaphysical achievement, and encapsulated in the doctrine of the real distinction between essence and existence in all created things and its identity in God. Philosophers schooled in analytical philosophy have regarded this doctrine as deeply flawed. Kenny says in his monograph devoted to Aquinas on being that 'it will be the aim of this book to show that on this crucial topic this first-rank philosopher was thoroughly confused'.[32] Kenny's close and painstaking reading of Aquinas's work, sifting through the main texts chronologically and distinguishing twelve different senses of being, results in three general criticisms. Firstly, Aquinas confuses being and existence. 'There is at no stage of Aquinas's career a clear awareness of the profound syntactic difference between the "there is" of specific existence and the other types of "is" he discusses'.[33] Secondly, there is an illicit celestial Platonism of a kind which Aquinas rightly rejects at a sublunar level. Thirdly, Aquinas's identification of God with subsistent being contains an ambiguity between common being and absolute being, neither of which options works as a way of explicating God's being.

To understand and evaluate Kenny's claims, it is useful to examine briefly the approach of Peter Geach, who has used insights from Gottlob Frege to elucidate Aquinas's work (which Kenny notes he encountered in 1955 and which 'has influenced my thinking ever since, and provides the background to much of the work in the present book').[34] Geach held that getting clear about reference, the different ways in which subjects and predicates have meaning, and distinguishing concrete and abstract reference have benefit in clarifying ontological claims. Geach argued that Aquinas changed his mind about essence and existence from his earlier to later works. In this early work, Aquinas contrasted one notion of existence with essence, whereas in his later work he expressly rejected this and contrasted essence with a different notion of existence. In *De Ente et Essentia*, Aquinas distinguished two senses of existence, which Geach has called the 'there is' sense and the 'actuality' sense. The 'there is', or 'propositional', sense is whatever can be expressed in an affirmative proposition, and includes things which are not actual, such as privations (e.g. there is evil in the world), whereas the 'actual' sense is about things which really exist. The kind of existence involved in the first kind is that expressed by the copula of propositions, and is constructed by the soul when it unites a subject and a predicate [ST 1.3.4ad2]. This kind of existence is ultimately dependent on the second kind, insofar as language supervenes on reality. Commenting on Aristotle, Aquinas says,

> [Propositional existence] is related to [Actual existence] as an effect is to a cause. For from the fact that something is in reality it follows that there is truth and falsity in a proposition and the intellect signifies this by this word 'is' being taken as a verb copula. [In Met 5.9.896]

Geach held that Aquinas initially contrasted the propositional sense of existence with essence, but later rejected this and contrasted the actuality sense. Whatever the evolution of his thought, what arguments does Aquinas use to support the distinction of the actuality sense of existence from essence? There is significant scholarly disagreement on the nature of these arguments.[35] A fundamental issue is whether Aquinas uses such arguments to get to God's existence or whether the essence/existence distinction is logically dependent on the prior establishment of God's existence. In earlier work, it seems as if the arguments are independent of God, whereas in later works they seem to presuppose God's existence. A crucial text in this respect is *De Ente et Essentia* ch. 4. Aquinas there seems to argue for a distinction between existence and essence in all creatures based on logical and metaphysical considerations. However, part of the puzzle of his argumentation is that he intrinsically involves God in it, as the sole case in which essence and existence are identical. His basic claim is fairly clear. When we understand the essence of a being, whether that being actually exists is not knowable by mere grasp of the essence. This is so for a human like Socrates but also for more exotic creatures such as phoenixes. Therefore, existence is not part of the essence of anything, and so existence comes to things from without (sometimes called the 'phoenix' argument). This basic point is made more complex by the observation that in all created things this distinction holds, but there is also the exceptional case of God, in which essence and existence are identical. Aquinas has set up three exhaustive and mutually exclusive options: existence is part of the essence of things (which he rejects on the basis of the 'phoenix' argument), existence is distinct from the essence of things (which he thinks true of creatures) and existence is identical with the essence of one reality (which he thinks true of God).

Is this distinction between essence and existence merely a conceptual distinction or something metaphysically weightier? The argument about whether existence is distinguishable from essence by virtue of exploration of the meaning of essence (the 'phoenix' argument) might seem to push in the direction of a conceptual distinction. A number of scholars have argued that Aquinas is influenced by Avicenna more in his earlier work than in his later work and gives more weight in the earlier to the idea of an essence absolutely considered – that is, abstracting from whether it exists in the world or in the mind.[36] In the later work, the metaphysical status of the essence (whether in reality or in the mind) is more emphasized, thereby avoiding the possibility of a Fregean 'third realm' of pure essences. This fits well with Geach's claim that Aquinas's earlier distinction of essence and existence is more conceptual, whereas it matures into a distinctive metaphysical claim. It might also be noted that the essence/existence distinction plays no explicit role in the official arguments for God's existence in ST and SCG, but rather is deployed in discussing God's nature. So it poses no conceptual problem to think of the distinction as logically presupposing God's existence – since that existence was established using other conceptual resources (the argument from motion, etc.). Given that Aquinas does make such a distinction and that it is interpreted as being metaphysically significant, what then of the three criticisms Kenny levels against Aquinas on existence?

The first is that Aquinas confuses the existence of kinds with the existence of individuals; there is a difference between saying that humans exist and that Socrates exists, which is muddied by Aquinas. The former is about the instantiation of a predicate, while the latter is not. Furthermore, a venerable tradition in contemporary philosophy seeks to assimilate the second kind to the first, with Bertrand Russell and W.V. Quine eliminating apparently referential proper names to definite descriptions or other referring expressions. They claim that surface grammar misleads one about the deeper logical structure. This is relevant here because Kenny thinks Aquinas is unclear whether the word 'God' operates as a predicate (a 'kind' word) or as a proper name picking out an individual. The mainstream tradition thinks that existence only operates as a marker for the instantiation of predicates, as Frege famously put it to deny the number zero of a predicate.[37] However, against this tradition, both Geach and Kenny think it intelligible and informative to posit existence of individuals. The lighthouse of Alexandria is not while the pyramids still are, and attempts to explain away the surface grammar of such sentences are strained and implausible. In this they are closer to Aquinas's position than Russell's. Yet Kenny thinks that Aquinas does not clarify this distinction of kind/individual in relation to God. If one thinks of God as a kind and deploys the essence/existence distinction, then there is the Avicennian problem that the kind has some sort of shadowy existence prior to receiving existence. On the other hand, if one thinks of God as an individual, to say that God's essence is to exist is to say something like Ex x (there is an x, such that x is...), which is not an intelligible statement. It is not a statement at all, being ill-formed and incomplete.

So does Aquinas confuse kinds and individuals in this way, and do the problems Kenny indicates arise for Aquinas? In general, Aquinas does not confuse individual existence and type existence. He is quite clear that types have a second-order existence (*esse intentionale*) which is dependent on the actual existence of tokens of that type. His rejection of Platonism is rooted in this distinction. Aquinas's mature work gives a central place to the existence of individuals. God is an individual (albeit of a unique kind). So I do not think this challenge can be seriously sustained. However, the two cited problems about essence/existence composition whether construed as type or individual remain. For types in general, the priority of existence to essence is not temporal. Creation involves the instantaneous existence of essence and existence. There is no spooky temporal priority of essence to existence. But given this, there can be other kinds of priority. Existence is prior in terms of actuality to essence as potentiality. Nevertheless, this is not relevant to discussing God's mode of existence, as God's existence is that of an individual. So how can the essence/existence discussion be sustained for God as an individual? Kenny argued that it results in nonsense. Existence is not the correct kind of feature to place in a predicate position (for some x, x is F, or ExFx). Aquinas would agree that this is so for every creature, but in the unique case of God, self-subsistent existence is a correct characterization.

I think this can be clarified by looking now at Kenny's third objection. The kind of existence attributed to God is either that which is common to all things, common existence (*esse commune*), in which case it is the thinnest possible descriptor and hence empty, or alternatively it is absolute existence, and the problem with this is that it also seems empty. The crux of the difference between Kenny and Aquinas lies in this. Aquinas clearly holds that *esse* not only is not empty but is that which is most profound (see above p. 53 for Aquinas's use of the term '*esse*'). If Kenny has a deflationist approach, Aquinas could be construed as having an inflationist approach. He makes such a contrast in *De Potentia*, rejecting the deflationist view and endorsing the inflationist one:

> Being [*esse*] as we understand it here, signifies the highest perfection of all...wherefore it is clear that being as we understand it here is the actuality of all acts and the perfection of all perfections. [QDP 7.2.ad9]

God, construed as pure actuality, is the cause of existence of everything else, but crucially also is the paradigm instance and fullness of existence. So exegetically there seems no confusion on this matter. However, it might be that this idea is simply incoherent. How can something have more or less existence; it just *is*? On this view, existence is something bipolar (on or off, as it were), while Aquinas thinks of it as scalar, that there are degrees of it. For Aquinas, the existence of something is always keyed to its essence. The essence 'contracts' the existence, gives it its shape 'because any created form thus subsisting has existence and is not identical with its existence, it is necessary that its own existence be received and restricted to a determinate nature' [1.7.2c]. The hierarchy of things which exist instantiates a hierarchy of essences with greater and lesser forms of existence. As co-principles of being, essence and existence are intimately related as potentiality to actuality, and God's existence is unlimited by virtue of the lack of distinction between essence and existence. Now whatever objections may be marshalled against this view, simply claiming that Aquinas is confused and that existence is not scalar is not very convincing. To reject the whole framework of potency and act would of course work – but this is not a strategy which Kenny himself deploys since he seems to think they have enduring value as concepts.

The notion that God exists most perfectly and that all creaturely existents are lesser instantiations is of a piece with Aquinas's fourth argument for God's existence. There he argued that God is the cause of existence, goodness and every other perfection in each thing. Such an argument clearly has a Platonic provenance and as such is rejected by Kenny. Yet what exactly is the problem with such a position? It does not commit one to abstract timeless entities such as Plato's forms. It is committed to the claim that God, who has no internal distinctions, contains in his perfection the source of all other things. The simple perfect existence which is God's essence contains within itself, in an undivided way, the ideas (prototypes) of all other things. In other things these exist as multiple effects of a single cause, but in God they are unified. 'All forms that are manifold in his effects are in his power as one thing, so that their multiplicity argues no composition in him' [QDP 7.1.ad8]. To reject this position again requires a stronger argument than merely labelling it 'Platonism'. So Kenny's three core criticisms can be countered. Yet there are other powerful objections to Divine Simplicity.

6.2.3 The incoherence challenge

Plantinga produced an influential attack on Aquinas's account of Divine Simplicity in his *Does God Have A Nature?* (1980). Plantinga's answer to this question is yes, but that God is not identical with this nature. He reads Aquinas as arguing that God is identical with his nature, which is the core claim of simplicity. The motivation for such a claim is to defend Divine Sovereignty and Divine Aseity. God is not dependent on anything else, and simplicity appears to be a way of explicating this. Yet Plantinga argues that simplicity does not explain anything and leads to various kinds of incoherence.

He identifies a variety of objections, including the fact that God does seem to have accidental properties (such as thinking of Adam), a situation which seems at odds with the claims of simplicity. And the response that this is not a property of God appears highly counterintuitive for Plantinga. Yet he places the force of his opposition on two further objections. Firstly, if God has all his properties essentially and these properties are identical with God, then these properties are identical with each other. Power collapses into goodness collapses into knowledge. Yet power, goodness and knowledge are different to each other, so this is incoherent. Secondly, even if this made sense, it would mean that God is identical with a single property, which would entail that God is an abstract entity. But being an abstract entity is not compatible with being alive, possessing knowledge, creating and all the other features traditionally attributed to God by theists. One way to dodge this conclusion is to deny that God is identical with the full Platonic universal of such properties, but rather is identical with his instantiation of such properties, that is, being identical with a state of affairs. But the same problem replicates, since a state of affairs is also an abstract entity. Another dodge is to hold that the relationship between God's instantiation of such a property and creaturely instantiations of such is 'analogical'; they are different. Why this is a dodge is that it invites scepticism – ignorance cuts both ways. One cannot have reason to postulate x of God and then claim that we do not know what x is – the ignorance of the second claim is sufficient to undermine the basis of the first claim.

The crucial aspect of this challenge to Aquinas is that it operates within a significantly different metaphysical framework, and therefore does not directly connect with Aquinas's views. Plantinga sets up the challenge in terms of properties, which seems intuitively plausible. However, he makes an assumption that the way properties operate in created reality is similar to the way they might operate in God. He compares property possession in Socrates with property possession in God (p. 51). This assumption is one which Aquinas clearly rejects. Socrates and God do not exist along the same continuum of being. The kind of metaphysical features exhibited by Socratic property instantiation are significantly different to those operative in God. Indeed, one might think of the doctrine of Divine Simplicity as a way of emphasizing this intuition – God is relevantly different to all other realities. The mode of being which is proper to God is one of perfection (4.1). Thus, properties which exist in the world and which are exemplified by Socrates (being, goodness, life) do exist in God, but in their perfected instances. The claim of Divine Simplicity is that the perfected version of these properties operates metaphysically differently to the creaturely instantiations of them. In God they are identical with God's essence. God is pure act, contains no potentiality and exhibits no composition. Using the distinction between mode of signification and reality signified (13.4), we can make distinctions among the Divine Attributes by virtue of their mode of signification. Relative to our cognition, we make distinctions among God's perfections. These are not merely conceptual or conventional distinctions. There is a real basis to them. However, the basis, as it is in itself and distinct from our cognition, has the feature of non-composition. While there is distinction and multiplicity in our thought, there is unity and simplicity in the reality thought about.

> But our intellect, since it knows God from creatures, in order to understand God, forms conceptions proportional to the perfections flowing from God to creatures, which perfections pre-exist in God unitedly and simply, while in creatures they are received divided and multiplied. [ST 1.13.4]

So it does not follow that simplicity entails that God is an abstract entity in the manner of a pure Platonic universal. Neither does it follow that goodness, knowledge and power collapse into each other as instantiated in the world. Now this defence, of course, relies on a commitment to analogy, which Plantinga has also challenged, saying it leads to scepticism.

Aquinas's strategy rests on a dialectic of affirmation and negation. The basic affirmation is causal. God causes the world to be, and this can be rationally demonstrated. Certain features of the cause are evident from such arguments – that God is unmoved, the first cause, the source of necessity, perfect and the source of order. Aquinas's negative strategy is to remove from this cause such features as apply to creaturely being. So there is an agnosticism or apophatic aspect to the negative part of the dialectic. Aquinas emphasizes that God is not fully knowable; our knowledge of him is deficient. Yet the positive aspect of the dialectic holds off a full agnosticism. There is a reality which is perfect and contains within itself the perfections of features of the world (being, goodness, knowledge and power). These exist in God in three significantly different ways to the way they exist in creatures. Firstly, in terms of universality – all perfections are in God, which are not united in any creature. Secondly, in terms of fullness, there is no defect in the way they exist in God. Finally, in terms of unity, these which in creatures are divided are united in God [S1.2.1.3]. It is also true that we do not understand how this is so. As Gerard Hughes nicely puts it,

> We know something about the truth-conditions for the application of such terms to God; for we know that those truth-conditions obtain. But we do not know what those truth-conditions consist in. In other words, we know something about the meanings of these terms used

analogically of God, since we know that they are related to the meanings of the same words used of ourselves; but we do not know what they mean when used of him.[38]

Hughes's mention of truth-conditions foreshadows recent defences of Aquinas on divine simplicity in terms of truth-maker theory. Such approaches seek to avoid the whole problematic of property talk by instead leaving open the ontological category which makes statements about divine simplicity true.[39] Whether such approaches are ultimately successful or not, what is clear is that discussions of divine attributes as properties are foreign to Aquinas's conceptual scheme and that objections to him based on such assumption miss the mark.

There are further objections to divine simplicity rooted in considerations that nothing religiously significant could be so constituted.[40] Something simple could not be a person, respond to prayer, care for the changing world and so forth. Since much of the discussion is relevantly similar to objections presented to God's being eternal, I shall postpone discussion of the objections to the next section.

6.3   Divine eternity

6.3.1   Relation to simplicity

In Aquinas's mature exposition of God's nature in the *Summa Theologiae*, divine simplicity plays a master role in determining the way the other attributes are to be understood. As has been shown, the core notion of simplicity is to deny composition of God. Referring back to Aquinas's conceptual scheme, the basic underlying kind of composition in all created things is that of potentiality and actuality, which can also be used as a way of making sense of matter/form and essence/existence composition. So simplicity entails that there is no potency in God. God is pure actuality. But how then does God, without having any potency, act, operate or cause change in anything else? Aquinas's answer is that God's actuality is not something inert, deficient or lacking in perfection. Attempting to explain how this is so is the primary way of responding to objections that Aquinas's conception of God is remote, philosophical and irreligious, objections that have already arisen in respect of immutability and simplicity. I shall discuss this in greater detail below in responding to objections to divine eternity.

That God is pure actuality emerges from the specific conclusions of the first and the third ways, as seen above. The first way had shown that whatever is moved has to be moved by another. This analysis is conducted in terms of potency and act. Were God to be moved, this would require some anterior act which would bring this about. So God is not moved, nor does God undergo *mutatio* (come to be or pass away), which is the result of the third way. Aquinas notes in 1.3.1

> because the first being must of necessity be in act, and in no way in potentiality. For although in any single thing that passes from potentiality to actuality, the potentiality is prior in time to the actuality; nevertheless, absolutely speaking, actuality is prior to potentiality; for whatever is in potentiality can be reduced into actuality only by some being in actuality. Now it has been already proved that God is the First Being. It is therefore impossible that in God there should be any potentiality.

In the specific question devoted to immutability [ST 1.9.1], Aquinas provides three arguments as to why God does not change. The first recapitulates the first way, noting that the first being does not have any potentiality, since potentiality is posterior to act, and so the first being would not be first if any potentiality existed in it. With no potentiality, there is no change. Secondly, drawing on the analysis of change (*motus*), he argues that anything which undergoes change remains the same in some respect and changes in a different respect. If this were so, it would be something composite, but simplicity rules out composition. Thirdly, when something changes, it takes on a new perfection, attaining something it previously did not have or, correlatively, losing a perfection. But God is such that this is not possible, containing the fullness of existence. Thus, God does not change.

However, Aquinas makes an important distinction between kinds of potentiality in ST 1.9.2. There is active potency which allows one to act in certain ways (which can also be called a power). God possesses active potency, although it is exercised in a unique way compatible with simplicity, which does not entail change, as I shall discuss below. On the other hand, passive potency is the capacity to change by being changed. God does not have this, but all creatures do. For physical beings, it is built into their metaphysical make-up with the possibility of generation and corruption. For non-physical beings it exists in terms of alteration of intellect, will and action. And for both physical and non-physical, their very existence can cease, since they exhibit metaphysical composition of essence and existence. Therefore, God's immutability is unique.

The objection that this is incompatible with biblical data is dealt with in two ways. Firstly, one might note that the data is underdetermined.

Biblical texts point both ways. Aquinas cites Malachi 3.6: 'I am God and I do not change', and James 4.8: 'Draw near to God and God will draw near to you'. Secondly, the texts which imply that God changes should be treated as metaphorical. There are many biblical passages which imply that God is physical (stretching forth his arm) or indeed flawed (forgetful, wrathful), and there is no hesitation for most readers to interpret these metaphorically. In fact one might usefully recall Richard Dawkin's observation that

> The God of the Old Testament is arguably the most unpleasant character in all fiction: jealous and proud of it; a petty, unjust, unforgiving control freak; a vindictive, bloodthirsty ethnic cleanser; a misogynistic, homophobic, racist, infanticidal, genocidal filicidal, pestilential, megalomaniacal, sadomasochistic, capriciously malevolent bully.[41]

However one might respond to this, it will typically involve appeal to metaphor or the requirement of not taking texts literally. So Aquinas's appeal to metaphor to dismiss the appearance of temporality in God is not a wholly unusual technique.

In fact the biggest problem with divine immutability is the alleged impossibility of God's acting and responding to creatures, on that view. If this can be shown not to follow, then there is good reason to treat the biblical data as not decisive and indeed metaphorical when implying change in God. If God is immutable, then eternity follows because of Aquinas's Aristotelian understanding of time. Time is understood as the measure of change, and if something does not change, then it is not in time. I shall discuss this further below when examining Aquinas on eternity at ST 1.10.

6.3.2   Influences

Augustine is a major influence on Aquinas's conception of divine eternity. Augustine's famous reflections on the nature of time in *Confessions* Bk.11 led directly to Augustine's articulation of God's mode of existence as being outside of time. He considered a variety of puzzles about time, beginning with the puzzle of what God was doing before creation [*Confessions* XI.12]. Why did God choose to create at this time rather than that? Such a question seems perfectly reasonable and natural, yet Augustine rejects it as conceptually confused. Time comes along with creation; it is part of what is created. Hence, it makes no sense to construe God as being in a temporal sequence and fixing on one point along that sequence to create the universe. Augustine's reflections on the nature of time led him to think of it as unreal in some sense. The past and future do not exist. One is gone, and the other is not yet [*Confessions* XI.14]. But the present has no extension, and rapidly becomes the past. Human existence, distended across time, exhibits a lack of presence to itself – our past and future are not present to us. In contrast, God's existence is one in which there is an immediacy of presence, a lack of gap or of distension. In eternity, 'all is at once present, whereas no time is all at once present' [*Confessions* XI.11].

For Augustine, then, what is most real is what exhibits this mode of presence in the highest degree. In this he accepts (with Aquinas) the Neoplatonist assumption that existence or reality comes in degrees. It is scalar, not bipolar. It is not sufficient simply to note a distinction between existence and non-existence, but rather one must think in terms of degrees or gradations of being.[42] For Augustine, what is more real is connected to the present and disconnected from past and future. Therefore, timeless beings will be more real than temporal beings, since they do not exhibit the connection to non-existence of beings caught in the flow from past to future. And lack of such a flow also entails immutability. So the mode of existence which is God's is changeless and timeless.

Another major influence on Aquinas is Boethius. In *The Consolation of Philosophy*, written while imprisoned, and before his execution in 524, Boethius articulated the classical definition of eternity. This was an important work for the transmission of Neoplatonic ideas to the medieval West. In bk 5, ch. 6, he begins his discussion of the divine nature and asserts that everyone who lives according to reason holds that God is eternal. However, the importance of Boethius's discussion lies in his definition and clarification of the notion of eternity, which set the framework for later thinkers. His definition states that

> Eternity, then, is the complete and perfect possession, all at once, of boundless life.
> [*Aeternitas igitur est interminabilis vitae tota simul et perfecta possessio.*][43]

At first glance, this seems an odd definition, since it does not refer to time at all, a factor which one might consider essential to thinking about eternity. However, Boethius is clear that time and eternity serve as contrasts. He explicitly states that the Platonic view, which says that the world has always existed in the past and always exists in the future, refers to the world's being perpetual (*perpetuum*), not eternal. Eternal, on his understanding, means timeless. To grasp what he means, each element in his definition must be taken in turn and examined.

The concept of 'life' is fundamental to his account. This can seem puzzling. Why does anything eternal have to be alive? Why can something not just exist forever? If we recall the explicit contrast between being perpetual and being eternal, it may be the case that something inert or non-living may be perpetual, while to have eternity, one has to have life. Why? No explicit argument is forthcoming, but one could imagine something along the following lines. In expressing the meaning of eternity, Boethius is explaining a form of being which is different to the form of being of temporal entities. On his view, eternity is a higher and more perfect form of being, and since living is more perfect than non-living, the life of an eternal reality follows. Other elements of his definition (particularly the notion of possession) imply that whatever is eternal possesses knowledge or awareness, and accordingly, whatever has knowledge must have life.

This life is boundless. There is no form of limitation to it. This introduces an interpretative problem into Boethius's account. One could conceive of boundless life as being static, like a point, or alternatively as having duration. On the former view, it seems inert and thereby non-living. On the latter, it is brought back into time and succession. Neither of these is appealing. By saying that it is alive, the inert approach is written off, and by saying it is eternal, the duration approach is blocked. What is required is the thought that it is alive, and alive in such a way that it is unconstrained and unlimited. If one can make sense of a notion of duration which is not extended in time, then that might apply to it. However, the meaning of duration, to many, is tied to being in time. So perhaps a different term could be coined, maybe even just 'duration*', to capture this notion of something non-static, alive, actual, unlimited, which is nevertheless not in the temporal flow.[44] This 'boundless life' is possessed – so there is a reality or entity which is the possessor of this boundless life. The kind of possession is 'whole', 'perfect' and 'all at once'. Taking these in turn, 'whole' entails that there are no parts involved (whole, not part possession). It is 'perfect' in that no better can be achieved; it is fully actualized. It is also 'all at once', indicating simultaneity. Another way of putting that is to deny succession, and so the possession of illimitable life is non-successive.

Indeed, one can think of 'whole' and 'all at once' as negations – denying parts and denying succession – which together give specifying content to the notion of perfection involved. This is quite an abstract conception of eternity. Could it not be illuminated by helpful examples?

No – because there is only one eternal being, God. In his definition of eternity, Boethius is specifying a form of being which is unique to God. Even if there were a being which never began and would never end, such a being would be perpetual (or sometimes called 'sempiternal'), not eternal. So a crucial facet of Boethius's definition is that eternity is not about time; rather, it is about a being which exists apart from time.

6.3.3 Aquinas ST 1.10

Aquinas' discussion of eternity in the *Summa Theologiae* [ST I.10] follows Boethius closely. Indeed, the very first article lacks Aquinas's characteristic phrase 'but against this...' (Latin: *sed contra*), normally used when citing an authoritative source. He omits this because his following argument is completely about the appropriateness of Boethius's definition, which serves in this case as the authoritative source. He endorses Boethius's definition and holds that God is eternal in precisely this sense. Aquinas notes that we learn about the unknown by means of the known. We understand the meaning of a 'point' by denying that it has parts [ST 1.10.1ad1]. We do so because it is natural to our way of understanding to think about things which have parts, and so we think about something lacking parts by first thinking about more familiar things that have parts, and then contrasting with them. We think about eternity by means of denying that it is like things in time. Things in time have successiveness, a before and an after. Two things characterize eternity:

- Anything eternal is unending; it lacks a beginning and an end.
- Anything eternal lacks successiveness; it exists as a simultaneous whole.

Aquinas closely links the eternity of God to his unchangeability [ST 1.10.2]. As noted above, God is unchangeable because there is no potency in him; he is fully actual. God is simple and has no parts, which he would have if he changed (temporal parts). It is also the case that God's eternity is not distinct from his essence. It is characteristic of how he is. From this it follows that God's eternity is unique to him. Other beings may come in some way to share in his eternity: by persisting in being and contemplating him. But strictly speaking, eternity is God's own being [ST 1.10.3].

In an important discussion, Aquinas contrasts time and eternity [ST 1.10.4]. He notes that some people distinguish between the two on the basis that time has a beginning and an end, whereas eternity has neither.

However, this is an accidental rather than an essential distinction. Even if time always existed and will never end (as Aristotle believed), there is still a crucial distinction between time and eternity. Time has succession, while eternity does not. Time measures changing existence, while eternity is a mark of unchanging existence.

So Aquinas clearly articulates and defends a version of the classical conception of God as eternal. However, such a conception is open to a wide range of objections. If God is unchanging, how can he respond to free human beings who act contingently? If God is outside time, how does he relate to time? Is not this picture of God one of a static metaphysical abstraction, rather than a genuinely religious conception? These kinds of objections must now be faced.

6.3.4   Objections

Two basic facets of the opposition to Aquinas's view are a) it is unmotivated; it is not forced on one and b) it is incoherent and leads to many problems. With respect to its lack of motivation, it is claimed that it forms part of a static, Platonic, picture of the deity. Insofar as few hold to Platonic positions nowadays, it is held that this also should be jettisoned. Eternity is tied to a picture of a God who is immutable and inert, a lifeless abstraction which kills genuine religious sensibility. From G.W.F. Hegel onwards, philosophers have explored ideas of the Absolute in which it is evolving and developing, dynamic and responsive.[45] In twentieth-century thought, Alfred North Whitehead (1861–1947) developed 'process metaphysics', which was developed into a 'process theology' by Charles Hartshorne (1897–2000).[46] Such a philosophical system, it is claimed, fits better with a biblical conception of God than does the classical view. Theologians such as Jürgen Moltmann have trenchantly made this case.[47]

In relation to the second kind of objection, there are several ways of claiming that Aquinas's position is incoherent. Assuming that God is eternal and immutable, there are two ways of thinking about his immutability. The first is that God's character remains unchanged – that God remains good and powerful and knowledgeable and so on. This is a weak form of unchangeability, as it is compatible with having changing ideas, acting sequentially, exhibiting consistent power in different ways at different times. A stronger form of unchangeability is that God does not change in any way whatsoever. This is the classical claim, and many imagine that it conflicts with the concept of divine freedom. If God cannot change in any way, then God cannot be free. Swinburne says a person immutable in the strong sense would be unable to perform any action at a certain time other than what he had previously intended to do. His course of action being fixed by his past choices, he would not be perfectly free.[48]

Swinburne thinks that being timeless does entail being immutable – so both should be jettisoned. However, this argument – that freedom and immutability are inconsistent – only works if you have already dropped the idea of divine eternity. Swinburne's argument assumes that freedom and immutability are inconsistent against a backdrop of time, of having one's present action determined by prior choices. However, if divine freedom is exercised in a continuous present (eternity), the issue of prior choices does not arise. Now, it may be that the notion of God's continuous present is incoherent, but that is precisely the point at issue here. By assuming temporality as a premise against it, this argument against eternity begs the question against the very coherence of eternity. So a different case would have to be made against God's eternity.

A second, stronger, argument says that in making sense of the notion of divine eternity, incoherence erupts into the very idea of time. Boethius had used a telling image of a person on a mountain looking down on travellers on a road.[49] From the perspective of the mountaintop, the person can see more than the travellers. The person on top can see all of the road at once, while those on the road can only see a bit. God, from eternity, sees all time at once, while we *in via*, in time, see only our own limited perspective. God is said to exist simultaneously with all points of time. So students starting to write an essay, their writing of it and their future finishing of it are all equally present to God in eternity. The limited perspective of human life only works in terms of past, present and future, but God knows them all, in an eternal 'now' (Latin: *nunc stans*).

However, if x is simultaneous with y and y is simultaneous with z, then x and z are simultaneous. So the view that God simultaneously knows the start of the writing of an essay and the end of writing it surely entails the odd conclusion that these are simultaneous with each other, simply by the logical law of transitivity (if 'a' is taller than 'b' and 'b' is taller than 'c', then 'a' is taller than 'c'). So defending divine eternity has the unwanted result of apparently making time collapse into a single point; hence, eternity is claimed to be an incoherent notion.[50]

A different assault on Aquinas's conception of divine eternity involves human freedom. It is claimed that God interacts with free human beings. For example, Moses was free to remain in Egypt or to lead the Hebrews out, and was free to accept or reject the covenant on Sinai. So, if God is atemporal and eternal, how does this work? If God knows in advance what Moses will do, since he is eternal, in what way was Moses free? In order for God to truly allow human freedom, it seems that he has to exist in time with human beings; otherwise, he constrains them by his eternal knowledge. Human freedom and eternity are incompatible.

6.3.5   Responses

The classical conception defends the view that eternity and time are distinct modes of being. Eternity is, by definition, timeless. The notion of 'the present' therefore has two distinct meanings. One refers to the timeless present of eternity – the present of the simultaneous and the perfect possession of illimitable life. The other refers to the present within the flow of time, bounded by the past and future on each side. The eternal present is not thus bounded, and is a different concept.

The objection levelled against the classical conception of eternity is that if an eternal being were simultaneously present to different temporal times, they would then be simultaneous with each other and hence time would collapse into a single present. To block this inference, one would need to show that the term 'simultaneous', when used in the context of eternity, means something different to the term 'simultaneous' when used in time. So saying that something is Eternal-Simultaneous (ES) is not to say that it is also Time-Simultaneous (TS). Saying that God is ES with the birth of Moses, with the battle of Waterloo and with today, does not mean that they are TS with each other – which is what the objection alleges.

To defend this claim, Eleanore Stump and Norman Kretzmann draw attention to the use of the notion of simultaneity in modern physics.[51] Imagine two flashes of lightning hitting a train at the same time, one at the front and one at the end. Do they really hit the train at the same time? Well, in physics, it depends on the perspective of the observer. Observers are in movement (you who are sitting and reading this page are, for example, moving at very high speed about the sun!). The train is in movement. For an observer moving at high speed away from the train (say, improbably, at half the speed of light), the two flashes will occur at different times. For another observer, one sitting on the train, they occur at the same time. Now, the question is, which one is right? And the answer is that space and time are relative to the position and speed of the observer. There is no absolute position, just position relative to others (as evidenced in the familiar phenomenon of not being able to tell whether your train or the other train is actually moving, unless you check with something else, say, the platform). So the notion of being simultaneous is a relativized notion – even in the context of time.[52] Stump and Kretzmann then argue that simultaneity is relativized further to Eternal Simultaneity and Time-Simultaneity. Being simultaneous with an eternal being is different to being simultaneous with a temporal being. God's E-simultaneity with all points in time does not lead to the temporal simultaneity of all points of time. If such a relativized notion of simultaneity is correct (as seems indicated by the use in physics), then this objection is defused.

Yet if this is so, there still remains the objection that an eternal being is unresponsive, inert and cannot interact with temporal beings. The classical view holds that God, as eternal, is present (ES) with each point in time. What happens in the course of history is present in an ongoing way (ET) to God, but only temporally present (Time-Simultaneous) to agents in history, as it ebbs away into the past. The mode of being of the eternal being is unlimited. God's power, knowledge and goodness are in full play at each instant of simultaneity – God is fully present at each point of history. The reason for this is God's causal sustenance of all things, whereby God's causal activity is present in every created effect.

Two distinctions may be used to help make some sense of this. The first is that of a single cause having multiple effects. God's single act of creation is understood as resulting in multiple effects in the spatio-temporal realm which are ES with God, but temporally spread out in history. The second distinction is of a single referent (God's simple act) having multiple senses. In distinguishing between God's goodness and God's power, God's justice and God's benevolence, our cognitive multiplicity picks out things that mark distinctions to our finite minds, but that are unified in themselves. The point of invoking these distinctions is to show that it is not incoherent to think about a simple, eternal reality interacting and responding (in some analogical sense of 'respond') to beings existing in time. It also affirms that we do not really understand this – we are attempting to stretch our concepts beyond their normal usages, and our grasp is always incomplete and partial.

In relation to the first kind of objection, that divine eternity is unmotivated, defenders of Aquinas could go on the offensive against those who want to argue that God exists in time. Firstly, they can show that if God exists in time, then time operates as a framework external to God, beyond God, encompassing both God and history. How can this framework be explained? How does one account for its explanatory priority relative to God? If God is, supposedly, the alpha and omega, the ultimate, then the act of postulating time in this way suggests that there is something beyond both alpha and omega. So the existence of time becomes a mystery in some way more ultimate than the mystery of God. Furthermore, since Albert Einstein, time is understood as being relative, not absolute, and also as being inextricably connected to space. Various physical theories account for the interaction of space and time, and speculate on the correct description of the 'space-time continuum'. But even those theists who want to argue that God is temporal are slow to say that he is also spatial. Yet that seems to follow inexorably from contemporary accounts of time, linking it to space. So if God is temporal, his spatiality follows, given contemporary physical theory. To resist this requires some substantial philosophical commitments (such as appealing to Cartesian dualism), a path few want to follow.

Also there is the theoretical systematicity of Aquinas's account. Solutions to the problem of the alleged incompatibility of divine omniscience and human freedom are available from this account of eternity which are not available to temporal theorists (as shall be addressed in the next chapter). Opponents argue that this alleged theoretical power exists only at the price of obscurity and ignorance. We do not know what eternity is like. We cannot imagine what a simple being is like. We might utter the words about a single infinite act of creation with multiple effects, but in fact we have no real idea of what we are saying. However, classical theorists such as Aquinas can accept this as a positive aspect of their position. Talking about God as an agent, operating in time, foreknowing and forestalling, intervening and planning is to anthropomorphize God – to create an idol. Classical theists clearly and unambiguously accept that we do not know what God is like. We use our concepts and ideas to point in the right direction, to rule out false ways, but ultimately none of these are adequate. In this respect, the classical conception, though using some of the most sophisticated philosophical hardware to articulate its case, defends a deep philosophical humility at its core. God remains a mystery.

7
God's Nature: The Way of Eminence

7.1 Divine goodness

7.1.1 *Via Eminentiae*

As discussed earlier, Aquinas's discussion of God's nature follows the dialectic of Denys the Areopagite's *triplex via*. Aquinas argues that demonstrations of God's existence are available. These constitute *demonstrationes quia*, arguments from effect to cause, rather than the full *demonstratio propter quid*, which is the standard form of acquiring *scientia*. Since God's nature is unknowable to us, this latter form of reasoning is not possible for us. Yet fully reasonable causal argumentation establishes the existence of something which is the first cause of motion, the source of necessity, the basis of teleology and so forth. The second phase of the dialectic argues that various features of creaturely being are not applicable to the reality so demonstrated. It is not in space or time; it is unique, immovable, impassible and not literally describable in anthropomorphic terms. Thus the boundaries of what such a reality might be are circumscribed. Valuable as such negative characterizations are, Aquinas holds that they are nevertheless insufficient. He critiques Maimonides's purely negative approach to God [ST 1.13.2], saying that it is not the case that terms predicated of God only serve to deny things of the divinity. On such an approach there would be no way to way to distinguish between terms one might want to say of God, such as 'God is good' and others one does not, such as 'God is a body'. If God is good merely serves to say 'God causes Goodness', then it would be legitimate to also say 'God is a body', since God causes bodies as well as good things. Furthermore, the sense of these words would apply to God only secondarily, with their primary signification referring to creatures, which is not what people who use religious language typically mean – 'when we say

"God is living" we intend something different than "God is the cause of life" or that God differs from inanimate bodies' [1.13.2c].

So such terms as 'good' do say something affirmative about God, albeit in an imperfect and partial way. However, where do they come from? How does Aquinas establish the list of things one can affirm of God? The progression of questions 3–5 in ST I helps make sense of this. As has been seen, ST 1.3 deals with divine simplicity, and in the process of doing so, Aquinas argues for self-subsistent existence as a basic designation of the divine nature. Granted humans do not grasp what this really means. It has been argued that at the least it introduces the idea of a hierarchy of existence. Rather than existence being simply an on/off phenomenon, it exhibits degrees. Aquinas's presentation of the fourth way in ST 1.2.3 rests on this sort of reasoning – 'there is something that is truest, best, noblest and consequently greatest in being'. Peter Geach thinks that Aquinas's analysis of gradations in intensity is a valuable intellectual innovation – explaining how to make sense of differences of intensity in property F without invoking other parallel properties G or H.[1] Instead he speaks of greater degrees of existence as the explanation of intensive difference. God is at the pinnacle of the degrees of existence. Aquinas's reason for this is given in ST 1.4, which directly touches on God's perfection. God is perfect insofar as God is fully actual – 'something is said to be perfect insofar as it is in actuality' [ST 1.4]. Also, Aquinas holds that existence is the 'perfection of all perfections' insofar as it is the manner in which actuality is realized: 'Existence is the most perfect of all things, for it is related to everything as to their actuality' [ST 1.4.1 ad3, see also QDP 7.2. ad9]. Because God is construed as self-subsistent existence, then all perfections pertain to the divinity.

> Thus since God is subsisting existence itself, nothing of the perfection of existing can be lacking in God. But the perfections of all things belong to the perfection of existing, for things are perfect inasmuch as they have existence in some way. Thus it follows that God does not lack the perfection of any thing. [ST 1.4.2]

Goodness is internally related to being, via the doctrine of the transcendentals.[2] Goodness brings out the aspect of desirability, which is not explicit in being itself. Being and goodness differ in meaning (in *ratio*), but not in reality [ST 1.5]. Hence goodness is internally connected to the very nature of God, through the identification of existence as the fundamental attribute of God and the sameness in being of goodness and existence. As possessing the fullness of being, God also possesses the fullness of goodness. Hence, it is not gratuitous that goodness follows the progression from simplicity to perfection. Yet what of other aspects of God's being – such as knowledge, power and so forth? Aquinas postpones discussion of these until after dealing with questions about how God is known by us [ST 1.12] and the names of God [ST 1.13]. The logic of this progression is that Simplicity, Goodness, Eternity and the rest pertain to God's essence, whereas knowledge and power are operations flowing from this essence (although such distinctions are *quoad nos*, since God's knowledge and power are God). Thus, I use Aquinas's sequence of treatment by following the order of divine goodness, divine knowledge and divine power.

One might finally note that although there is an internal logical deductive structure to the order of treatment, Aquinas is of course drawing on extra-philosophical sources in this work. The inherited tradition of Christian reflection on God has constantly taught God's goodness, God's knowledge and God's power. Looking at the *Sed Contra* citations in the articles of questions 3–6 in ST 1 is instructive in this respect as Aquinas cites scriptural and patristic sources for his views: 'You must be perfect as your heavenly father is perfect' [Matthew 5.48] 1.4.1; 'God is good to those who hope in him, to the soul seeking him' [Lamentations 3.25] 1.6.1; 'Augustine says in *On the Trinity* that the Trinity of divine persons "is the highest good which is discerned by the most purified minds"' [PL42.822] 1.6.2. These quotations illustrate how Aquinas puts into practice his views on the harmonious interaction of faith and reason, of theology and philosophy.

7.1.2 The metaphysics of goodness

Topics addressed above in meeting the problem of evil are also relevant to making sense of God's goodness, and I shall briefly recap which are the major ones for Aquinas. A basic point to note is that Aquinas's views flow from his fundamental conceptual scheme, the analytical framework of substance and accident, essences, four causes, potency and act (above 2.4). From this he develops an account of God's goodness, which has several wide-reaching and surprising consequences. These include that God is not a moral agent (in the sense humans are) and that God causes all human actions, thereby being incompatible with what is known as the 'free-will defence' to the problem of evil (while nevertheless committing himself to the claim that humans act freely). The metaphysical account of God's goodness allows Aquinas to have a response to the naturalistic fallacy challenge (which denies that moral norms can be derived from facts) and also to the Euthyphro dilemma – whether goodness is dependent on God's will or not. I shall discuss the naturalistic fallacy and the Euthyphro problem later in this section, but first I shall indicate the connections between his account of goodness and his general metaphysical system.

As noted above, goodness and being are transcendental features of anything which exists. That is, these are co-extensive; they pertain to the same things, but have different intentions, or mean different things. Goodness can be understood as meaning 'attractive' – it is what attracts our wills – while there is no reference to this in talk of being. This quality of attractiveness also explains how someone can be mistaken in moral judgement – one can be attracted to what is an apparent good rather than what is actually good. 'Good' is also what Geach calls an attributive rather than a predicative adjective.[3] One needs to know the kind of thing involved, to know what is meant by saying it is good. Goodness manifests in radically different ways in different things. A linguistic test for the difference between attributive and predicative properties is to consider how one makes a double predication of some entity, that is, saying it is AB. If the property is predicative, one can say X is A and also X is B. For example, 'this is a hot drink' yields 'this is hot' and 'this is a drink'. However, attributive properties do not allow such inferences. Saying 'this is a big mouse' does not yield 'this is big' and 'this is a mouse'. Bigness is relative to the kind of thing in question. So too with goodness – whatever counts as good is relativized to the kind of thing in question. So while goodness is co-extensive with being, it also exhibits the kind of pluralism and diversity exhibited by being. As being is divided into kinds, so also the ways in which things are good are indexed to the kind of thing in question.

Goodness is also related to the teleological structure of creation. As Aquinas's explanatory schema makes use of 'form' as a key notion, the notion of an end is internally related to form. Final causation shapes efficient and formal causation (p. 44 above). Jean Porter summarizes this well:

> formal causes and teleological explanation, or in other words, explanations in terms of final causes, are inextricably linked. The proper form of a given kind of living creature can only be adequately understood by reference to some idea of a paradigmatic instance of the form, that is to say, a healthy and mature individual of the kind in question. It is only by reference to this paradigm that we are able to identify immature, sick or defective individuals of this kind as such, that is to say, as (less than perfect) representatives of the kind.[4]

The final cause of creation is God's goodness. In Aquinas's discussion of order in nature, he argues for a pervasive structure of final causality to explain physical processes. And since God also causally sustains all beings in existence, there is no aspect of the created realm which is not implicated in this framework of causal interactions of different kinds – whether efficient, formal or final.

This is the reason why the 'free will defence' does not fit with Aquinas's account of God's relationship with the world. Aquinas believes that human beings act freely, but he also believes that God causes human actions at the same time. This assumption is rejected by both defenders and critics of the free will defence alike. In a classic discussion,[5] John Mackie wonders why God could not have created human beings such that they, in fact, always freely do good. Alvin Plantinga argues that this does not make sense. It could only mean that God either causes human actions (in which case they are not free) or else he does not (in which case Mackie's challenge becomes unmotivated and puzzling). In contrast, Aquinas holds that God causes human action, but in a way which is a precondition for freedom. Without God's causal sustenance, human existence, cognition, intention and action could not be [ST 1.22.1], and so all human actions are causally dependent on God. Nevertheless, God's causal role is not like the causal roles of other creaturely causes. It is not as if God works like antecedent physical causes, for example, like a drug. Such causes would impact on the freedom of the action, rendering it unfree. God's causal action is in another framework, a precondition for the web of causes in the world [ST 1.8.1]. So while God causes all things, some are free, some not (just as some are necessary, some not). Thus, for Aquinas, God's causal role does not rule out human freedom, but actually makes it possible. With these preambles stated, it is now time to turn to the way in which Aquinas thinks of God as being good.

7.1.3   God is goodness itself

The manner in which goodness is exemplified in God is different from the way in which goodness is exemplified in any other being, for Aquinas. This is directly due to the doctrine of divine simplicity, which I described above as the master concept governing how all other features must be thought about in God. In fact, to say that goodness is exemplified in God is not strictly correct, as that implies a common scale along which God could be measured in relation to other creaturely forms of goodness. God is construed as the fullness of the perfection, goodness, as the model, archetype or paradigm of all forms of goodness. Other forms of goodness are related to God's as their source, cause and model, but are distinct by virtue of the full actuality and perfection of God's goodness. Aquinas gives a general rationale for this in ST 1.4.3, discussing whether creatures can resemble God. There is an analogical connection between creaturely attributes and God – but they do not belong in the same framework:

> the same things can be like and unlike to God: like, according as they imitate Him, as far as He, Who is not perfectly imitable, can be imitated; unlike according as they fall short of their cause, not merely in intensity and remission, as that which is less white falls short of that which is more white; but because they are not in agreement, specifically or generically.

This raises questions about how Aquinas thinks we use terms such as 'good' – and requires an account of how he construes the truth-maker for such propositions as 'God is good' and how this might differ from the truth-maker for a proposition such as 'God is creator'. The former proposition is necessary, but the latter seems contingent (since God freely creates), so how can the same thing make them true? I shall begin by discussing Aquinas's general account of universals, turning then to see how this dovetails with God as source of perfection. Then I shall examine Aquinas's account of God as a truth-maker.

Goodness is an instance of a universal predicate. To what does such a term refer? Realists postulate an abstract entity as the referent for such terms. Aquinas believes that this is the result of failing to observe appropriate distinctions in philosophy of language. In subject-predicate propositions, the subject refers in a material sense, the predicate in a formal sense. What is picked out by the subject term is characterized in some fashion by the predicate term – but the predicate does not refer in the same way as the subject. Geach draws a parallel between Aquinas and Gottlob Frege's doctrine of Object (*Gegenstand*) and Concept (*Begriff*).[6] There is a fundamental distinction in reality between individuals and properties they may have. Aquinas does not speak of 'properties', but does speak of 'form'. Forms (at least on Earth) do not exist as subsistent entities, but rather exist in individuals. The wisdom of Socrates exists only in Socrates. Geach suggests an analogy with the notion of a mathematical function – something which is incomplete and requires filling-in to have full reference. Speaking of 'wisdom' as a universal requires intellectual abstraction. The features exhibited by the universal – being one over many, instantiability in multiple individuals – come from the nature of mind. When I say 'Socrates is good', I apply the common nature 'goodness' to the individual 'Socrates' and pick out the individuated form which is dependent on Socrates, the individual referred to by the subject term, the form designated of that individual by the predicate term.

What happens when I say 'God is good'? By the predicate term I refer to the form 'goodness', and to the way it is in God. The way in which it exists in God is different to the way it is instantiated in creatures, yet there is a connection, as the cause and perfection of creaturely goodness. Hence it is an analogical usage. But what of the problem which arises due to divine simplicity – that God's goodness is no different from God's existence or knowledge and so forth? As noted above, Plantinga believes this is incoherent (p. 171 above).

Jeffrey Brower has recently employed truth-maker theory to defend Aquinas's view.[7] The problem stated by Plantinga arises if one thinks that what makes propositions true are individuals and properties, for example, Socrates and his wisdom. However, one might substitute the notion of truth-maker for property on this account. A truth-maker is a functional term which picks out whatever it is which makes the proposition true. It makes no commitment to the ontological type involved; it may be an individual or a property. John F. Fox[8] gives a classical definition of the truth-maker axiom::

If p, some x exists such that x's existing necessitates that p.

What makes the proposition 'God is good' true is the truth-maker, *God*. This makes the proposition 'God is powerful' also true, but a unitary truth-maker can make multiple propositions true. Brower (p. 115) gives the following list made true by the same truth-maker – Socrates himself (and note how the propositions may have different modal features).

Socrates is human
Socrates is an animal
Socrates is a material object
Socrates exists
Socrates is identical with himself

The truth-maker of 'God is good' and 'God is powerful' and so forth is God and God's perfections, which exist in reality in a unified simple manner, but which exist in our thought and language in a multiplicity of descriptions. It does not follow from this that the referent of such sentences has to be an abstract entity or a bare property. On Aquinas's account the referent is the most ontologically rich reality there is. His metaphysical account of existence, with goodness as one of its transcendental properties and the idea that there are gradations of perfection, yields the following account of goodness in God:

> Moreover, each good thing that is not its goodness is called good by participation. But that which is named by participation has something prior to it from which it receives the character of goodness. This cannot proceed to infinity, since among final causes there is no regress to infinity, since the infinite is opposed to the end [*finis*]. But the good has the nature of an end. We must, therefore, reach some first good, that is not by participation good through an order toward some other good, but is good through its own essence. This is God. God is, therefore, His own goodness. [SCG 1.38.4]

7.1.4   The naturalistic fallacy

An influential objection to this view is what is called 'the naturalistic fallacy' associated with David Hume and G.E. Moore.[9] The basic insight underlying their position is that one cannot have something in the conclusion of an argument which is not contained in the premises. Factual premises, it is argued, do not have evaluative components in them and hence do not yield normative conclusions. Therefore, talking about goodness as if it were connected to facts about reality is to commit a mistake. If one accepts this critique, one might seek to root ethics in human emotional responses (Hume), or in intuitions of good as a non-natural feature of reality (Moore) or as a kind of expression of an attitude (A.J. Ayer). But thinking that goodness is connected to being was thought to be deeply flawed. And hence Aquinas's conception of God as goodness itself would be a gross violation of the principle that 'Ought' is not derivable from 'Is'.

Part of the background to this debate is the widespread opposition to metaphysics advanced by empiricists, which proved dominant in mid-twentieth-century philosophy. Renewed interest in metaphysics allows a fresh look at this debate. Anthony Lisska has given a detailed and convincing analysis of the assumptions underlying Moore's rejection of ethical naturalism.[10] Moore's conception of ontology, akin to that of Bertrand Russell and Ludwig Wittgenstein in the era of Logical Atomism, is that the most fundamental elements in philosophical analysis are ontological simples. In such a system it is indeed hard to see how one might derive any ethical mileage from consideration of the fundamental entities which exist. However, the basically Aristotelian ontology used by Aquinas has a significantly different approach to reality. The most fundamental entities are not simple elements, but are structured and exhibit complexity.[11] Individual concrete entities – such as human beings or animals – are the paradigms of substances for Aristotle. These exhibit not only features which make them individuals (matter) but also features making them members of kinds (form). There is a functional organization which characterizes their identities, and such functional organization is understood teleologically, exhibiting intelligible end-oriented dispositional processes. Hence, it is possible to argue that there is an internal connection between the factual descriptive structures evident in the natural world and value or purpose exhibited by their functions. The problem of the derivation of 'Ought from Is' makes sense in an ontology of simples, but does not find purchase in a different ontology in which goodness is construed as the fulfilment of potential, the actualization of essence. Aquinas's God stands as the final cause in such an ontological system. One may challenge this by rejecting metaphysics simpliciter, or rejecting the teleologically oriented metaphysics deployed by Aquinas, but the mere statement of the naturalistic fallacy does not have force against the kind of metaphysics underpinning Aquinas's position, which does allow the derivation of value statements from factual ones.

7.1.5   The Euthyphro dilemma

As Socrates faced trial in Athens, he met with a religious expert, Euthyphro, and ironically declared his delight in meeting such a person, since he was being charged with 'impiety' – a religious fault. However, as is familiar in Socratic dialogue, Euthyphro found the ground shifting beneath him and was discomfited by the questions put to him by Socrates. The crucial question raised in the dialogue is whether things are loved by the gods because they are good, or are they good because they are loved by the gods? Despite the original context of polytheism, the question is one which also raises acute problems for monotheistic views of God. The crux is that the question offers a dilemma. If one says that things are good by virtue of God's loving them, then it seems as if the nature of goodness is somehow arbitrary. It is the willing of God, or the brute choice of God, which makes good things good and evil things evil. It could have been otherwise. There is nothing intrinsic about goodness or evil which makes them so. On the other hand, if one says that God loves good things because they are antecedently good, then it seems as if God is forced to love them by virtue of some external structure. This seems to compromise God's independence and power, and leaves inexplicable where goodness comes from and how it governs God's choices. The simple question seems either to make morality arbitrary or else to impugn God's independence, neither an attractive option.

Some medieval philosophers opted for the horn of the dilemma which made goodness dependent on God's will.[12] The background assumption which makes this attractive is the thought that will is a superior faculty to intellect in God (because will is directed by love, which is superior to truth, which directs the intellect). Thus, it is ultimately God's will which determines the inner nature of goodness, and it is logically and metaphysically possible that the nature of goodness could be other than it is. A descendent of this view is Divine Command Ethics, which roots ethical normativity in the commands of God. Certainly this seems to be consonant with many scriptural passages in which God issues commands. Yet the standard objection to such a position seems to be that there seems to be something about theft, murder, torture and so on which could not be just reversed by God's command, magically making them to be good.

Aquinas does not directly address this dilemma, but a response is clearly evident in the account of divine goodness he gives. He can reject both horns and escape between them. There does not exist a standard of goodness independent of God's making things good. Neither is it simply God's arbitrary willing which makes them good. Rather, God wills in accordance with God's own nature, and this is not something arbitrary. God is the paradigm, model and standard of goodness. In creating the world, God creates beings which exhibit a structured tele-ologically oriented existence. Goodness is inscribed, so to speak, in their structure, and as they seek to develop and perfect themselves, they operate in a good fashion. Evil has been discussed above as a defect in the functioning of such structures. Evil suffered is the causal impact on a subject of the operation of another subject's good (the lion and the lamb example), whereas evil performed is itself a defect within the moral operation of an individual capable of reasoning and choosing the good. Eleanore Stump[13] characterizes Aquinas's position as offering a Grand Unified Theory of Goodness – presenting a metaphysical account of the deep nature of goodness in his account of God's nature, connected to the rest of creation in a teleological system which operates in human beings as a virtue ethics. Lisska argues that theories which fail to give a rational metaphysical basis to judgements of value (such as Rawlsian veil of ignorance considerations), ultimately fall foul of the Euthyphro problem.[14] On such accounts there is no good account of what makes X good, other than that it is chosen to be so by a group of people.

7.2   Divine knowledge

Aquinas discusses God's knowledge as the first operation of the divine substance [ST 1.14 *prooemium*]. These operations are distinguished into those which are immanent (intellect and will) and those which result in external results (power). In giving an analysis of his account of God's intellect, it is useful to begin with a brief account of human cognition, which will serve as a contrast for characterizing divine knowledge. I shall then present Aquinas's account of divine cognition as deriving from his position on God's immateriality and perfection, and show how divine simplicity shapes his account, notwithstanding his endorsement of divine ideas. There is then the thorny issue of what might be the objects of God's knowledge. Aquinas argues that among what God knows are individuals, propositions, evil and future contingent propositions, each of which raises conceptual problems.

7.2.1   Human cognition

Aquinas follows Aristotle in arguing that all human cognition begins in sensory knowledge.[15] However, what distinguishes human rationality from animal cognition is the human capacity to abstract general concepts from sensible particulars. So, for example, when presented with ten different red things, I can note certain common features – for example, that each is an individual, each is red, each is different in some respect to the others and so on. All this information is explicable in terms of recognizing different forms and different aspects of forms along with the associated matter. Aquinas employs the distinction between 'agent intellect' and 'possible intellect' to explain the mechanics of the process of how intelligible patterns are recognized from patterns of sensory inputs. Aquinas's account of intentionality (the mind-world relationship) is based on the distinction between form as instantiated in real things and form as existing in the mind. He argues that there is an isomorphism, an identity in form, between, for example, my laptop as it exists before me and how it exists in my mind as I think of it. In reality it is instantiated in metal and plastic, but in my mind its form is divested of its matter. The link between world and mind is causal. At first, there is a causal interplay between objects in reality and my senses. My senses receive sensible forms. That is, they are impacted upon by features of the environment in such a way that information is transferred. Such sensory inputs are then converted into intelligible forms, which have universal features. What is common to the ten, red, objects is grasped through the universal concept 'red' formed by my intellect. Therefore, basic sensory inputs, which are causally stimulated by the environment, lead to more abstract forms of cognition.

Aquinas's account of cognition makes use of his conceptual scheme, using the tools of matter and form, potency and act. Forms existing in reality in things are potentially available to human cognitive powers and become actual in the intellect as concepts are formed. Concept formation is gradual – there are initially hazy concepts which get sharpened and more precise as they are reflected on. Aquinas's account has been characterized as a form of semantic externalism about concepts.[16] Conceptual content in the mind is causally produced by the environment physically impacting on the person. There are various stages in cognition. Concept formation is the first, making judgements using these concepts is the second stage and reasoning from such judgements to further truths is a third stage [In PA prol]. Hence human reasoning is discursive, involving making distinctions, making inferences, moving step by step through reasoning processes. The human way of knowing is grounded in sensory inputs, is causally related to the environment, is sequential and spread out over time.

7.2.2 Divine cognition

Divine cognition works significantly differently to human cognition. God does not use sensory inputs, is not causally acted upon. God's intellect is not sequential and does not exist in time. The fundamental insight guiding Aquinas is that God's cognition operates according to God's mode of being, which is dramatically different from the human mode of being. One might wonder, then, what remains of the notion of 'cognition' after such a thorough transformation? In what way is there any continuity in meaning between human thinking and divine thought? Yet Aquinas does find some common ground. Rationality in humans is a feature of the soul, the latter of which has both intellectual and appetitive powers. Acting well is governed by rationality, as is also thinking well. However, the more specifically intellectual part of the soul (*intellectus*) is distinguished from the will in being primarily oriented towards truth rather than action. Human rational activity is discursive and sequential, as noted above, following inferences and drawing conclusions. Nevertheless, there is a more fundamental aspect of human reasoning, which is not discursive itself, but is a precondition for discursive thought. This is the capacity to grasp first principles, known to Aristotle as *nous* and to Aquinas as *intellectus*. It is a direct, immediate grasp of basic truths, such as the principle of non-contradiction or that the whole is greater than the part. While the ensemble of human thought is sequential and comprises parts, this feature is unified, direct and immediate. And this is the kind of cognition which is closest to the kind God has. When God thinks, there are no parts, no inferences, no sequence, no process; rather, there is a single act. What are Aquinas's reasons for positing this of God and what is known by God in such an act?

Aquinas devotes ST 1.14 to God's knowledge and works systematically through the issues of whether God has knowledge, how it is related to God's nature, what kind is this knowledge, what kind of things are known (this is paralleled in SCG 1.44–71). His argument for the existence of knowledge in God in 1.14.1 is somewhat unexpected. He argues from God's immateriality to God's knowledge, drawing on his general account of cognition. The difference between things which are capable of cognition and those which are not is that those capable of cognition are able to receive forms in a non-material way into themselves. Things lacking cognition are more limited than those capable of cognition. Material things may receive forms in various ways – stones in a very limited physical way, wax in a less limited way, senses in a higher manner in which forms are received without the matter, intellect in a higher way still. Matter is what hampers the acquisition of form by mind, and that which is immaterial in the highest degree has knowledge in the highest degree. Since God is immaterial in the highest degree, God has the highest form of knowledge. Thus God's immateriality entails God's intellect.

Aquinas also presents an argument from perfection, described by Norman Kretzmann as the most effective and important of Aquinas's several sorts of arguments for intellect in God.[17] I quote the argument here:

> Then, too, as was shown above, no perfection found in any genus of things is lacking to God. Nor on this account does any composition follow in Him. But among the perfections; of things the greatest is that something be intelligent, for thereby it is in a manner all things, having within itself the perfections of all things. God is, therefore, intelligent. [SCG 1.44]

In this argument, 'perfection' seems best glossed as 'form', since perfections are ranked in genera and so part of the general classificatory scheme of things. To say that no form of any thing is lacking to God seems odd at face value. How are forms of material things in God – say, cats, dogs, quarks and fleas? Obviously they do not exist in the same way in which they exist in those things – so they must exist intentionally in God. Aquinas cites Aristotle's famous comment in *De Anima* III.8 that the soul is in some sense all things, insofar as it can receive the form of all things. This is the manner in which forms exist in God, and so intellect must be predicated of God. However, this multiplicity of forms does not result in composition. The manner in which these forms exist in God, even intentionally, is simple, which will be examined below. It is interesting to note that Aquinas characterizes intelligence as the greatest of all perfections. He does not offer a reason for this, but one can imagine it has to do with the idea that greater powers and abilities are available to intelligent rather than non-intelligent entities. Aquinas, therefore, has argued that intellect exists in God by virtue of God's immateriality and God's perfection. Yet this intellect is simple and not distinct from God's own substance, so how does Aquinas seek to explain these features of divine cognition?

7.2.3   God's nature

Given that Aquinas has earlier argued, on the basis of the argument from motion, that God is pure actuality and has no potentiality, his account of God's cognition has to conform to this. And this is what seems most incomprehensible to Aquinas's critics, since God's unchangingness, impassivity and eternity seem to cut against God's knowing actual individuals changing in time. However, Aquinas argues that God does indeed know temporal individuals as individuals, so it remains to see how this is possible. The two central planks of his argument are that God knows other things in knowing God's own self and that God's knowledge is causal. Unlike human cognition, in which the environment impacts on the knower in a causal fashion, the causal direction is reversed in God's knowledge. Things exist insofar as God knows them, not vice versa [ST 1.14.8].

God's pure actuality is the feature which governs the whole discussion. Human cognition moves from potential knowing to actual knowing, from having the capacity to form concepts, to actualizing this. Thus, process and moving from potency to actuality characterize human cognition, and one can draw a distinction between concepts in the mind and the mind which entertains these concepts. Since God exhibits no potential, God's mind is fully actualized, and the ideas are not different from God's mind itself – which is not how things work in human cognition [ST 1.14.2]. That is, because of God's actuality, there is no real distinction to be drawn between the content and nature of God's mind. Because God is fully actual, God's knowledge is fully comprehensive – there is no deepening of God's knowledge. God's power to know is equal to God's actuality in existence – which is maximal [ST 1.14.3]. If it were otherwise and God's knowledge changed, or the object of God's knowledge were not God's own substance, then this would not be compatible with God's pure actuality. To reject this picture of divine cognition is to reject the account of God's actuality – but to defend God's actuality and simplicity leads inevitably to this account of divine cognition. Since there is no distinction of essence and existence in God, 'it follows from all the foregoing that in God, intellect and the object understood, and the intelligible species, and His act of understanding are entirely one and the same' [ST 1.14.4].

God's self-knowledge is complete and does not lack anything. But in knowing God's self, God knows that to which God's power extends. God is the source of existence of all things, and so God's knowledge also extends to all things.

> But the power of anything can be perfectly known only by knowing to what its power extends. Since therefore the divine power extends to other things by the very fact that it is the first effective cause of all things, as is clear from the aforesaid, God must necessarily know things other than Himself. [1.14.5]

Aristotle had argued that there is an exclusivity involved in the objects of God's cognition – either God knows the world or else knows God's own self.[18] For Aquinas, this is a false dichotomy. God knows the world *through* knowledge of self. The power of God, which extends to all, is known thoroughly by God, and hence all things are also known as sustained by this power. Hence the connection between God and the world is power sustaining all things in existence, and God knows all things through self-knowledge of this power. Nevertheless, the problem remains as to how the multiplicity of things known is compatible with God's simplicity. Aquinas accepts that there are many divine ideas [1.15.2], so surely this is blatantly inconsistent with simplicity.

As an initial clarification, it is useful to clarify what Aquinas understands by 'idea'. He does not mean that an idea is something subjective or psychological, but rather he conforms to Platonic usage – he says '"*Idea*" in Greek corresponds to "*forma*" in Latin' [ST 1.15.1]. Ideas therefore are patterns, exemplars, paradigms or forms. Aquinas employs the image of an architect using the pattern of a house to understand actual houses [ST 1.15.2], and he employs the term *ratio* to capture this notion. As noted above, he accepts Aristotle's criticism of Plato's forms as separated. It makes no sense to think of such things as existing on their own, as it were. Yet Aquinas notes in commenting on Aristotle 'even though this argument does away with the separate exemplars postulated by Plato, it still does not do away with the fact that God's knowledge is the exemplar of all things' [In Met 1.15. 233]. The problem with Plato's position is that it postulated universals as existing outside the mind. Aquinas accepts the existence of paradigmatic instances of forms, but not existing as separate individuals but rather as ideas within the mind of God. Aquinas makes a twofold distinction in the function of a form existing apart from the thing of which it is a form. In one way, it can be a pattern and operate without any conscious input on behalf of the agent – for example, in reproduction, where species replicate their forms. In another way, the form can exist in an intellectual way in an agent (e.g., the architect and the house), and is produced by means of conscious choice. Ideas exist in the mind of God in the latter way, and they are the likenesses (*similitudo*) by which things are made in the world.

But how does this not compromise simplicity, since 'ideas' imply multiplicity? To clarify this, it is useful to look again at Aquinas on the cause of multiplicity in the world. In ST 1.47.1, he says

> the distinction and multitude of things come from the intention of the first agent, who is God. For He brought things into being in order that His goodness be communicated to creatures, and be represented by them; and because his goodness could not be adequately represented by one creature alone.

Goodness, which is simple and uniform in God, is multiple and divided in creatures. Aquinas affirms again in his discussion of divine ideas that God's essence is simple. He says

> 'Idea' is not the name for the divine essence as such, but in so far as it is the likeness or intelligible nature of this or that thing. Hence there are said to be many Ideas in so far as the one essence provides the intelligibility of many natures. [ST1.15.2 ad1]

One way of making sense of this is to argue that the relations between God and created things do not exist in God, but only in created things. Following Geach, one could call them merely Cambridge properties in

God; the genuine multiplicity is in the world, not in God. However, Aquinas explicitly rejects this way out. If ideas in God are constituted by temporal creatures, then they do not exist from eternity in God [ST.1.15.2 ob4]. So these relations have to exist in some sense in God. Aquinas argues that they are, however, not real relations but intellectual relations. What is this distinction among relations, and what is the significance of its use?

In analysing the notion of relation, Aquinas follows Aristotle's account in the *Categories* and holds that four of the ten categories are more basic than the others [In Met 5.9. 891]. Substance states what a subject is (and is 'said of' a subject). Quantity and quality are in a subject absolutely, deriving from the matter and form of the subject respectively. Relation is not in a subject absolutely, but with reference to something else. Some kinds of relation are completely extrinsic to the subject – for example, when Socrates is clothed. Other forms of relation have some internal connection to the subject – and these are either in terms of action (the subject acts on something else) or passion (the subject is acted upon by something else).

Aquinas uses two distinctions to clarify different kinds of relation. One is the distinction between Predicamental Relations (*relationes secundum esse*) and Transcendental Relations (*relationes secundum dici*) [SS I.1.33.1ad1; QDP 7.10.ad 11; ST 1.13.7ad1]]. The term 'predicamental relations' refers to the relation itself and not to the things related (the relata) (e.g. the valley between two mountains). The term 'transcendental relations' refers to the things related (the mountains). Aquinas also uses another distinction between Real relations (*relationes reales*) and Logical relations (*relationes rationis*), with which it should not be confused. Real relations have a basis in extra-mental reality [QDP 7.9.ad1], whereas logical relations derive from the mind. Aquinas points out that some predicamental relations (picking out the relation itself) are in fact logical (e.g. right and left of a pillar). And some transcendental relations (picking out the relata) signify real relations (for example, knowledge) [QDP 7.10.11]. The reason that one acknowledges real relations at all is from the natural order of things to each other, and so he denies the anti-realist view that relations are all mind dependent. He further distinguished a third type of relation (as discussed above p. 161), characterized by the mixed relata involved. Given there are purely logical (Logical-Logical) and purely real (Real-Real) relations, there are also mixed relations (Real-Logical). Mixed relations happen when one of the relata is not of the same order as the other. Aquinas's example of this is knowledge. The side of the relation in which knowledge occurs is real, but is merely logical on the side of the thing known. So when I know that my computer is before me, one side of that relation, in me, is a real feature of me, but it is not a real feature in the computer, despite falling under the same relation.

What is God's relationship to creation? God is the cause of nature, but while this is real in the creature, it is logical in God [QDP 3.3; ST 1.13.7]. However, God's creative act is also God's knowledge. Aquinas says

> Now it is manifest that God causes things by His intellect, since His being is His act of understanding; and hence His knowledge must be the cause of things, in so far as His will is joined to it. [ST 1.14.8]

Note that this is the reverse of human cognition, in which extra-mental things cause human mental content. God's creative intellect causes everything else outside the divine mind.

> Natural things are midway between the knowledge of God and our knowledge: for we receive knowledge from natural things, of which God is the cause by His knowledge. Hence, as the natural objects of knowledge are prior to our knowledge, and are its measure, so, the knowledge of God is prior to natural things, and is the measure of them. [ST 1.14.8ad3]

The relationship of God to world is therefore one of knower to known, causer to caused. God knows many things, but knows them in a single act of knowledge. Aquinas makes a terminological clarification which removes the appearance of contradiction between divine simplicity and God's having many ideas [ST 1.15.2ad1]. There are many ideas in God in the sense that God knows many things. But there is only one means by which God knows – God's knowledge of the divine essence, which is perfect and known in all the ways in which it is knowable, including all the ways in which it can be participated. The core claim on which Aquinas's position rests is that a multiplicity can be understood in a simple, undifferentiated, perfect, eternal act of knowledge. Of course, there is no example of this available to us, since God's cognition is definitionally beyond anything humans can grasp. Nevertheless, some analogies from computational theory might be suggestive of ways in which a great deal of complexity is capturable in simpler form, which fits with the spirit of what Aquinas says.

7.2.4 Objects of divine knowledge

There are a number of potential objects of knowledge for God which raise conceptual problems given Aquinas's account of divine cognition.

If God's knowledge is the cause of things, can God know things which do not exist? If God knows evil, is God not thereby the cause of evil? Does God know individuals (if God's knowledge is of exemplar ideas)?

Things which do not exist can be distinguished into two classes – those which exist at some point in time and not at others, and those which never exist [ST 1.14.12] Those which exist at some point in time exist potentially as producible by God or by some creature, and are known by God in that way. Things which could be in existence, but never actually exist, are nevertheless known by God. The general principle governing Aquinas's treatment here is that things which do not exist in extra-mental reality may nevertheless exist in a different manner in the divine intellect. God's knowledge does assure the existence of everything possible and imaginable in the divine intellect, but not all of that comes into actual existence in creation. It also follows that God knows changing things, knows that some propositions are true at some times and false at others, but does so in an unchanging way [ST 1.14.16].

If God knows evil, is God not the cause of evil? Aquinas answers that evil is known through goodness, just as darkness is known by light, and so God's knowledge does not cause evil, but rather goodness. But, the objection goes, this is an imperfect form of knowledge (knowing indirectly), and hence it attributes imperfection to God. In response, Aquinas notes it would only be an imperfection if it were possible to know evil directly, but the nature of evil makes it such that it can only be known indirectly, so no imperfection arises [ST 1.14.10].

God knows individuals, according to Aquinas, but rejects certain possible ways in which this might be explained. They are not known through universal causes (via a kind of inference), because this would not yield genuine knowledge of individuality, and also God's knowledge is not inferential. Rather, God's knowledge extends as far as God's causation, and so God knows both form and matter, the latter of which is the principle of individuation. So God knows individuals in their individuality. Thus these objects of divine cognition do not pose problems for his account. However, the issue of God's knowledge of future contingent propositions is a significant problem for accounts of divine cognition.

7.2.5 Future contingents

One especially thorny puzzle about God's knowledge had been labelled the problem of future contingent propositions. These are sentences referring to some undetermined future event, which may go one way or another. If God knows the truth about, say, whether there will be a sea battle tomorrow, then it seems as if there is already a fact of the matter about this. Knowledge entails truth, and for God to know the truth-value of 'there will be a sea battle tomorrow' requires there to be a truth-maker – some fact which makes it true. Thus God's knowledge of the future seems to require the existence of the set of future facts, which makes the future determinate. An especially problematic consequence of this for Aquinas would be that it makes human free choice impossible. There seems to be an incompatibility between holding God's knowledge of future contingent truths on the one hand and human free choice on the other hand. Aquinas wants to hold both, so is this possible?

He tackles this in ST 1.14.13 (also SCG 1.67; QDV 2.12; QDM 16.7 and In PH 1.14). Firstly, he establishes that contingent events do exist in the world. Even though God is a necessary cause, it does not follow that every effect is necessary, since intermediate causation allows space for contingent effects in creation. So on an ontological level, he holds that contingency is a real feature of reality and also that God has knowledge of such a feature. The problem with God's knowledge of such contingent events is illustrated in the following inference: 'If God knew that this is going to happen, it will happen' (*Si Deus scivit hoc futurum esse, hoc erit*). God's knowledge seems to determine the future event – this proposition is necessary.

Aquinas rejects a number of possible solutions to this problem. One such appeals to a distinction between hard and soft facts about the past, hard being fully determinate (there was a sea battle in 1805), soft having an as yet undischarged future reference (God knew there will be a sea battle tomorrow). He denies that this option removes the problematical necessity involved. Another tries to replicate the appeal to intermediate causes as a way of blocking the necessity between God's knowing and the event having to happen. Aquinas, while accepting that intermediate causes can allow genuine indeterminacy in reality, denies that it is relevant in the logical context of the relation of antecedent to consequent in a proposition.

His own solution to the problem uses two key distinctions. He distinguishes knowledge from the perspective of eternity and knowledge from a temporal perspective, and he also distinguishes two different kinds of necessity – in things (*de re*) and in language (*de dicto*). If one considers any contingent event from the perspective of eternity, it is actual, present, determinate and the object of certain, necessary knowledge. The same event viewed from the perspective of its being future is potential, future, indeterminate and the object of conjectural knowledge. When such an event becomes present, for example, 'there is a sea battle happening now', it is actual, present, determinate and necessary. But our present, actual, determinate and necessary knowledge of the sea battle, does not mean that the sailors had no options or that it was predetermined. Similarly, Aquinas argues that God's knowledge from eternity, while it is necessary, is necessary in the same way as my knowledge that I am now typing is necessary. It leaves it causally open that I chose to do so. I might have chosen not to.

Thus the kind of necessity involved in God's knowledge of contingent events is *de dicto*, a kind of logical or definitional knowledge which is metaphysically different to the kind of deterministic necessity *de re* which would block free choice. A bachelor's being an unmarried man is true *de dicto*, but this does not mean that the poor man cannot get married by virtue of some deep *de re* condition that makes it necessary that he be unmarried. The necessity is definitional rather than real. Likewise, God's knowledge is necessary in a *de dicto* way, from the vantage point of an eternal present, but this does not determine contingent events, in particular human free choice. So Aquinas's solution to the problem of future contingent propositions makes essential use of his position on divine eternity.

7.3 Divine power

7.3.1 Introduction

In contemporary philosophy of religion, the topic of God's power is discussed under the title 'Omnipotence'.[19] Defining what exactly constitutes omnipotence has become a rather technical and detailed debate, invoking various distinctions and terms of art. An intuitive notion is 'God can do anything'. This is rooted in scriptural citations and also in the metaphysics of theism, a development of the idea of a reality which is purely actual, simple, eternal, good and intelligent. Yet there are obvious difficulties with such a definition, and it invites in response a shopping list of things which God clearly cannot do – for example, sin, sit down, fail, die. And this does not include more recondite puzzles such as whether God could create a stone too heavy to lift, or how God's power relates to God's goodness or human freedom.[20] So it seems there are many things which God cannot do, or which at the least constrain divine power. Does this then mean there is no omnipotence? Not necessarily. Various distinctions and adjustments to the definition need to be made. For example, one might think that God's not being able to sit down is a trivial objection, since it is not possible for a disembodied being to sit. However, this solution raises rather difficult questions about God's relationship to modality. How does God relate to necessity and possibility? Indeed, more pressingly, how does God relate to logic? If God is governed by logic, how does that impact on what is meant by God's omnipotence? Because few contemporary philosophers of religion defend the full classical theistic position, approaches to omnipotence vary greatly among them and differ to the approach of Aquinas. If God exists in time (is not eternal), is capable of being acted upon (is not impassible), can change (is not immutable) and has genuine internal complexity (is not simple), then the account of omnipotence will differ greatly from that of a theorist who accepts the classical position.

As I have constantly emphasized, Aquinas articulated a strong version of the classical position. I shall begin this analysis of his position on omnipotence with a discussion of what Aquinas understands by power and how it is instantiated in God. Indeed, he thinks that a distinct argument is required to show that God is omnipotent, having initially argued for power in God. Since it is an important part of his strategy to dissolve apparent objections by showing that they arise from contradictions, I also need to examine Aquinas's view of the relationship between God and logic. Furthermore, I shall examine the distinction between failure and success and look at the question of God's freedom. Finally, there is the interesting puzzle about whether God can change the past.

7.3.2 Power

Aquinas has a detailed discussion of what he means by power (*Potentia*), as one might expect, in the opening section of *De Potentia* [QDP 1.1]. There he draws a connection between power and act (*Actus*): 'we speak of power in relation to act'. Act is divided into two kinds. The most obvious form of act is operation, where some process is undertaken. Strictly speaking, an operation is an immanent activity in an agent (such as willing or thinking), whereas the term 'action' (*Actio*) is reserved for the transitive activity of acting on something else. But Aquinas does not distinguish between action and operation in this context.

A less obvious kind of act is form. Aquinas holds that form is the principle and the end of operation. That is to say, whenever something acts (e.g. fire burns wood), the kind of operation which occurs is constituted by the structure of the agent. That fire burns and ice freezes are examples of operations (heating and freezing) being established in virtue of the inner structure (form) of the agents causing the operation. This leads to an important distinction between two kinds of power. The kind of power associated with operation is active power, while the kind of power associated with form is passive power. His account becomes a little more complex in that form is ultimately the basis of both active and passive power. A thing can operate on something else by virtue of its form (I can manipulate this computer), and also it can be acted upon by something else in virtue of its form (I can get a headache from too much use of the computer). The important upshot of this discussion is that Aquinas distinguishes between active power, which operates on something else, and passive power, which allows something to be acted upon. While I have the passive power to be given a headache by the computer, my glasses (which are part of that same causal chain) do not.

Aquinas has consistently argued that God is to be characterized in terms of active power. God is the source of being for all other things, and as such is the source of actuality in everything else [SCG 2.7]. The causal arguments for God's existence are all established within a framework of potentiality and actuality, and God emerges from these as purely actual, not having any kind of potentiality – which view is the leitmotif of Aquinas's whole discussion of God's simplicity, immutability, impassibility, eternity, and so forth. Active power is linked to the perfection of any thing, and since God is maximally perfect, God exhibits maximal active power.

Yet there is the possibility of some confusion given the use of the same word (*Potentia*) for God's *power*, which Aquinas affirms, and *potential*, which Aquinas denies of God. The first objection to God's having power in the *Summa Theologiae* treatment is based on this equivocation [ST 1.25.1ob1]. It denies that God has *Potentia*, because there is no potential in God. In response, Aquinas clarifies that there are two kinds of power – active and passive. God has active power in a maximal way (*'in Deo maxime sit potentia active'*) and in no way has passive power.

A further worry is that this account of power is not compatible with divine simplicity. Since power has been characterized as a principle of operation, it seems that there is a distinction between God's essence and God's power, as between a principle and that which flows from it. If God's act is a manifestation of God's power, there seems to be a distinction between God's act and God's power, or between God's active power as productive of the being of others and God's power, the source of that action [QDP 1.1ad1]. Aquinas attributes the apparent complexity involved here to the human mode of thinking. There is absolutely no complexity involved in the divine essence, so no talk of a principle of the divine essence makes sense. It does make sense to speak of the principle of the divine operation, but this is a manner of speaking due to the mode of thinking for humans. A logical distinction exists between the divine essence and divine operation in human cognition, but this distinction does not pick out any real distinction in God.

In QDP 1.1ad10, Aquinas elaborates on how logical distinctions arise in this way. Concepts relate to reality in two ways. The first way is immediate, in which whatever the concept designates exists in extramental reality, for example, a human being or a stone. In the second way, the mind reflects on its own structures and generates concepts which do not pick out entities in reality, but rather capture something of the intelligible structure of thought, which is nevertheless rooted in reality. Aquinas's example is the general notion of 'animal'. What exists in reality are cats, dogs, cows and so forth, but the concept of 'animal' is generated by reflection on the common features of these various species. The concepts of such genera are mediate. They connect to reality, but not immediately in the manner of first-order concepts.

As humans reflect on God, this process operates. Human cognition thinks of creatures as being dependent on the creator, which is something real in reality. However, to think of this relation of creature to creator, human cognition poses the other side of the relation in God. God is construed as the first principle, and so God's power is seen as the principle of the effects evident in creation. Yet for Aquinas, this side of the relation is logical, arising from the human mode of thought. In reality, in God's essence, there is no distinction between essence, principle and act. 'God's activity, however, is not distinct from his power; each is the divine essence, identical with the divine existence' [ST 1.25. ad2].

7.3.3   Omnipotence

Brian Leftow has recently noted two key questions in relation to omnipotence. The first is about the degree of power God might have, and the second is about the scope of that power.[21] Aquinas engages with the first question by relating God's power to infinity. He has already argued that God is infinite [ST 1.7], and as I shall discuss below, this is directly connected to the denial of composition in God. He distinguishes two different ways of thinking about infinity [QDP 1.2]. The first is associated with privation and found in quantities – it connotes something unbounded, but deficient by virtue of this unboundedness. The key instance of this is prime matter, which lacks form. Its lack of form makes it both infinite and deficient [SCG 1.43]. The second kind of infinity is associated with qualitative magnitude, and is negative rather than privative. That is, it denotes a lack of boundedness or limit, which is not something missing, but rather a kind of perfection. In God, this kind of infinity comes from simplicity. The existence of each thing is bounded by its essence. For example, the kind of existence a horse has is contracted or bounded by the form of horse. However, in God there is no distinction between essence and existence, and therefore God's existence is unbounded; it is infinite. This is clearly to be understood in the manner of intensive magnitude discussed above – God's existence is the perfection of all other kinds of existence [QDP 1.2, ST 1.25.2]. That God is infinite in this way allows Aquinas to answer the question above about what degree of power God has – it is infinite.

In the *Summa Theologiae*, Aquinas initially discusses the meaning of power and how God's power is infinite, before broaching the question of God's omnipotence [ST 1.25.1–3]. He notes there that it is difficult to come to a clear definition of what one means by God's omnipotence. In QDP 1.7, he gives an interesting analysis as to why it is that such a definition is difficult. He argues there that instead of giving a definition (*ratio*) of God's power, theorists tend to confuse this definitional process with either giving a cause of God's omnipotence (which is God's infinity) or discussing the perfection of God's power (God's impassibility) or the way in which God has power (God can do whatever God wills essentially and by nature). The problem with such approaches is that they miss the relation between an operation and its object. That is, they do not attend to the link between God's active power and the objects to which it extends. For Aquinas, this link is captured by invoking the notion of non-contradiction. God can do whatever does not imply a contradiction, and this answers Leftow's second question, about the range of God's power.

To make sense of Aquinas's views on omnipotence and contradiction takes one to his views on modality. This topic has arisen in a variety of places earlier in this book. Scientific knowledge, for Aquinas, is of what is necessary, and the logical sequence of scientific propositions mirrors the underlying structure of reality [see above p. 68]. The Third Way rests on contingency and necessity, and the meaning of these terms was discussed, showing how Aquinas's account of God's necessity differs from that of, for example, Gottfried Leibniz [see above p. 149]. In uncovering the latent resources Aquinas has for responding to naturalism, the difference between logical and metaphysical necessity was addressed [see above p. 167].

In discussing God's omnipotence, Aquinas needs to clarify the notion of possibility, since he uses this notion to analyse the meaning of contradiction. God can make to exist whatever is possible, but possibility can be understood in a variety of ways [QDP 1.3.corp]. If possibility is viewed as a relative notion, it must be considered in respect of some particular power. One might say that God can do whatever is possible to any creature, but theists want to say that God can do much more than this (and Aquinas's rejection of this approach would put him at odds with those current theorists who speak of maximal power construed in a relational fashion).[22] However, if one says that God can do that which is possible for God's power to do, this is uninformative and circular, so Aquinas rejects relative possibility as an option. Absolute possibility on the other hand is captured in propositions in which the predicate is not incompatible with the subject, and in ST 1.25.3 this is the way Aquinas seeks to explain omnipotence – God can do whatever is absolutely possible, or putting it another way, God can do whatever does not imply a contradiction.

One might note here how this differs from another approach to omnipotence, that associated with René Descartes.[23] Descartes holds that God has power even over the laws of logic and mathematics and can alter them, and hence is not bound by contradiction. However, as with the Euthyphro dilemma discussed above [p. 193ff], Aquinas does not think that logic (like goodness) is something which can be arbitrarily changed. But this is not because there is a source of normativity independent of God, but rather that logic and goodness are internally connected to God's nature. Since goodness, truth and being are transcendental concepts crossing all the categories and existing in God in a pre-eminent way, there is an internal connection between the principles of logic (which are actually principles of being) and God's mode of existence.

Geach has insightfully distinguished different ways of articulating omnipotence.[24] The first is one in which absolutely anything can be done by God, including bringing about contradictions (the Cartesian view stated above) – this is clearly not Aquinas's position. The second is that God can do anything that is describable in a logically consistent proposition. However, there are a number of logically consistent propositions which one would want to deny of God – God sins, God fails, God creates something too heavy to lift. Now, given that these scenarios make logically consistent propositions while associated with creatures (unlike, say, making a round square), these scenarios are not consistent with being done by God, given God's nature. So Geach gives a third account of omnipotence in which 'God can do x' is true only when 'God does x' is logically consistent. This rules out sinning, failing, and so forth. The nature of God is part of the package, which includes the logical content of the proposition in determining whether the whole is consistent or not. So, for example, 'X sins' is logically possible when X is a human, but not when X is God.

The paradox of the stone, discussed by Denys the Areopagite and Averroes and made classic in a series of discussions in the 1970s, is a stock objection to divine omnipotence.[25] Can God create a stone so heavy it cannot be lifted? If yes, then there is something God cannot do, namely create such a stone. If no, then there is something God cannot do, namely lift such a stone. The upshot of this semantic paradox is that it seems omnipotence is an incoherent notion. How might Aquinas respond to such an objection? It is clear that his way of dealing with such issues is to hold that divine power is not impugned if one says that God cannot do something because it leads to a contradiction. God cannot create a square circle because the subject and predicate of such a proposition are incompatible with each other, and so there is nothing to create there. How might this fit the paradox of the stone case? Aquinas believes that God cannot limit the scope of God's power. Is that inability not a lack, or a constraint? Aquinas deploys the distinction between failure and achievement [ST 1.25.3ad2] to argue that whatever implies a deficiency is not compatible with God's nature. God does not tire, fail, sin, die, precisely because God is omnipotent – God's not being able to do these things does not compromise omnipotence. If we apply this to the case of the stone, the paradox arises because one action of God leads to an incapacity to perform another act. But such self-limitation is incompatible with God's nature. Recall that all the divine attributes, for Aquinas, are governed by divine simplicity. Hence there is no composition in God's act – the kind of complexity involved in one part of an action negating a different part is ruled out by the governing intuition of simplicity. This could well be an instance of a theoretical advantage of simplicity, despite its apparently counterintuitive status.

If this solution works against the paradox of the stone, there are further problems with omnipotence. Geach himself objects to this third way of characterizing omnipotence and thinks it is not Aquinas's full position, due to an example he takes from ST 1.25.4, which involves paradox arising from God's relation to time. I shall now turn to issues emerging for divine omnipotence which involve the notion of time.

7.3.4 Omnipotence and time

Can God change the past? Aquinas is clear that this is not possible [ST 1.25.4]. Yet in an objection, he notes a quite powerful argument against this. God can bring sight to the blind or the dead to life – things which are against physical possibilities in nature. And whether Socrates stands or sits is a contingent possible state of affairs, so why cannot God alter such a contingent past state of affairs, making Socrates to have sat instead of stood? In response, he observes that the kinds of natural impossibilities noted in the objection are relative impossibilities – impossible relative to the physical circumstances, but not absolutely impossible – whereas Aquinas believes that changing the past entails an absolute impossibility, a contradiction. To change the past is to make a state of affairs both exist and not exist at the same time in the same manner, and so is impossible. But one might reasonably query this.[26] By changing the past, surely God has obliterated the earlier state of affairs and so there is no contradiction. If God were to change the timing of the Battle of Clontarf from 1,000 years ago today to 999, surely there would be no trace of the original event left to generate the contradiction?

It is clear that Aquinas does not accept this. In numerous locations in his work he affirms that God cannot change the past [e.g. SCG 2.25; QDP 1.3; In NE 6.2], and follows Aristotle and Augustine on this. The above objection to his view arises from the perspective of belonging to the temporal sequence. And indeed the whole problem of altering the past arises from existing in time. God, however, does not exist in time and relates to the temporal sequence from eternity in a relationship of simultaneity [see above p. 182]. Therefore, every event in the temporal sequence is eternally present to God. On this understanding, to change a past event would be to have a contradiction present to God in eternity – that Clontarf is both happening and not happening to God in the same eternal present. And furthermore, for Clontarf to cease to occur in 1014 would be to change God's eternal knowledge, which is not an option for Aquinas. So perhaps this is his background reasoning.

But what then of future contingent events? Does not the same consideration apply, such that God cannot change future contingent events? Well, to God they occur as present, but contingent in their nature and causes. To humans they are future and not determined, by virtue of the chains of contingent causes leading to them. God does not change such events, inasmuch as God does not change – they are also eternally present. So in one way of answering the question, God cannot change the future, in the sense that God's eternal act is once and for all, and creation with its temporal unfolding is instantaneously and eternally present to the divine mind – God knows tensed propositions, even though the divine knowledge is unchanging [ST 1.14.15ad3]. But this is not a lack in God's power, as distinct from a feature of the way in which God's power operates, eternally and unchangingly. Humans are aware of the past and its fixity qua past, even though the events had been contingent. God is aware of the future, and its fixity as eternally present, even though the events are contingent. But this fixity then raises a question about God's freedom – does God act freely or is God's acting necessitated in some way?

7.3.5   Omnipotence and freedom

As has been seen, for Aquinas, God's power extends to all creation. But did God *have* to create the world? Some considerations from Neoplatonic philosophy seem to point in this direction. A common maxim derived from Neoplatonism is that goodness tends to extend itself, *'bonum est diffusionem sui'*. Aquinas cites this in his discussion of goodness, but links the operative power of goodness to final causation, rather than efficient causation, which seems to have been the way it was understood in Neoplatonism [ST 1.5.4ad2]. When Plotinus speaks about the derivation of everything else from the One (the ineffable metaphysical source of reality), he speaks of 'emanation', which seems to be a kind of natural process, sometimes metaphorically characterized as a kind of 'boiling over', a spilling of being into the rest of reality. Whether this is actually Plotinus's view or not,[27] Aquinas rejects such a conception of creation. He distinguishes between natural causes, which operate solely according to their nature, yielding determinate results (e.g., frogs begetting frogs), and intelligent causes, who operate with choice and who may produce a wide variety of results [ST 1.19.1]. God's power is like the latter, and Aquinas, to speak of God's power, uses the metaphor of the architect's making objects on the basis of plans [ST 1.27.1ad3].

As seen above, God's absolute power is such that God can create anything which does not lead to a contradiction. But Aquinas draws a distinction between God's absolute power and God's ordered power, which is God's power as actually exercised [ST 1.25.5ad.1]. God's absolute power ranges over all logically possible states of affairs, while God's ordered power relates to what actually exists, as established by God's choice. In God there is will and intellect. I have discussed above Aquinas's reasons for postulating intellect of God. Will follows naturally from the establishment of intellect – as God knows the divine goodness, God also desires it, which is the nature of the will. However, there is no logical need for God to create anything at all; God from eternity is self-sufficient. Hence, the decision to create (from eternity, which implies no change in God) is completely free [ST 1.19.4]. One of the implications of such a free choice is that there is no metaphysical necessity to God's creating the world. This is at the basis of Aquinas's refusal to accept that there are good philosophical arguments to show that the world cannot be eternal. It is philosophically an open question whether the world has always existed or not. Now this is a different point from whether creation occurs at all – since even if the world existed from eternity, it would be constituted in such a way that it lacks an explanation for its existence within itself, and requires the existence of a further principle to explain it. So there would still be creation of an everlasting world. The question whether the world started or not is not capable of being rationally deduced, and the reason for this is that it rests on God's free choice.

There are some constraints on how God creates, but these are based in the general constraint discussed above of not entailing contradiction. Could God have created different things? Certainly [ST 1.25.5]! But God could not have created, for example, humans without also creating rational souls (which are essential to them). This is of a piece with the thought that God could not create triangles without three inner angles, or have made the number four greater than it is. These are formal constraints on the nature of things, the denial of which would lead to contradiction (and go further to emphasize the way in which, for Aquinas, logic is not merely about the structure of our thoughts but is world-involving). But it is open to God to have created different kinds of things to those which were actually created. So Aquinas does not believe in the notion of the 'best of all possible worlds', associated with Leibniz.[28] The world could always be better in a multiplicity of ways. Geach rejects the notion of the 'best of all possible worlds', arguing that, like 'the highest number', it does not make sense.[29]

Finally, God's power obviously also extends to human beings, but not in such a way that human freedom is impugned. As already noted, Aquinas thinks that God's causal power sustaining humans in existence is a precondition of free action – so God's causal role is compatible with human freedom. He nevertheless does speak of predestination, citing St Paul and Augustine in presenting his views. To make sense of his views on predestination, one needs to consider his account of providence. He thinks of God's providence as underpinning the basic structure of reality [ST 1.22.1]. The inner dynamic structure of each thing, internally ordered by form, which has an intrinsic connection to teleology and which exists from eternity in the exemplar ideas of God, constitutes an overall pattern working towards an end. Some structures in the world are necessary, some are contingent, some work in a determinate way, some make free choices, but all are governed by this pattern. God is the end of the whole system, but creatures tend towards that end in two ways [ST 1.23.1]. In one way they do so in accord with their own nature, actualizing themselves and seeking to perfect themselves in a natural manner. However, another way is to achieve the vision of God which is beyond the capacity of any creature on its own power. The planned sending of any rational creature to that end is called predestination. However, human free choice is still operational in this structure. Some people can reject God, but this is on account of their own freely chosen actions. So Aquinas thinks that some people experience reprobation, the loss of eternal life. But he is explicit that the causal process in reprobation differs from predestination [ST 1.23.3.ad2]. The path away from God is caused by human free action (which nevertheless requires God's causal input even to exist). Aquinas uses a distinction between God's antecedent will and God's consequent will [ST 1.19.6] – the former is present in God's general desire for all rational creatures to achieve eternal life, while the latter is God's will in interaction with the facts of free human choice. He uses the image of a judge who wills a prisoner to die, even though he would in general want the prisoner to live. Those who fail to achieve eternal life are akin to such a prisoner, willed to reprobation by God, but on the basis of their own free choice.

Conclusion

The details of Aquinas's account of predestination led into impenetrable theological thickets and pitched battles between Molinists and Thomists at the start of the seventeenth century, which resulted in a forced truce, and I shall not even attempt to chart the course of that debate. However, it is significant to note, at this point, that the discussion moves into more properly theological territory with this question. The question of grace, the issues of the Incarnation, the Trinity, the Church, sacraments, and so on all play a role in Aquinas's developed response to questions about how humans relate to God. So even though I have ended this presentation of Aquinas's philosophy of religion with some reflection on how God's power operates concurrently with human freedom, the full articulation of Aquinas's thought leads inevitably into the realm of theology. By no means does he abandon philosophy when he presents his theological vision, but there he uses resources which methodologically he thought not available to philosophers qua philosophers. Exploring Aquinas's philosophical theology is the task of a different book.

Notes

1 Philosophy and Theology

1. Russell (2004) p. 427.
2. Kenny (1969a) p. 2.
3. In NE 5.11, 1013.
4. ST 2–2.95.5.
5. ST 1–2. 105.4.
6. *De Regno ad regem Cypri*.
7. ST 2–2.11.3.
8. I have in mind here work such as the magisterial Wippel (2000), which engages with nothing outside of Aquinas's texts, sources and commentators. It is interesting to contrast this approach with the equally impressive Stump (2003), who relates Aquinas's work to relevant parts of Daniel Dennett, Harry Frankfurt, Alvin Plantinga, Oliver Sacks, Sydney Shoemaker and Richard Swinburne, among others.
9. *'quia studium philosophiae non est ad hoc quod sciatur quid homines senserint, sed qualiter se habeat veritas rerum'*. In DC 1.22.8.
10. For more on this topic, see O'Grady (2002) and Baghramian (2004). This objection was pressed on me by Prof Baghramian.
11. See Rhees (1981) p. 159 and see also Kerr (2008) ch. 2. Dawkins (2006) p. 77.
12. See, for example, Rea and Crisp (2009).
13. Kenny (2006) pp. 47–48.
14. BonJour (1997) Katz (2000).
15. See, for example, Everitt (2003), Nagasawa (2011), Oppy (2009).
16. See, for example, Hoffman and Rosenkranz (2002), Hughes (1995), Swinburne, (1993).
17. Hick, (2004) p. 153
18. Ganeri (2007) and O'Grady (2005b).
19. Tugwell (1988) p. 203.
20. Throughout this book I shall use the English Dominican translation of the *Summa Theologiae*, single-handedly produced by Laurence Shapcote op in the early twentieth century, as it is consistent and stays close to the Latin.
21. There was a longstanding debate in medieval philosophy as to whether being in general or the supreme being is the subject matter of metaphysics. Note how Aquinas in these texts points to God as the principle or source of being, and hence as strictly outside the scope of the object of the science. See Wippel (2000) ch. 1.
22. One might note a contrast with continental philosophy of religion on these issues. See Caputo (2007) or Kearney (2011) for examples.
23. Gale (1993), Rowe (1998), Swinburne (2004).
24. ST 1.2.2, SCG 10–11.
25. See Plantinga (1983) for a classic statement of what has become known as 'reformed epistemology'.

26. See e.g. ST 1.13.2.
27. See e.g. QDV 2.2 on Empedocles; Super Heb 1.6 on Eriugena.
28. See Popper (2002) for the distinction between context of discovery and context of justification.
29. Jordan (1993).
30. ST 1.1.8 ad2.
31. For the debate on the purpose of SCG – see Weisheipl (1983), Jordan (1986), Tugwell (1988), Te Velde (1994), Gauthier (2002), Torrell (2005).
32. See Kretzmann (1997).
33. Kerr (2002a) and (2003).
34. Velecky (1994).
35. Kerr (2002a) p. 56.
36. Kerr (2002a) p. 64.
37. Kerr (2002a) p. 65 (One wonders how this fits with Aquinas's crediting Aristotle, Avicenna and Maimonides with natural theology).
38. See Pasnau (2002) p. 30ff for Aquinas on ancient philosophy.
39. See ST 1.13.4 and O'Callaghan (2003) ch.1 for a detailed account.
40. In PA 1.4 'For a definition expresses what a name signifies…. But we take the signification of a name from what those who use the name generally intend to signify by it.
41. See O'Grady (2000).
42. See Carnap (1967) for the original usage of the term and Chalmers (2012) for a recent development of the idea.
43. Te Velde (2006).
44. Te Velde (2006) p. 171.
45. Te Velde (2006) p. 4.
46. Te Velde (2006) p. 38.
47. Te Velde (2006) p. 2.
48. Te Velde (2006) p. 172.
49. See ch. 6.1 for the triplex via.
50. 'I entitle *transcendental* all knowledge which is occupied not so much with objects as with the mode of our knowledge of objects in so far as this mode of knowledge is to be possible *a priori*. Kant (1989) A12/B25.
51. Kant (1989) A23/B37 ff.
52. Kant (1989) A236/B295 ff.
53. Kant (1989) A 204/B249 ff.
54. Chignell (2009).
55. Loux and Zimmerman (2003).
56. For a brief introduction to Karl Barth (1886–1968), see Kennedy (2010).pp. 69–84; for a longer study see Webster (2004).
57. For a survey, see Caputo (2007).
58. Kant (1989) A631–2/B659–60. See Wolterstorff (2009) for a helpful discussion.
59. Wittgenstein (1975), 3.031, 5.123, 6.372 ,6.432.
60. See Rhees (1981) p. 159.
61. Arrington (2001) p. 177–178.
62. See, for example, Kenny (1993) and McCabe (1969, 2008). For a study of McCabe's contribution, see O'Grady (2012).

2 Aquinas's Contexts

1. For a good overview of the main strands of medieval thought, see Kenny (2005).
2. Dante (1996) IV.131.
3. The main biographical source on Aquinas is Torrell (2005), which has replaced Weisheipl (1975) as the standard biography. Also very useful is Tugwell (1988).
4. Kretzmann (1997) p. 2.
5. Boyle (1982) is an influential study of the intended audience of the ST.
6. See Te Velde (2006).
7. Anscombe and Geach (1961) p. 69.
8. Such an interpretation of Plato can be found in Aristotle's *Metaphysics* Bk 1, ch. 6, and was influential on Aquinas. See his In Met 1.10.
9. See Barnes (2002) ch. 8.
10. See Garfield (1995) p. 103ff.
11. See Danto (1965) ch. 1.
12. See Moran (1999) ch. 11.
13. See Simons (2011).
14. See Barnes (2002) ch. 9.
15. See Radhakrishnan and Moore (1967).
16. See *Metaphysics* Bk1 for Aristotle's discussion of his predecessors' views on change and identity.

3 Reason and Faith

1. See Broadie (2009).
2. Russell (1993) p. 138.
3. Dawkins (2006).
4. Putnam (1981) ch. 5.
5. 'A rule of thinking which would absolutely prevent me from acknowledging certain kinds of truth if those kinds of truth were really there, would be an irrational rule'. James (2003) *The Will to Believe* Section X.
6. Dawkins (2006), p. 308.
7. Tertullian (1951) ch. 7.
8. See Evans (1998) chs. 6–7.
9. See Cantwell Smith (1998) ch. 1.
10. For a good exploration of the issues associated with fideism, see Evans (1998).
11. This distinction originates with Wilfred Sellars. See O'Shea (2007) ch. 5.
12. Evans (1998).
13. See Tugwell (1988) p. 279ff for a discussion of the intellectual aspect of contemplation.
14. Plantinga (2000) ch. 3.
15. Although one might not be able to offer reasons for all of one's beliefs.
16. Plantinga (1993) ch.1.
17. For a representative account, see Audi (2010).
18. See MacDonald (1993) and Stump (2003) for contrasting interpretations.
19. Wittgenstein (1969) passim.

20. Putnam (1981) chs. 1–2.
21. See SCG 1.4, 1.8, ST 1.1.
22. See Jordan (1993) for a good discussion of the transformation of Aristotelian virtue theory into theology.
23. Strictly speaking, Aquinas thinks we know that the proposition 'God exists' is true, since we do not actually know God's existence, since it exceeds our intellectual grasp.
24. McCabe (2008) p. 79.
25. See Hick (2004) and Cantwell Smith (1998).
26. For example, QDV 2.5.ad7; QDV 2.12.ad7; ST 1.12.4; ST 1.14.1ad3.
27. Cantwell Smith (1998) p. 12.
28. Ibid. p. 87.
29. *Summa Theologiae*, Vol. 31, Blackfriars edn, p. 82, n.i.

4 Arguments for God's Existence

1. See texts cited in Ch.1 above, pp. 10–11.
2. ST 1.3. proem 'Having recognized that a certain thing exists, we have still to investigate the way in which it exists, that we may come to understand what it is that exists. Now we cannot know what God is, but only what he is not, we must therefore consider the ways in which God does not exist, rather than the ways in which he does'.
3. This position is sometimes called 'evidentialism'. See Plantinga (2000) p. 70ff for a discussion.
4. Quine (1969) p. 83.
5. Rowe (1998) p. 255ff.
6. See Craig (1980) p. 158.
7. SS, 1.d.3.q.1; SCG 1.13,15; CT 3; ST 1.2.3.
8. In Phys 7.2, 8.9; In Met 12.5.
9. Super Io, prol; Super Rom I, l.6.
10. QDV 5.2; QDP 3.5.
11. DEE ch.4.
12. Kenny (2005) p. 189.
13. See ST 1.2.2, but also QDV 10.12 where Anselm is mentioned.
14. Kretzmann (1998) p. 2.
15. Representatives would include Maritain, (1955), Gilson (1957), and Reith (1958).
16. Kenny (1969) p. 1.
17. Mackie (1982).
18. Swinburne (2004) p. 136.
19. See Kretzmann (1998), Davies (1985, 1992, 2011), MacDonald (1991), Stump (2003), Hughes, G. (1995), Hughes, C. (1989).
20. *Prima autem et manifestior via est, quae sumitur ex parte motus. Certum est enim, et sensu constat, aliqua moveri in hoc mundo. Omne autem quod movetur, ab alio movetur. Nihil enim movetur, nisi secundum quod est in potentia ad illud ad quod movetur, movet autem aliquid secundum quod est actu. Movere enim nihil aliud est quam educere aliquid de potentia in actum, de potentia autem non potest aliquid reduci in actum, nisi per aliquod ens in actu, sicut calidum in actu, ut ignis, facit*

lignum, quod est calidum in potentia, esse actu calidum, et per hoc movet et alterat ipsum. Non autem est possibile ut idem sit simul in actu et potentia secundum idem, sed solum secundum diversa, quod enim est calidum in actu, non potest simul esse calidum in potentia, sed est simul frigidum in potentia. Impossibile est ergo quod, secundum idem et eodem modo, aliquid sit movens et motum, vel quod moveat seipsum. Omne ergo quod movetur, oportet ab alio moveri. Si ergo id a quo movetur, moveatur, oportet et ipsum ab alio moveri et illud ab alio. Hic autem non est procedere in infinitum, quia sic non esset aliquod primum movens; et per consequens nec aliquod aliud movens, quia moventia secunda non movent nisi per hoc quod sunt mota a primo movente, sicut baculus non movet nisi per hoc quod est motus a manu. Ergo necesse est devenire ad aliquod primum movens, quod a nullo movetur, et hoc omnes intelligunt Deum.

21. QDV 5.2; SCG 1.13; QDP 3.5; In Phys 7.2; In Met 7; Comp 3.
22. Aquinas elaborates on the meaning of *motus* in In Phys 7.8.
23. Te Velde has an interesting discussion of the meaning of *motus* and whether it is observational or conceptual. Te Velde (2006) p. 55ff.
24. Kenny (1969) p. 22.
25. Russell (1993) p. 140.
26. See for example Mackie (1982) p. 87ff.
27. ST I.46.2.
28. ST 1.46.2.
29. ST 1.46.2.
30. Smart and Haldane (2002) p. 117.
31. ST 1.2.3 second way.
32. Sadowsky (2000) p. 239.
33. Optics Bk 3, Part 1.
34. MacDonald (1991).
35. *Tertia via est sumpta ex possibili et necessario, quae talis est. Invenimus enim in rebus quaedam quae sunt possibilia esse et non esse, cum quaedam inveniantur generari et corrumpi, et per consequens possibilia esse et non esse. Impossibile est autem omnia quae sunt, talia esse, quia quod possibile est non esse, quandoque non est. Si igitur omnia sunt possibilia non esse, aliquando nihil fuit in rebus. Sed si hoc est verum, etiam nunc nihil esset, quia quod non est, non incipit esse nisi per aliquid quod est; si igitur nihil fuit ens, impossibile fuit quod aliquid inciperet esse, et sic modo nihil esset, quod patet esse falsum. Non ergo omnia entia sunt possibilia, sed oportet aliquid esse necessarium in rebus. Omne autem necessarium vel habet causam suae necessitatis aliunde, vel non habet. Non est autem possibile quod procedatur in infinitum in necessariis quae habent causam suae necessitatis, sicut nec in causis efficientibus, ut probatum est. Ergo necesse est ponere aliquid quod sit per se necessarium, non habens causam necessitatis aliunde, sed quod est causa necessitatis aliis, quod omnes dicunt Deum.*
36. See Wippel (2000) p. 462ff. for a survey of interpretations of this argument.
37. See Melia (2003) ch. 1 for a discussion.
38. See Boghossian (1999).
39. See Klima (2002).
40. See MacIntosh (1998).
41. Note the distinction between eternity and eternality. Eternity means existing outside of time, and eternality means existing within infinite time.
42. Geach (1970).
43. Davies (2001).

44. Owens (1980).
45. Lovejoy (1990) ch. 3.
46. ST 1.46.2.
47. DEE 4.7. See Maurer (1983) p. 20n33 for a survey of the scholarship.
48. Maurer (1983) p. 26.
49. Kretzmann (1997) pp. 88, 97.
50. *Quinta via sumitur ex gubernatione rerum. Videmus enim quod aliqua quae cognitione carent, scilicet corpora naturalia, operantur propter finem, quod apparet ex hoc quod semper aut frequentius eodem modo operantur, ut consequantur id quod est optimum; unde patet quod non a casu, sed ex intentione perveniunt ad finem. Ea autem quae non habent cognitionem, non tendunt in finem nisi directa ab aliquo cognoscente et intelligente, sicut sagitta a sagittante. Ergo est aliquid intelligens, a quo omnes res naturales ordinantur ad finem, et hoc dicimus Deum.*
51. See for example Davies (2004) ch. 4.
52. William Paley *Natural Theology*, excerpted in Davies (2000) pp. 253ff.
53. Davies (2004) p. 75.
54. David Hume, *Dialogues Concerning Natural Religion*, excerpted in Davies (2000) pp. 260ff.
55. Davies (2004) p. 76.
56. Swinburne (2004).
57. QDV 5.2.
58. Boethius (1973) p. 166.
59. ST 1.22.2 ad1.
60. Gjertson (1989) p. 223.
61. Gjertson (1989) p. 225.
62. See John Carriero (2009) for an excellent study.
63. *Meditations* 4.6.
64. Molière *La Malade Imaginaire*, 3rd Intermission.
65. Oderberg (2008) p. 269.
66. Geach (1961) p. 101ff.
67. Kenny (1969) pp. 104–105.

5   Objections to God's Existence

1. Hume (2008) p. 100.
2. See Smart (1998) ch. 9 for a discussion.
3. Such as Advaita Vedanta. See Radhakrishnan and Moore (1967).
4. Adams and Adams (1990) p. 1.
5. Mackie (1971).
6. Plantinga (1971) and Draper (2009) p. 335 on the influence of Plantinga.
7. See Howard-Snyder (1996).
8. See Plantinga (1971) for a classic statement, and McCabe (2007) ch. 6 offers a good analysis of how this relates (or rather does not relate) to Aquinas's position.
9. Swinburne (2004) ch. 11.
10. See Philips (2012).
11. See Davies (2011) ch. 9 for a clear account.
12. Hume (1978) p. 469.
13. Moore (1903) pp. 46–58.

14. There is not a full conceptual mapping of *malum culpae* onto what is known as natural evil, since Aquinas did not believe it existed prior to the fall of Adam, hence the name 'evil of blame'.
15. There is a further complication in that Aquinas believes, for theological reasons, that evil did not exist before the fall of Adam, and so the 'world we live in' refers here to the post-lapsarian world. See Davies (2003a) pp. 43–48 for an account.
16. See Stump (2003) ch. 9 for a good overview.
17. Geach rather unkindly refers to 'Hume's logically sluttish ways', while challenging the simple acceptance of a Humean account of the logic of causation. Geach (1969) p. 76.
18. See Davies (2003b) for a discussion of the differences.
19. Austin (1962) p. 68n.1.
20. McDermott (2011)
21. See ST 1.1.8ad2, ST 1.62.5c.
22. Camus (1955).
23. Davies (2011) p.129.
24. Kenny (2006) p. 24.
25. McCabe (2008) p. 123.
26. Blackfriars edition of ST, Vol. 16, p. xv.
27. Rea (2002) p. 1.
28. See Richardson (2008), O'Grady (1999).
29. Spade (1982) p. 188.
30. See above p. 18.
31. Quine (1953) p. 22.
32. MacDonald (1993) p. 169.
33. O'Callaghan (2003).
34. Jacobs (2002).

6   God's Nature: The Way of Negation

1. See Rogers (2000) for a thorough overview.
2. See above p. 99.
3. Hume (2008) Part V.
4. Mackie (1971).
5. Pascal (1995) p. 178.
6. See Davies (2003b) for a useful discussion.
7. Swinburne (1993) ch. 12.
8. Plantinga (1980).
9. Davies (2003b) p. 380.
10. Plantinga (1980) p. 47.
11. Kenny (2002) p. 193.
12. For an authoritative overview, see Kerr (2002a).
13. Kerr (2002a) ch. 4.
14. See for example Knasas (2006) and Shanley (2006b).
15. Kretzmann (1997) ch. 3.
16. For a classic discussion of the origin of the ST, see Boyle (1982).
17. O'Rourke (1992) pp. 14ff.
18. Shanley (2006a) p. 202.
19. See for example ST 1.79.9, QDV.15.2.

20. Herbert McCabe remarks in his notes on Vol. 3 of the Blackfriars edition of the ST, 'In the opinion of the present translator too much has been made of St. Thomas's alleged teaching on analogy', p. 106.
21. See McInerny (1996) ch. 1 with the self-explanatory title, 'Where Cajetan Went Wrong'.
22. See Plantinga (1980), Woltertorff (1991), Davies (2003b).
23. See Plotinus (1991) VI.9. O'Meara (1995) has a good discussion in ch. 5.
24. Augustine (2003) XI.10.
25. Anselm (1998) *Monologion* ch. 16.
26. Kenny (2002) p. 165.
27. In Met 1.10. 151ff; ST 1.6.4.
28. Gilson (1957).
29. Fabro (1963) and Geiger (1953). For more recent work, see O'Rourke (1992) and Boland (1996).
30. Rocca (2004), p. 283.
31. See Casey (1987), McInerny (1990).
32. Kenny (2002) p. v.
33. Ibid.p. 192.
34. Kenny (2002) p. vi.
35. See Wippel (2000) p. 137n14; Rocca (2004) p. 248.
36. Rocca (2004) pp. 247–248.
37. Frege (1974) section 53.
38. Hughes, G. (1987) p. 51.
39. See Brower (2009).
40. Wolterstorff (1991).
41. Dawkins (2006) p. 31.
42. How fine-grained the degrees are is open to question. A minimal set of grades is Fully Existent (Eternal), Partially Existent (Temporal) and Non-Existent.
43. Boethius (1973) p. 422.
44. A significant interpretative debate on whether duration makes sense in relation to eternity has raged, with Kretzmann and Stump (1981), Fitzgerald (1985), Leftow (1991), Rogers (2000) offering different ways of reading Boethius and Aquinas. Fox (2006) makes a convincing case for different meanings of eternity being in play in the thirteenth century, one extensional, the other not, depending on the kind of being of the entity under discussions . He cites SS 1.8.2.1ad6 in support of the view that Aquinas rejects a certain kind of duration in God: 'duration means a certain kind of distension and since one should not understand any such sort of distension in the divine existence, Boethius does not posit duration, but possession...', see p. 300n50. However, he also argues that duration can be seen as analogical, having extensional and non-extensional meanings, and that the latter could be attributed to God, thus explaining Aquinas's apparent endorsement of duration in God in ST 1.10.1ad2.
45. See Collins (1967).
46. See Griffin (1997).
47. See Moltmann (1981).
48. Swinburne (1993) p. 222.
49. Boethius (1973) p. 426.
50. See also Kenny (1969a) p. 264.
51. Stump and Kretzmann (1981).

52. Granted that no relativism ensues once an agreed framework is fixed. The point, however, is that there is no unique framework.

7   God's Nature: The Way of Eminence

1. Anscombe and Geach (1961) p. 93.
2. See above p. 125.
3. Geach (1956).
4. Porter (2005) p. 101.
5. See Mackie (1971), and Plantinga (1971).
6. Geach (1969) p. 45ff.
7. Brower (2009).
8. Fox (1987) p. 189.
9. Hume (1739) p. 469; G.E. Moore (1903) pp. 46–58.
10. Lisska (1996) p. 195ff.
11. Aquinas allows for the existence of elements, but thinks of them being sub-fundamental, so to speak, indicating that 'fundamental' here refers to appropriate level of priority in explanation, not to being atomic simples.
12. See Rogers (2000) p. 127ff for a useful discussion with references to Scotus and Ockham.
13. Stump (2003) p. 90.
14. Lisska (1996) p. 192, drawing on the work of Henry Veatch.
15. For detailed accounts of Aquinas on cognition, see Kenny (1993), Kretzmann (1993), Pasnau (2002).
16. Jacobs (2002) p. 116.
17. Kretzmann (1997) p. 181.
18. Aristotle, *Metaphysics* Bk. 12, ch. 9 1074b15ff.
19. See Leftow (2009) for a good, contemporary survey.
20. See, for example, Savage (1967), and Rowe (2006).
21. Leftow (2012) p. 187, Leftow (2009) p. 167.
22. See Hoffman and Rosenkrantz (2002) ch. 8.
23. For a thorough discussion with textual references to Descartes, see Hughes (1995) p. 132ff.
24. Geach (1973). Geach rejects the use of the term 'omnipotence' with God and prefers 'almighty'.
25. See Averroes (1969) sections 529–536; Pseudo-Dionysius (1987) section 893B; Savage (1967).
26. See Hughes (1995) p. 117.
27. Plotinus (1991), *Enneads* 5.1.6, 5.3.1, 5.4.1 support the view of a natural process, whereas 6.8 argues for will and intellect and hence choice. See O'Meara (1995) p. 68.
28. Leibniz *Theodicy*, Part 1.8.
29. Geach (1961) p. 120.

Bibliography

Works by Thomas Aquinas

The definitive text of Aquinas's works is being established by the Leonine Commission (although Kenny's observation that the Leonine Edition is incomplete and inconvenient to use is correct – Kenny (2002) p. 205). An accessible Latin text of all of Aquinas's work can be found at the Corpus Thomisticum website, with various critical tools [www.corpusthomisticum.org]. In the following I list the works used in this study and give an English translation when available. LC refers to the Leonine Edition Volume, where available.

Compendium theologiae ad fratrem Raynaldum. LC 42 (1979): 83–205. *Compendium of Theology*, (2009), Richard J. Regan, (trans.), Oxford: Oxford University Press.

De aeternitate mundi. LC 43 (1976): 85–89. *On the Eternity of the World*, in McInerney, (1998), pp. 710–717.

De ente et essentia. LC 43 (1976): 369–381. *On Being and Essence*, in McInerney, (1998), pp. 30–49 and McDermott, (1993), pp. 90–113.

De principiis naturae. LC 43 (1976): 39–47. *On the Principles of Nature*, in McInerney, (1998), pp. 18–29 and McDermott, (1993), pp. 67–79.

Expositio libri Boetii De hebdomadibus. LC50 (1992): 267–282. *How are Things Good? An Exposition of On the Hebdomads of Boethius,* in McInerney, (1998), pp. 142–162.

Expositio libri Peri hermenias. LC1 (1882). *Aristotle on Interpretation: Commentary by St Thomas and Cajetan,* (1962), J.T. Oesterle, (trans.), Milwaukee: Marquette. Section 1.14, in McDermott (1993) pp. 277–283.

Quaestiones de quodlibet I–XII. LC 25 2 vols. Partial translation in *Quodlibetal Questions 1 and 2* (1983), S. Edwards, (trans.), Toronto: PIMS.

Quaestiones disputatae De malo. LC 23 (1982). *On Evil*, (2003), Richard Regan, (trans.), Brian Davies, (ed.), Oxford: Oxford University Press.

Quaestiones disputatae De veritate. LC 22 3 vols. (1970–1976). *The Disputed Questions on Truth*, (1952–1954), R.W. Mulligan, J.V. McGlynn, R.W. Schmidt, (trans.), 3 Vols. Chicago: Regnery.

Scriptum super libros Sententiarum. Books 1–2, *Scriptum super Sententiis*, vols.1–2, P. Mandonnet, (ed.), Paris: Letheilleux.

Sententia libri De anima. LC 45/1 (1984). *Commentary on Aristotle's De Anima*, (1994), Kenelm Foster and Silvester Humphries, (trans.), Notre Dame: Dumb Ox Books.

Sententia libri Ethicorum. LC47 2 Vols. (1969). *Commentary on Aristotle's Nicomachean Ethics*, (1993), C.I. Litzinger, (trans.), Notre Dame: Dumb Ox Books.

Sententia super Metaphysicam. (1950), M.R. Cathala and R.M. Spiazzi (eds), Turin: Marietti. *Commentary on Aristotle's Metaphysics*, (1995), John P. Rowan, (trans.), Notre Dame: Dumb Ox Books.

Sententia super Physicam. (1884), LC 2. *Commentary on Aristotle's Physics*, (1963), R.J. Blackwell, R.J. Spath and W.E. Thirlkel, (trans.), London: Routledge and Kegan Paul.

Summa Contra Gentiles. LC 13–15 (1918–1930). *On The Truth of the Catholic Faith*, (1955–57), A.C. Pegis, J.F. Anderson, V.J. Bourke, C.J. O'Neil, (trans.), 5 vols. Garden City, NY: Doubleday.

Summa Theologiae. LC 4–12 (1888–1906). *Summa Theologiae*, (1964–1981), (various trans.), 61 vols. London: Eyre and Spottiswoode [The Blackfriars Edition]. An older literal English translation is available at http://www.newadvent.org/summa/.

Super Boethium De Trinitate. LC 50 (1992): 75–171. *Faith Reason and Theology*, (1982), A. Maurer, Toronto: PIMS, (translation of qq. 1–4). *The Division and Methods of the Sciences*, (1986), A. Maurer, Toronto: PIMS, (trans- lation of qq. 5–6). 'On Natural Science, Mathematics and Metaphysics', in McDermott (1993) pp. 1–50 (translation of qq. 5–6).

Super librum De causis, (1955), C.Pera, (ed.), Turin: Marietti. *Commentary on the Book of Causes*, (1996), V. Guagliardo, C. Hess, R. Taylor, (trans.), Washington, DC: Catholic University of America Press.

Super librum Dionysii De divinis nominibus, (1950), C. Pera, (ed.), Turin: Marietti.

Adams, Marilyn McCord, and Adams, Robert M., (1990), *The Problem of Evil*, Oxford: Oxford University Press.

Adamson, Peter and Taylor, Richard C., (2005), *The Cambridge Companion to Arabic Philosophy*, Cambridge: Cambridge University Press.

Aertsen, Jan, (1993), 'Aquinas's Philosophy in Its Historical Setting', in *The Cambridge Companion to Aquinas*, Kretzmann, N. and Stump, E., (eds), Cambridge: Cambridge University Press, pp. 12–37.

Anscombe, G.E.M., and Geach, Peter, (1961), *Three Philosophers*, Oxford: Basil Blackwell.

Anselm, (1998), *Anselm of Canterbury: The Major Works*, Davies, Brian and Evans Gillian, (eds), Oxford: Oxford University Press.

Arrington, Robert L., (2001), '"Theology as Grammar", Wittgenstein and Some Critics', in *Wittgenstein and the Philosophy of Religion*, Arrington, Robert L. and Addis, Mark, (eds), London: Routledge, pp. 167–183.

Ashworth, E. J., (1991), 'Analogy and Equivocation in Thirteenth Century Logic: Aquinas in Context', *Mediaeval Studies*, 54, pp. 94–135.

Audi, Robert, (2010), *Epistemology: A Contemporary Introduction to the Theory of Knowledge*, 3rd edn., London: Routledge.

Augustine, (2002), *Confessions*, Pine-Coffin, R.S., (trans.), Harmondsworth: Penguin.

Augustine, (2003), *City of God*, Bettenson, Henry (trans.) rev. edn., Harmondsworth: Penguin.

Austin, J. L., (1962), *Sense and Sensibilia*, Oxford: Oxford University Press.

Averroes, (1969), *Tahafut al-Tahafut (The Incoherence of the Incoherence)*, Simon Van Der Bergh, (trans.), London: Luzac & Company.

Avicenna, (2005), *The Metaphysics of Healing*, Michael Marmura (trans.), Provo, UT: Brigham Young University Press.

Baghramian, Maria, (2004), *Relativism*, London: Routledge.

Barnes, Jonathan, (2002), (new edn.), *Early Greek Philosophy*, London: Penguin Classics.

Boethius, (1973), *The Consolation of Philosophy*, in *Boethius: The Theological Tractates and The Consolation of Philosophy*, Stewart, H.F, Rand, E.K., and Tester, S.J., (eds), Cambridge, MA: Harvard University Press.

Boghossian, Paul, (1999), 'Analyticity', in *A Companion to the Philosophy of Language*, Hale, Bob, and Wright, Crispin, (eds), Oxford: Blackwell, pp. 331–368.

Boland, Vivian, (1996), *Ideas in God According to Saint Thomas Aquinas: Sources and Synthesis*, Leiden: Brill.

BonJour, Laurence, (1997), *In Defense of Pure Reason: A Rationalist Account of A Priori Justification*, Cambridge: Cambridge University Press.

Boyle, Leonard, (1982), *The Setting of the Summa Theologiae of Saint Thomas*, Toronto: PIMS.

Boyle, Leonard, (2002), 'The Setting of the *Summa Theologiae* of St. Thomas – Revisited', in *The Ethics of Aquinas*, Pope, Stephen, J., (ed.), Washington, DC: Georgetown University Press.

Broadie, Sarah, (2009), 'Aristotle', in *Ancient Philosophy of Religion*, Oppy, G. and Trakakis, N.N. (eds), Durham: Acumen.

Brower, Jeffrey, (2009), 'Simplicity and Aseity', in *The Oxford Handbook of Philosophical Theology*, Flint, T., and Rea, M. (eds), Oxford: Oxford University Press, 105–128.

Brower, Jeffrey, (2012), 'Matter, Form and Individuation', in *The Oxford Handbook of Aquinas*, Davies, B., and Stump, E., (eds), Oxford: Oxford University Press, pp. 85–103.

Brower, Jeffrey, (2013), 'Medieval Theories of Relations', *The Internet Encyclopedia of Philosophy*, Zalta E., (ed.).

Brown, Patterson, (1966), 'Infinite Causal Regression', in *Aquinas: A Collection of Critical Essays* Kenny, Anthony, (ed.), London: Macmillan, pp. 214–236.

Brown, Patterson, (1969), 'St. Thomas's Doctrine of Necessary Being', in *Aquinas: A Collection of Critical Essays*, Kenny, Anthony, (ed.), London: Macmillan, pp. 157–174.

Brown, Stephen, F., (2002), 'The Theological Virtue of Faith: An Invitation to the Ecclesial Life of Truth', in *The Ethics of Aquinas*, Pope, Stephen, J., (ed.), Washington, DC: Georgetown University Press pp. 221–231.

Burrell, David, (1979), *Aquinas, God and Action*, Notre Dame: University of Notre Dame Press.

Burrell, David, (1986), *Knowing the Unknowable God, Ibn Sina, Maimonides, Aquinas*, Notre Dame: University of Notre Dame Press.

Burrell, David, (1993), 'Aquinas and Islamic and Jewish Thinkers', in *The Cambridge Companion to Aquinas*, Kretzmann, N. and Stump, E., (eds), Cambridge: Cambridge University Press, pp. 60–84.

Camus, Albert, (1955), *The Myth of Sisyphus and Other Essays*, New York: Alfred A. Knopf.

Caputo, John D., (2007), 'Atheism, A/theology and the Postmodern Condition', in *The Cambridge Companion to Atheism*, Martin, Michael, (ed.), Cambridge: Cambridge University Press.

Carnap, Rudolf, (1967), *The Logical Structure of the World*, Berkeley: University of California Press.

Carriero, John, (2009), *Between Two Worlds: A Reading of Descartes's* Meditations, Princeton: Princeton University Press.

Casey, Gerard, (1987), 'An Explication of the De Hebdomadibus of Boethius in the Light of St. Thomas's Commentary', *The Thomist* 51, pp. 419–434.

Catan, John R., (ed.), (1980), *St. Thomas Aquinas on the Existence of God: Collected Papers of Joseph Owens*, Albany: State University of New York Press.

Ceausescu, Gilles-Jérémie, (2008), *Thomas d'Aquin: Sur La Vérité*, Paris: CNRS Éditions.

Chalmers, David, (2012), *Constructing the World*, Oxford: Oxford University Press.

Chignell, Andrew, (2009), "'As Kant has Shown...': Analytic Theology and the Critical Philosophy", in *Analytic Theology: New Essays in the Philosophy of Theology*, Rea, Michael and Crisp, Oliver, (eds), Oxford: Oxford University Press, pp. 117–135.

Collins, J., (1967), *The Emergence of Philosophy of Religion*, New Haven: Yale University Press.

Copleston, Frederick, (1955), *Aquinas*, Harmondsworth: Penguin.

Craig, William Lane, (1980), *The Cosmological Argument*, New York: Harper and Row.

Dante, (1996), *The Divine Comedy of Dante Alighieri, Vol.1, Inferno*, Robert M.Durling, (ed. and trans.), Oxford: Oxford University Press.

Danto, Arthur, (1965), *Nietzsche as Philosopher*, New York: Columbia University Press.

Davies, Brian, (1985), *Thinking About God*, London: Geoffrey Chapman.

Davies, Brian, (1992), *The Thought of Thomas Aquinas*, Oxford: Clarendon Press.

Davies, Brian, (2001), 'Aquinas's Third Way', *New Blackfriars*, 82, pp. 450–466.

Davies, Brian, (ed.), (2002), *Thomas Aquinas: Contemporary Philosophical Perspectives*, Oxford: Oxford University Press.

Davies, Brian, (2003a), 'Introduction' to *On Evil, Thomas Aquinas*, Oxford: Oxford University Press.

Davies, Brian, (2003b), 'Letter from America', *New Blackfriars* 84, pp. 371–384.

Davies, Brian, (2004), 3rd edn., *An Introduction to the Philosophy of Religion*, Oxford: Oxford University Press.

Davies, Brian, (2011), *Thomas Aquinas on God and Evil*, Oxford: Oxford University Press.

Davies, Brian, and Stump, Eleanore, (eds) (2012), *The Oxford Handbook of Aquinas*, Oxford: Oxford University Press.

Davis, Stephen T., (1997), *God, Reason and Theistic Proofs*, Edinburgh: Edinburgh University Press.

Dawkins, Richard, (2006), *The God Delusion*, London: Bantam.

Dolezal, James E., (2011), *God without Parts: Divine Simplicity and the Metaphysics of God's Absoluteness*, Eugene, OR: Pickwick Publications.

Draper, Paul, (2009), 'The Problem of Evil', in *The Oxford Handbook of Philosophical Theology*, Flint, T., and Rea, M., (eds), Oxford: Oxford University Press, pp. 332–351.

Evans, C. Stephen, (1998), *Faith Beyond Reason*, Edinburgh: Edinburgh University Press.

Everitt, Nicholas, (2003), *The Non-Existence of God*, London: Routledge.

Fabro, Cornelio, (1963), *La nozione metafisica di partecipazione secondo S. Tommaso d'Aquino*, 3rd edn., Turin: Societa editrice internazionale.

Feser, Edward, (2009), *Aquinas: A Beginner's Guide*, Oxford: Oneworld.

Fitzgerald, Paul, (1985), 'Stump and Kretzmann on Time and Eternity', *Journal of Philosophy*, 82, pp. 260–269.

Fox, John F., (1987), 'Truthmaker', *Australasian Journal of Philosophy*, 65:2, pp. 188–207.

Fox, Rory, (2006), *Time and Eternity in Mid-Thirteenth Century Thought*, Oxford: Oxford University Press.

Frege, Gottlob, (1952), *Translations from the Philosophical Writings of Gottlob Frege*, P. Geach and M. Black (eds and trans.), Oxford: Basil Blackwell.

Frege, Gottlob, (1974), *The Foundations of Arithmetic*, J.L. Austin (trans.), 2nd edn., Oxford: Basil Blackwell.

Gale, Richard, (1993), *On the Nature and Existence of God*, Cambridge: Cambridge University Press.

Gallagher, David M., (2002), 'The Will and Its Acts', in *The Ethics of Aquinas*, Pope, Stephen, J., (ed.), Washington, DC: Georgetown University Press, pp. 69–89.

Ganeri, Martin, (2007), 'Knowledge and Love of God in Ramanuja and Aquinas,' *Journal of Hindu-Christian Studies*: 20:6, pp. 3–9.

Garfield, Jay, (1995), *The Fundamental Wisdom of the Middle Way: Nagarjuna's 'Mulamadhyamikakarika'*, Oxford: OUP.

Gaskin, J.C.A., (1988), *Hume's Philosophy of Religion*, 2nd edn. Basingstoke: Macmillan.

Gauthier, R-A., (2002), *Introduction a la Somme Contre les Gentiles de Saint Thomas d'Aquin*, Paris: Vrin.

Geach, Peter, (1950), 'Subject and Predicate', *Mind*, 59:236, pp. 461–482.

Geach, Peter, (1956), 'Good and Evil', *Analysis*, 17, pp. 32–42.

Geach, Peter, (1969), *God and the Soul*, London: Routledge and Kegan Paul.

Geach, Peter, (1970), Review of Anthony Kenny *The Five Ways*, in *The Philosophical Quarterly*, 20, pp. 311–312.

Geach, Peter, (1973), 'Omnipotence', *Philosophy*, 48:183, pp. 7–20.

Geiger, Louis Bertrand, (1953), *La Participation dans la philosophie de S. Thomas d'Aquin*, 2nd edn., Bibliotheque thomiste 23, Paris: Vrin.

Gilson, Etienne, (1957), *The Christian Philosophy of St Thomas Aquinas*, London: Victor Gollancz.

Gjertsen, Derek, (1989), *Science and Philosophy: Past and Present*, Harmondsworth: Penguin.

Griffin, David Ray, (1997), 'Process Theology', in *A Companion to the Philosophy of Religion*, Quinn, Philip, L., and Talieferro, Charles (eds), Oxford: Blackwell, pp. 136–142.

Haldane, J., (ed.), (2002), *Mind, Metaphysics and Value in the Thomistic and Analytical Traditions*, Notre Dame: University of Notre Dame Press.

Helm, Paul, (1988), *Eternal God: A Study of God Without Time*, Oxford: Oxford University Press.

Henninger, M., (1989), *Relations, Medieval Theories 1250–1325*, Oxford: Clarendon Press.

Hick, John, (2004), *An Interpretation of Religion* 2nd edn., Basingstoke: Palgrave Macmillan.

Hoffman, Joshua and Rosenkrantz, Gary S., (2002), *The Divine Attributes*, Oxford: Blackwell.

Honnefelder, Ludger, (2012), 'God's Goodness', in *The Oxford Handbook of Aquinas*, Davies, B., and Stump, E., (eds), Oxford: Oxford University Press, pp. 147–157.

Howard-Snyder, D., (1996), (ed.), *The Evidential Argument from Evil*, Bloomington: Indiana University Press.

Hughes, Christopher, (1989), *On A Complex Theory of a Simple God*, Ithaca: Cornell University Press.

Hughes, Gerard, (1987), 'Aquinas and the Limits of Agnosticism', in *The Philosophical Assessment of Theology*, Hughes, G., (ed.), Washington, DC: Georgetown University Press, pp. 35–63.

Hughes, Gerard, (1995), *The Nature of God*, London: Routledge.

Hume, David, (1978), *A Treatise of Human Nature*, Selby-Bigge, L.A., (ed.), Oxford: Oxford University Press.

Hume, David, (2008), Gaskin, J.C.A., (ed.), *Dialogues Concerning Natural Religion*, Oxford: Oxford University Press.

Jacobs, Jonathan, (2002), 'Habits, Cognition, and Realism', in *Mind, Metaphysics and Value in the Thomistic and Analytical Traditions*, Haldane, J., (ed.), Notre Dame: University of Notre Dame Press, pp. 109–124.

Jalbert, Guy, (1961), *Nécessité et Contingence chez saint Thomas d'Aquin et chez ses Prédécesseurs*, Ottowa: Editions de l'Universite d'Ottowa.

James, William, (2003), *The Will to Believe and Human Immortality*, New York: Dover Publications.

Jenkins, John, (1997), *Knowledge and Faith in Aquinas*, Cambridge: Cambridge University Press.

Jordan, Mark D., (1986), 'The Protreptic Structure of the *Contra Gentiles*', *The Thomist*, 60, pp. 173–209.

Jordan, Mark D., (1993), 'Theology and Philosophy', in *The Cambridge Companion to Aquinas*, Kretzmann, N. and Stump, E., (eds), Cambridge: Cambridge University Press, pp. 232–251.

Kant, I., (1989), *The Critique of Pure Reason*, Smith, N.K. (trans.), Basingstoke: Palgrave Macmillan.

Katz, Jerold J., (2000), *Realistic Rationalism*, Cambridge, MA: MIT Press.

Kearney, Richard, (2011), *Anatheism: Returning to God after God*, New York: Columbia University Press.

Kennedy, Philip, (2010), *Twentieth Century Theologians: A New Introduction to Modern Christian Thought*, London: I.B. Tauris.

Kenny, Anthony, (ed.), (1969a), *Aquinas: A Collection of Critical Essays*, London: Macmillan.

Kenny, Anthony, (1969b), *Aquinas, The Five Ways*, London: Routledge and Kegan Paul.

Kenny, Anthony, (1980), *Aquinas*, Oxford: Oxford University Press.

Kenny, Anthony, (1993), *Aquinas on Mind*, London: Routledge.

Kenny, Anthony, (2002), *Aquinas on Being*, Oxford: Oxford University Press.

Kenny, Anthony, (2005), *A New History of Western Philosophy Vol.2: Medieval Philosophy*, Oxford: Clarendon Press.

Kenny, Anthony, (2006), *What I Believe*, London: Continuum.

Kent, Bonny, (2002), 'Habits and Virtues', in *The Ethics of Aquinas*, Pope, Stephen, J., (ed.), Washington, DC: Georgetown University Press, pp. 116–130.

Kerr, Fergus, (2002a), *After Aquinas: Versions of Thomism*, Oxford: Blackwell.

Kerr, Fergus, (2002b), 'Aquinas after Wittgenstein', in *Mind, Metaphysics and Value in the Thomistic and Analytical Traditions*, Haldane, J., (ed.), Notre Dame: University of Notre Dame Press, pp. 1–17.

Kerr, Fergus, (2003), *Contemplating Aquinas: Varieties of Interpretation*, Notre Dame: University of Notre Dame Press.

Kerr, Fergus, (2008), *'Work on Oneself': Wittgenstein's Philosophical Psychology*, Arlington, VA: The Institute for Psychological Sciences Press.

Klima, Gyula, (1996), 'The Semantic Principles Underlying Saint Thomas Aquinas's Metaphysics of Being', *Medieval Philosophy and Theology*, 5, pp. 87–141.

Klima, Gyula, (2002), 'Aquinas' Theory of the Copula and the Analogy of Being', in *Logical Analysis and History of Philosophy*, 5, pp. 159–176.

Klima, Gyula, (2002), 'Contemporary "Essentialism" vs. Aristotelian Essentialism', in *Mind, Metaphysics and Value in the Thomistic and Analytical Traditions*, Haldane, J., (ed.), Notre Dame: University of Notre Dame Press, pp. 175–194.

Knasas, John F.X., (2006), 'Haldane's Analytic Thomism and Aquinas's Actus Essendi', in *Analytical Thomism: Traditions in Dialogue*, Paterson, Craig, and Pugh, Matthew S., (eds), Aldershot: Ashgate, pp. 233–252.

Kretzmann, Norman, (1993), 'Philosophy of Mind', in *The Cambridge Companion to Aquinas*, Kretzmann, N. and Stump, E., (eds), Cambridge: Cambridge University Press, pp. 128–159.

Kretzmann, Norman, (1997), *The Metaphysics of Theism: Aquinas's Natural Theology in* Summa Contra Gentiles I, Oxford: Clarendon Press.

Kretzmann, Norman, (1999), *The Metaphysics of Creation: Aquinas's Natural Theology in* Summa Contra Gentiles II, Oxford: Clarendon Press.

Kretzmann, Norman and Stump Eleanore, (1993) *The Cambridge Companion to Aquinas,* Cambridge: Cambridge University Press.

Leftow, Brian, (1991), *Time and Eternity*, Ithaca: Cornell University Press.

Leftow, Brian, (2009), 'Omnipotence', in *The Oxford Handbook of Philosophical Theology*, Flint, T., and Rea, M., (eds), Oxford: Oxford University Press, pp. 167–198.

Leftow, Brian, (2012), 'God's Omnipotence', in *The Oxford Handbook of Aquinas*, Davies, B., and Stump, E., (eds), Oxford: Oxford University Press, pp. 187–198.

Lisska, Anthony J., (1996), *Aquinas's Theory of Natural Law: An Analytic Reconstruction*, Oxford: Clarendon Press.

Lonergan, Bernard, (1968), *Verbum: Word and Idea in Aquinas*, London: Darton, Longman and Todd.

Loux, Michael J., Zimmerman, Dean W., (2003), *The Oxford Handbook of Metaphysics*, Oxford: Oxford University Press.

Lovejoy, Arthur O., (1990), *The Great Chain of Being*, new edn., Cambridge: Harvard University Press.

MacDonald, Scott, (1984), 'The Esse/Essentia Argument in Aquinas's *De esse et essentia*', *Journal of the History of Philosophy*, 22, pp. 157–172.

MacDonald, Scott, (1991), 'Aquinas's Parasitic Cosmological Argument', *Medieval Philosophy and Theology*, 1, pp. 119–155.

MacDonald, Scott, (1993), 'Theory of Knowledge', in *The Cambridge Companion to Aquinas*, Kretzmann, N. and Stump, E., (eds), Cambridge: Cambridge University Press, pp. 160–195.

Macintosh, J.J., (1998), 'Aquinas on Necessity', *American Catholic Philosophical Quarterly* 72:3, pp. 371–403.

MacIntyre, Alasdair, (2006), *The Tasks of Philosophy, Vol. 1, Selected Essays*, Cambridge: Cambridge University Press.

Mackie, John L., (1971), 'Evil and Omnipotence', in *Philosophy of Religion*, Mitchell, B., (ed.), Oxford: Oxford University Press, pp. 92–104.

Mackie, John L., (1982), *The Miracle of Theism*, Oxford: Clarendon Press.

Maimonides, Moses, (1995), *The Guide of the Perplexed*, Rabin, Chaim, (trans.) Indianapolis: Hackett.

Marenbon, John, (1987), *Later Medieval Philosophy*, London: Routledge and Kegan Paul.

Maritain, Jacques, (1955), *Approaches to God*, London: Allen and Unwin.

Martin, Christopher, (1988), *The Philosophy of Thomas Aquinas: Introductory Readings*, London: Routledge.

Martin, Christopher, (1997), *Thomas Aquinas: God and Explanations*, Edinburgh: Edinburgh University Press.

Martin, Michael, (ed.), (2007), *The Cambridge Companion to Atheism*, Cambridge: Cambridge University Press.

Maurer, Armand, (1983), 'Introduction', in *St Thomas Aquinas: On Being and Essence*, Toronto: Pontifical Institute of Medieval Studies.

McCabe, Herbert, (1969), 'Categories', in *Aquinas: A Collection of Critical Essays*, Kenny, Anthony, (ed.), (1969a), London: Macmillan, pp. 54–92.

McCabe, Herbert, (2007), *Faith within Reason*, Brian Davies (ed.), London: Continuum.

McCabe, Herbert, (2008), *On Aquinas*, Brian Davies (ed.), London: Continuum.

McCabe, Herbert, (2010), *God and Evil in the Theology of St. Thomas Aquinas*, Brian Davies (ed.), London: Continuum.

McDermott, Timothy, (1993), *Thomas Aquinas: Selected Philosophical Writings*, Oxford: Oxford University Press.

McDermott, Timothy, (2011), Review of Mark Vernon, *How to Be an Agnostic*, *Times Literary Supplement*, 16 September 2011.

McInerny, Ralph, (1990), *Boethius and Aquinas*, Washington, DC: Catholic University of America Press.

McInerny, Ralph, (1996), *Aquinas and Analogy*, Washington, DC: Catholic University of America Press.

McInerny, Ralph, (1998), *Thomas Aquinas: Selected Writings*, Harmondsworth: Penguin.

Melia, Joseph, (2003), *Modality*, Chesham: Acumen.

Michon, Cyrille, (2004), *Thomas D'Aquin et la controverse sur L'Éternité du monde*, Paris: Flammarion.

Miller, Barry, (1992), *From Existence to God, A Contemporary Philosophical Argument*, London: Routledge.

Miller, Barry, (2002), *The Fullness of Being: A New Paradigm for Existence*, Notre Dame: University of Notre Dame Press.

Moltmann, J., (1981), *The Trinity and the Kingdom of God*, London: SCM Press.

Moore, G.E., (1903), *Principia Ethica*, Cambridge: Cambridge University Press.

Moran, Dermot, (1999), *An Introduction to Phenomenology*, London: Routledge.

Nagasawa, Yujin, (2011), *The Existence of God: A Philosophical Introduction*, London: Routledge.

Normore, Calvin, (1982), 'Future Contingents', in *The Cambridge History of Later Medieval Philosophy*, Kretzmann, N., Kenny, A., Pinborg, J., (eds), Cambridge: Cambridge University Press, pp. 358–382.

O'Callaghan, John P., (2003), *Thomist Realism and the Linguistic Turn: Towards a More Perfect Form of Existence*, Notre Dame: University of Notre Dame Press.

Oderberg, David S., (2002), 'Hylomorphism and Individuation', in *Mind, Metaphysics and Value in the Thomistic and Analytical Traditions*, Haldane, J., (ed.), Notre Dame: University of Notre Dame Press, pp. 125–142.

Oderberg, David S., (2007), *Real Essentialism*, London: Routledge.

Oderberg, David S., (2008), 'Teleology: Inorganic and Organic', in *Contemporary Perspectives on Natural Law*, Gonzalez, A.M., (ed.), Aldershot: Ashgate, pp. 259–280.

O'Grady, Paul, (1999), 'Carnap and Two Dogmas of Empiricism', *Philosophy and Phenomenological Research*, 59:4, pp. 1015–1027.

O'Grady, Paul, (2000), 'Anti-Foundationalism and Radical Orthodoxy', *New Blackfriars*, 81:951, pp. 160–176.

O'Grady, Paul, (2002), *Relativism*, Chesham: Acumen.

O'Grady, Paul, (2005a), 'Aquinas, Philosophical Theology and Analytic Philosophy', in *The Theology of Thomas Aquinas*, Van Niewenhove, R. and Warwykof, J., (eds), Notre Dame: University of Notre Dame Press, pp. 416–441.

O'Grady, Paul, (2005b), 'Form and Emptiness: Aquinas and Nagarjuna', *Contemporary Buddhism*, 6:2, pp. 173–188.

O'Grady, Paul, (2008), *Philosophical Theology*, Dublin: Priory Institute.

O'Grady, Paul, (2011), 'Finding Consolation in God: Boethius and *The Consolation of Philosophy*', in *The Consolations of Philosophy: Reflections in an Economic Downturn*, O'Grady, Paul, (ed.), Dublin: Columba Press, pp. 20–34.

O'Grady, Paul, (2012), 'McCabe on Aquinas and Wittgenstein', *New Blackfriars*, 93:1048, pp. 631–644.

O'Meara, Dominic, (1995), *Plotinus: An Introduction to the Enneads*, Oxford: Clarendon Press.

Oppy, Graham, (2009), *Arguing about Gods*, Cambridge: Cambridge University Press.

O'Rourke, Fran, (1992), *Pseudo-Dionysius and the Metaphysics of Aquinas*, Leiden: Brill.

O'Shea, James, (2007), *Wilfred Sellars: Naturalism With A Normative Turn*, Cambridge: Polity.

Owens, Joseph, (1980), '*Quandoque* and *Aliquando* in Aquinas's *Tertia Via*', *New Scholasticism* 54, pp. 447–475.

Owens, Joseph, (1993), 'Aristotle and Aquinas', in *The Cambridge Companion to Aquinas*, Kretzmann, N. and Stump, E., (eds), Cambridge: Cambridge University Press, pp. 38–59.

Pascal, B., (1995), *Pensées and Other Writings*, Levi, A. (ed.), Oxford: Oxford University Press.

Pasnau, Robert, (2002), *Thomas Aquinas on Human Nature*, Cambridge: Cambridge University Press.

Pasnau, Robert and Shields, Christopher, (2004), *The Philosophy of Aquinas*, Boulder, CO: Westview Press.

Paterson, Craig and Pugh, Matthew S., (2006), *Analytical Thomism: Traditions in Dialogue*, Aldershot: Ashgate.

Pawl, Timothy, (2012), 'The Five Ways', in *The Oxford Handbook of Aquinas*, Davies, B., and Stump, E., (eds). Oxford: Oxford University Press, pp. 115–134.

Phillips, D.Z., (2012), *The Problem of Evil and the Problem of God*, London: SCM Press.

Plantinga, Alvin, (1971), 'The Free Will Defence', in *Philosophy of Religion*, Mitchell, B., (ed.), Oxford: Oxford University Press, pp. 105–120.

Plantinga, Alvin, (1980), *Does God Have a Nature?*, Milwaukee: Marquette University Press.

Plantinga, Alvin, (1983), 'Reason and Belief in God', in *Faith and Rationality: Reason and Belief in God*, Plantinga, A., and Wolterstorff, N., (eds), Notre Dame: University of Notre Dame Press pp. 16–93.

Plantinga, Alvin, (1993), *Warrant and Proper Function*, Oxford: OUP.

Plantinga, Alvin, (2000), *Warranted Christian Belief*, Oxford: OUP.

Plotinus, *Enneads*, (1991), Dillon, John, (ed.), Harmondsworth: Penguin.

Pope, Stephen J., (ed.), (2002), *The Ethics of Aquinas*, Washington, DC: Georgetown University Press.

Popper, Karl, (2002), *The Logic of Scientific Discovery*, 2nd edn., London: Routledge.

Porter, Jean, (2005), *Nature as Reason*, Grand Rapids, MI: William Eerdmans.

Pouivet, Roger, (2006), *After Wittgenstein, St. Thomas*, South Bend, IN: St Augustine's Press.

Pseudo-Dionysius, (1987), 'Divine Names', in *Pseudo-Dionysius: The Complete Works*, Colm Luibheid (trans.), Mahwah, NJ: Paulist Press.

Pugh, Matthew S., 'Kenny on Being in Aquinas', in *Analytical Thomism: Traditions in Dialogue*, Paterson, Craig, and Pugh, Matthew S., (eds), Aldershot: Ashgate, pp. 263–282.

Putnam, Hilary, (1981), *Reason, Truth and History*, Cambridge: Cambridge University Press.

Quine, W.V., (1953), *From a Logical Point of View*, Cambridge, MA: Harvard University Press.

Quine, W.V., (1969), *Ontological Relativity and Other Essays*, New York: Columbia University Press.

Rea, Michael C., (2002), *World without Design: The Ontological Consequences of Naturalism*, Oxford: Clarendon Press.

Rea, Michael, and Crisp, Oliver, (2009), *Analytic Theology: New Essays in the Philosophy of Theology*, Oxford: Oxford University Press.

Reith, Hermann, (1958), *The Metaphysics of St. Thomas Aquinas*, Milwaukee: The Bruce Publishing Company.

Rhees, Rush, (ed.), (1981) *Recollections of Wittgenstein*, Oxford: Oxford University Press.

Richardson, Alan W., (2008), *Carnap's Construction of the World: The Aufbau and the Emergence of Logical Empiricism*, Cambridge: Cambridge University Press.

Rocca, Gregory P., (2004), *Speaking the Incomprehensible God*, Washington, DC: The Catholic University of America Press.

Rogers, Eugene F., Jr. (1995), *Thomas Aquinas and Karl Barth: Sacred Doctrine and the Knowledge of God*, Notre Dame: University of Notre Dame Press.

Rogers, Kathleen A., (2000), *Perfect Being Theology*, Edinburgh: Edinburgh University Press.

Roland-Gosselin, M.D., (1948), *Le 'De Ente et Essentia' De S. Thomas d'Aquin*, Paris: Vrin.

Ross, James F., (1969), *Philosophical Theology*, Indianapolis: The Bobbs-Merill Co.

Rota, Michael, (2012), 'Causation', in *The Oxford Handbook of Aquinas*, Davies, B., and Stump, E., (eds), Oxford: Oxford University Press, pp. 104–114.

Rowe, William, (1998), *The Cosmological Argument*, New York: Fordham University Press.

Rowe, William, (2006), 2nd edn., *Can God Be Free?*, Oxford: Oxford University Press.

Russell, Bertrand, (1993), *Why I Am Not a Christian*, London: Routledge.

Russell, Bertrand, (2004), *A History of Western Philosophy*, London: Routledge.

Radhakrishnan, Sarvapelli, and Moore, Charles (1967), *A Source Book of Indian Philosophy*, Princeton: Princeton University Press.

Sadowsky, James, (2000), 'Can There Be an Endless Regress of Causes?', in *Philosophy of Religion: A Guide and Anthology*, Davies, Brian, (ed.), Oxford: Oxford University Press, pp. 239–241.

Savage, C. Wade. (1967), 'The Paradox of the Stone', *Philosophical Review*, 76:1, pp. 74–79.

Sertillanges, A. (1940), *La philosophie de saint Thomas d'Aquin*, Paris, Aubier.

Shanley, Brian, (2006a), *The Treatise on the Divine Nature: Summa Theologiae 1.1–13*, Indianapolis: Hackett.

Shanley, Brian J., (2006b), 'On Analytical Thomism', in *Analytical Thomism: Traditions in Dialogue*, Paterson, Craig, and Pugh, Matthew S., (eds), Aldershot: Ashgate, pp. 215–224.

Sillem, Edward, (1961), *Ways of Thinking about God: Thomas Aquinas and Some Recent Problems*, London: Darton, Longman and Todd.

Simons, Peter, (2011), 'Whitehead: Process and Cosmology', in *The Routledge Companion to Metaphysics*, Le Poidevin, Robin, Simons, Peter, McGonigal, Andrew, Cameron, Ross (eds), London: Routledge, pp. 181–190.

Smart, J.J.C., and Haldane, J.J. (eds), (2002), 2nd edn., *Atheism and Theism*, Oxford: Blackwell.

Smart, Ninian, (1998), *The World's Religions*, 2nd edn., Cambridge: Cambridge University Press.

Smith, Wilfred Cantwell, (1998), *Faith and Belief: The Difference between Them*, Oxford: Oneworld.

Spade, Paul Vincent, (1982), 'The Semantics of Terms', in *The Cambridge History of Later Medieval Philosophy*, Kretzmann, N., Kenny, A., Pinborg, J., (eds), Cambridge: Cambridge University Press, pp. 188–196.

Stump, Eleanore, (2003), *Aquinas*, London: Routledge.

Stump, Eleanore and Kretzmann, Norman, (1981), 'Eternity', *Journal of Philosophy*, 78, pp. 429–458.

Swinburne, Richard, (1993), rev. edn., *The Coherence of Theism*, Oxford: Clarendon Press.

Swinburne, Richard, (2004), *The Existence of God*, 2nd edn., Oxford Clarendon Press.

Taylor, Richard, C., (2005), 'Averroes: Religious Dialectic and Aristotelian Philosophical Thought', in *The Cambridge Companion to Arabic Philosophy*, Adamson, Peter and Taylor, Richard, C. (eds), Cambridge: Cambridge University Press, pp. 180–200.

Tertullian, (1951), *On Prescription against Heretics*, in *The Ante-Nicene Fathers*, Vol. III, Roberts, A., and Donaldson, J., (eds), Grand Rapids, MI: William Eerdmans.

Te Velde, Rudi, (1994), 'Natural Reason in the *Summa Contra Gentiles*', *Medieval Philosophy and Theology* 4, pp. 42–70.

Te Velde, Rudi, (2006), *Aquinas on God: The 'Divine Science' of the* Summa Theologiae, Aldershot: Ashgate.

Torrell, Jean-Pierre, (2003), *St Thomas Aquinas Vol .2 Spiritual Master*, Washington, DC: The Catholic University of America Press.

Torrell, Jean-Pierre, (2005), rev. edn. *St Thomas Aquinas Vol. 1 The Person and His Work*, Washington, DC: The Catholic University of America Press.

Tugwell, Simon, (ed.), (1988) *Albert and Thomas: Selected Writings,* Mahwah, NJ: The Paulist Press.

Turner, Denys, (2004), *Faith, Reason and the Existence of God*, Cambridge: Cambridge University Press.

Turner, Denys, (2013), *Thomas Aquinas: A Portrait*, New Haven: Yale University Press.

Van Steenburghen, Fernand, (1980), *Le probleme de l'existence de Dieu dans les écrits de s. Thomas d'Aquin*, Louvain-La-neuve: Éditions de l'Institut Supérieur de Philosophie.

Velecky, Lubor, (1994), *Aquinas' Five Arguments in* The Summa Theologiae *1a 2,3*, Kampen: Kok Pharos Publishing House.

Webster, John, (2004), *Karl Barth*, London: Bloomsbury.

Weidemann, Hermann, (2002), 'The Logic of Being in Thomas Aquinas', in *Thomas Aquinas: Contemporary Philosophical Perspectives*, Davies, Brian, (ed.), Oxford: Oxford University Press, pp. 77–96.

Weigel, Peter, (2008), *Aquinas on Simplicity: An Investigation into the Foundations of His Philosophical Theology*, Frankfurt: Peter Lang.

Weisheipl, James, (1983), *Friar Thomas D'Aquino: His Life, Thought and Works*, Washington, DC: Catholic University of America Press.

Wieland, George, (2002), 'Happiness', Grant Kaplan (trans.), in *The Ethics of Aquinas*, Pope, Stephen, J., (ed.), Washington, DC: Georgetown University Press, pp. 57–68.

Williams, C.J.F., (1981), *What Is Existence?*, Oxford: Clarendon Press.

Williams, C.J.F., (1997), 'Being', in *A Companion to the Philosophy of Religion*, Quinn, Philip, L., and Talieferro, Charles, (eds), Oxford: Blackwell, pp. 223–228.

Wippel, John, (1988), 'Essence and Existence', in *The Cambridge History of Later Medieval Philosophy*, Kretzmann, N., Kenny, A., Pinborg, J., (eds), Cambridge: Cambridge University Press, pp. 385–410.

Wippel, John, (1993), 'Metaphysics', in *The Cambridge Companion to Aquinas*, Kretzmann, N. and Stump, E. (eds), Cambridge: Cambridge University Press, pp. 85–127.

Wippel, John, (2000), *The Metaphysical Thought of Thomas Aquinas*, Washington, DC: Catholic University of America Press.

Wisnovsky, Robert, (2005), 'Avicenna and the Avicennian Tradition', in *The Cambridge Companion to Arabic Philosophy*, Adamson, Peter, and Taylor, Richard C., (eds), Cambridge: Cambridge University Press, pp. 92–136.

Wittgenstein, Ludwig, (1969), *On Certainty*, G.E.M. Anscombe and G.H. von Wright (eds), D. Paul and G.E.M. Anscombe (trans.) Oxford: Basil Blackwell.

Wittgenstein, Ludwig, (1975), *Tractatus Logico-Philosophicus,* Pears, D. and McGuinness, B., (trans.) London: Routledge and Kegan Paul.

Wittgenstein, Ludwig, (1980), *Culture and Value*, G.H. von Wright and H. Nyman (eds), P. Winch (trans.), Oxford: Basil Blackwell.

Wolterstorff, Nicholas, (1991), 'Divine Simplicity', in *Philosophical Perspectives 5, Philosophy of Religion*, Tomberlin, James, (ed.), Atascadero: Ridgeview Publishing Co, pp. 531–552.

Wolterstorff, Nicholas, (2009), 'How Philosophical Theology Became Possible within the Analytical Tradition of Philosophy', in *Analytic Theology: New Essays in the Philosophy of Theology*, Rea, Michael and Crisp, Oliver (eds), (2009), Oxford: Oxford University Press, pp. 155–170.

Index